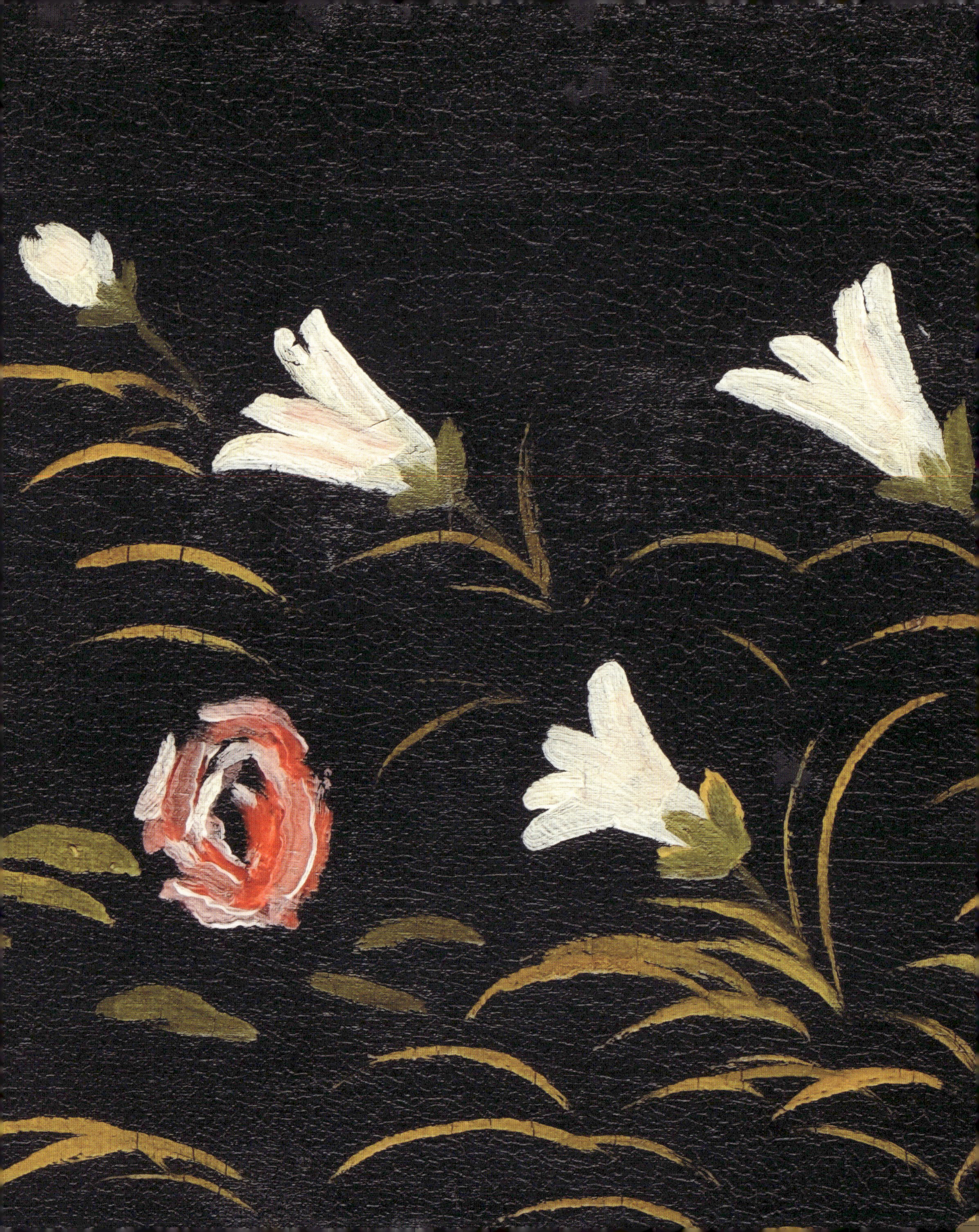

NIKO PIROSMANI

BLACK LIGHT

CONTENTS

ROE DEER AND LANDSCAPE. 1913

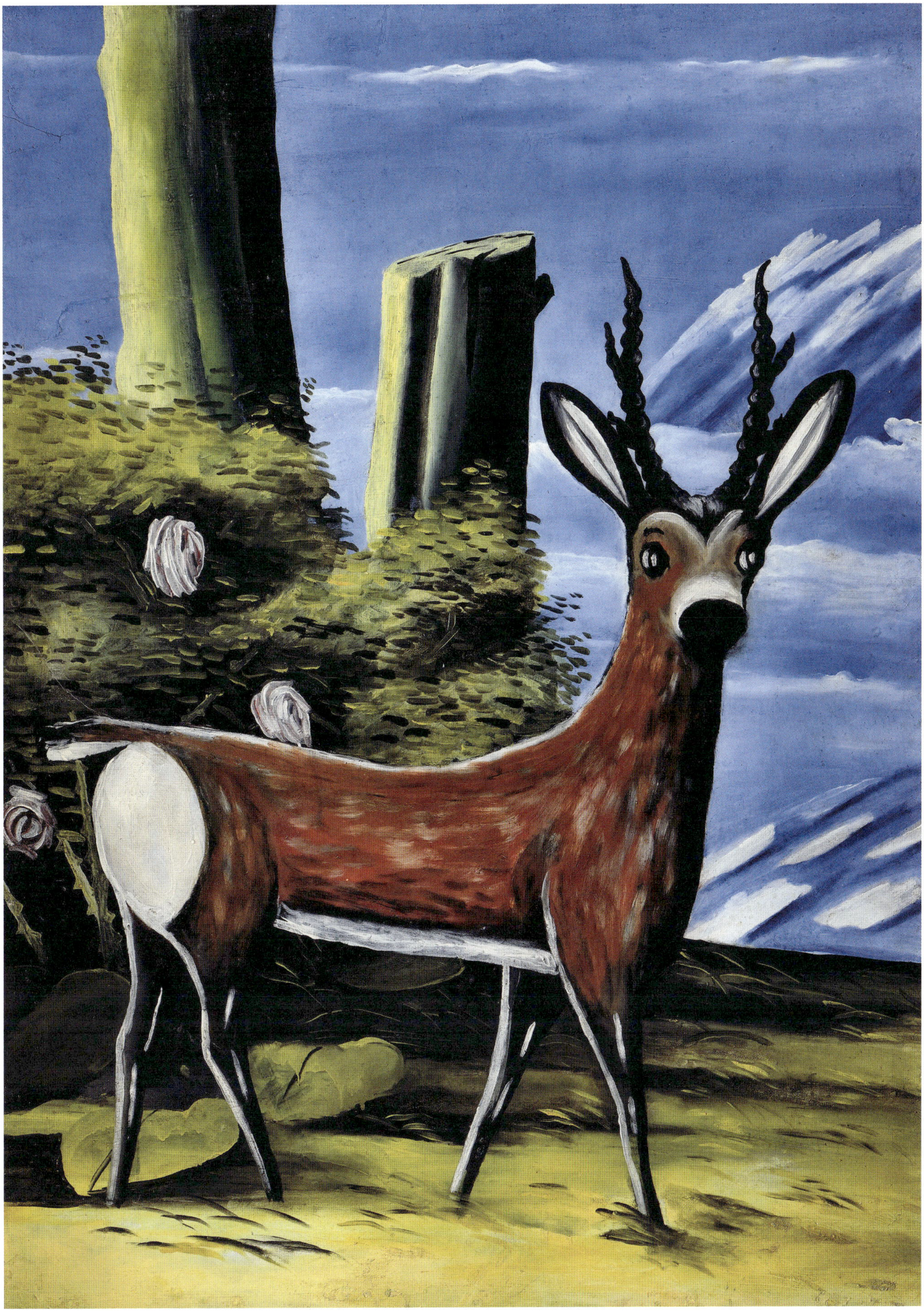

BLACK LIGHT

FOREWORD

POUL ERIK TØJNER

I Her name is Margarita, the woman on the cover of this catalogue – and she's looking at you across a distance of over a hundred years. How can she know that you're right there? She can't, of course, but the artist – Niko Pirosmani – has reckoned on your attendance. It's there in the image like a watermark. The viewer is anticipated – not just as someone looking at the picture, but as someone being looked at. In this case, by Margarita.

She's an actress. It says so in Russian in the lower left corner. She has given what she can to those who were there, there in that room – right up until this moment, now, as she stands with a bouquet of flowers in her hand. That's what you get once you've performed your act – that and the applause. Is she on a stage? The nature scene behind her resembles a backdrop, and the painter has placed her completely flat in the picture, at its bottom edge. Then there are the birds, golden sparrows, moving in the other direction. They're there in the air, but not as ornaments. All of a sudden the sky is open, this blue space, this angel's exit – because standing there she sure is angelic, almost a figure of Christ. And while we're here, look at the tree stumps, which are like something out of the annals of Byzantine iconography, as the 'colour' of the sparrows perhaps is too – from the same place the Danish artist Per Kirkeby (1938-2018) frequented in his later work. Truncated, they're like luminous hearts in the landscape's earthen gloom; there's not much growth here, only the cut flowers. There is a little, though, at the edge of the horizon, where the white wind gently rustles the flora. The bouquet seems to be brimming with eyebrows where the artist's hand has been a little loose, as it has in the tulle of her skirt and in the floral fringe of her décolletage. In Margarita's face, though, all calm is restored. She's looking at you. And it's you who blinks first. Not her.

II What *sort* of picture is this, Margarita? And it's entirely deliberate that we dwell a little on the anatomy of the painting before we come to the man behind it, the self-taught Niko Pirosmani (1862/63-1918). Not least since, in my case, this is where it began, and because for visitors to the Louisiana it most certainly cannot begin anywhere else – because no one here has heard of Niko Pirosmani, from Georgia – where no one has *not* heard of him. In Tbilisi he is an omnipresence, even though he and some 50 of his masterpieces are here 50 now in Humlebæk.
Is this picture about nature? Unlikely. There's a little too much staffage, perhaps with a nod to art history – the icons, as mentioned, or Albrecht Dürer's (1471-1528) grassy bank. Already at this point I can divulge a fundamental flaw in any theory regarding Pirosmani: we have no idea. Is it a sensitive portrait of a particular person? Yes and no. It has its caption – 'Actress. Margarita' – so yes. But is it here, in its fine strokes of characterisation, that the painting reveals its power? No. Not at all.

The painting's power comes from the presence it has as an image. It speaks to anyone who passes in front of it – and that's essentially how it is with Pirosmani. The power of his paintings lies in the way they function, the same as it is with Andy Warhol (1928-1987) – if you will forgive my lack of poetics and this skimming of pebbles over history. Even if Pirosmani is acclaimed as the painter of the Georgian soul, culture and folklore, there isn't the slightest clue for archaeologists to pursue. This is modern art that understands what it means for something to *be*, regardless of its archaic expression – or rather, precisely by virtue of that expression.

Never change a winning team – from tavern signs to church frescoes, Pirosmani knew perfectly well what his craft was capable of: contact! Or as the unobservant would be reminded: 'de te fabula' – the story's about you – the principle behind every parable.

Margarita stands there, and you stand here. Pirosmani isn't the only one to master this gaze, this glimpse of the eye, but his art, his work, refines it and does so in so many different ways. His work is infused with an immediacy – but that isn't quite the right word. It veers too far towards 'spontaneity', which is entirely inaccurate because every brushstroke in these paintings is calculated. The words 'naive', 'naivism' and 'primitive' put us on the wrong foot too. Then there is 'confrontation', which has its roots in the words 'face' or 'forehead' – thus actually face to face or forehead to forehead – but this is a little too conflictual. So we'll stick with the word 'direct', as in 'without an intermediary'. No distractions, perhaps not even any interpretation at all – the sign painter's very measure of success, by the way, since if a sign requires interpretation – well, the ship has already sailed.

III Niko Pirosmani was in fact a sign painter – just like Edward Hopper (1882-1967) or Ed Ruscha (born 1937) were too – and that's one of the few things about him we do know. He lived in the latter half of the 19th century, but only revealed himself as an artist in the first two decades of the 20th. He was born in the countryside and spent his early years there; he later came to Tbilisi, the capital of Georgia, which was flush with cosmopolitan energy, poetry, opera and salon culture, and he lived and worked there as an urban wayfarer with his painting kit in a suitcase.

Jobs: everything from walls to pictures to signs. And he was proficient. He painted quickly, but without yielding entirely to conventional wishes – throughout his work, his line is his own, he has stated.

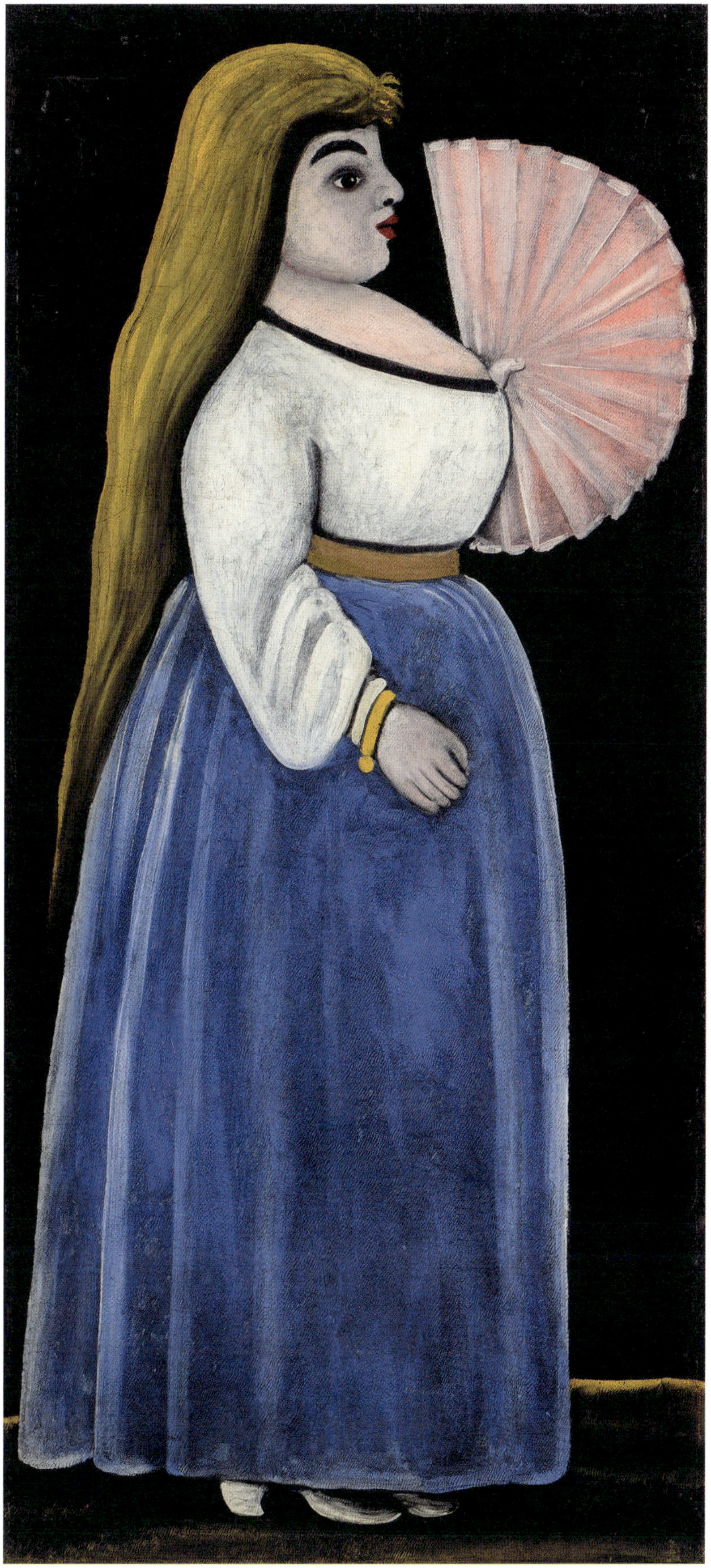

And you notice it immediately: a formidably assured hand, original in his cropping – clear in his communication, we would say today. Few colours, and he used the back of a black oilcloth as a canvas (his own invention, not just ordinary oilcloth), which lends his colours a fascinating and utterly unique lucidity – black light with a luminescence that sometimes resembles that of stained glass. And it works.

All confirmed biographical facts about him can be written on the back of a napkin, but in his paintings we see that he was an attentive observer of and participant in Tbilisian life. In many ways his art is applied art, at least at first glance; he painted because he needed the money, board and lodging included, but also because his clients needed his pictures – for decoration, as we say, or more correctly: in order to preserve the lives being lived, as icons of the fellowship of peoples and cultures, for mutual edification and collective memory. Nothing is private with Pirosmani; all of it is all we share in common when we look at each other and the world around us. His paintings are thus not just about communities; communities also form around them in the spaces where they hang – not unlike the imagery of the Christian church, which is absolutely central to Georgian culture and was there from very early on in ecclesiastical history. It's the same with Margarita, who calls upon you with her gaze: when Pirosmani depicts men gathered around a table for a feast, there's a spot for you on the other side.

IV His biography, then, does not drag out with the protraction of a Tolstoy novel. The succinctness of the short story suffices, and readers can learn about his circumstances in a little more detail elsewhere in this catalogue. On the other hand, it must be said that this biographical minimalism has opened the door for an anecdotal and mythologising maximalism, so that – similary to our relationship with an artist like Vincent van Gogh (1853-1890) – it can be difficult to approach Pirosmani's paintings merely as paintings. The legend mounts up, and does so in inverse proportion to the bedrock of concrete facts.

ORTACHALA BELLE WITH A FAN

We do know one thing, however, and that is how Pirosmani entered art history, and that in contrast to Van Gogh, it occurred while he was still alive. He was discovered as an artist *by* artists. In the second decade of the 20th century, avant-garde circles in St. Petersburg and Moscow oriented themselves away from the salon aesthetics of the academies and looked towards expressions, artistic practices and traditions that might subvert the stiff tastes of the period. Artists like Mikhail Larionov (1881-1964), Natalia Goncharova (1881-1962) and others – a certain Wassily Kandinsky (1866-1944) – mastered a balancing of the books between abstraction and folk art that managed to throttle the life out of academicism, from the bottom up, so to speak, in a kind of pincer movement.

In 1913, a handful of Pirosmani's works wound up at the renowned *Mishen* (Target) exhibition. It's really not difficult to understand why, once one casts aside the art-political interest in self-taught culture, in the applied arts. Several of Pirosmani's pictures are so simplified – but in the most elegant way, namely through conscious artistic choices – that you don't have to fiddle much with the knobs before they sort of bleed over into abstraction, or at least into a Cézanne-like combination of basic geometric forms, cones, circles, etc. – Paul Cézanne (1839-1906), who also painted the familiar out towards the frontiers of abstraction.

See, for example, the wonderful painting *Ortachala Belle with a Fan* (p. 5). During that time, she was presumably known to the guests at the Tbilisian garden restaurant Eldorado as a 'fallen woman' and elsewhere more optimistically as a 'pleasure girl' (the pleasure, naturally, never being on the woman's behalf). She is enshrined in the pictorial space, and yes, she embodies it with a statuesque presence and an iridescence that is utterly beautiful. Pirosmani has given her dignity, and to that extent the picture derives its power from the balance between its elements and channels this back to the woman as one of her qualities.

We don't know who she is, but her body – unlike the expropriation to which it has been subjected – inspires respect and admiration. She is at ease and, perhaps for the first time, almost inviolable. Later in history, when the Stalinist regime took hold and cut off Pirosmani from the ever-dwindling circle of acceptable company, the (art) police would presumably argue that the picture lacked class analysis and promoted a spurious humanism.

V The avant-garde's feeling for Pirosmani is understandable. His pictures take effect – without taking tangents. And they take effect on the world around them in the same way as the paintings of *Le Douanier*, France's Henri Rousseau (1844-1910) – to whom Pirosmani is often compared. He, too, had a sudden breakthrough among the contemporary avant-garde and then with the surrealists. But whereas Rousseau works with the stuff of dreams, almost like René Magritte (1898-1967) would later do, there is a different presence to Pirosmani's pictures. And presence is a key word in Pirosmani's universe, the reason why we're obliged to take another tour around the sign painter and his sign, though without making an explanatory mechanism of the artist's socio-economic (mis)fortunes. It is more a question of the picture's function in society.

A sign is a means of orientation – 'Where am I, where am I going?' – and there are thus at least two kinds of signs in the world, one that promises Café Paradise around the corner, 300 metres away, and one telling you that you have arrived. In other words, some signs tell you what *isn't* there while others simply put a label to a fact. Pirosmani painted plenty of the latter; often on tin until it fell into short supply during the First World War, and then on wood – only a few have been preserved. Pirosmani's signs are entirely conventional declarations of time and space – 'This is where you are and this and that are available' – but well painted and well composed. He was the best. Because of course the signs were borne by a greater artistic talent, even though Pirosmani had no compunction about putting chalk to a wall from time to time.

For the last 15 years of his life he (apparently) had no fixed abode, meaning he lived hand to mouth – and yet he used the finest English colours it was possible to obtain.

As a social functionary (as it would later be known), through his presentation of types, of scenes from daily life, of festivities and especially in his few, notably large, multi-episodic panoramas where several things are happening all at once and in conspicuous proportion, he helped put words and images to popular custom. A man with a camel, a waterboy, a ferryman, a woman with a tankard of beer, poor folk with children and rich folk without, a widow on the move – some were or became genuine typologies, others had a precursor in biography. It must be clear to anyone who saw our exhibition *The Cold Gaze* (2022-2023) featuring German photographer August Sander (1876-1964) how, in his delicate balance of universalism and local colour, Pirosmani also does his part to plot human geography. So it's not all intense personal presence like it is with Margarita, the actress with whom Pirosmani was reportedly so smitten that he bought every bouquet of flowers in Tbilisi and strewed them across the street to her 'hotel', which, unfortunately, she had just vacated. Perhaps. She was French – and she had gone. But by Pirosmani's hand, she returned.

VI Nevertheless it is this particular feature – presence in Pirosmani – that holds us in its grasp, estranged as we may be from Georgian culture and tradition.
And that holds true whether it is animals that Pirosmani has painted, or people.
The animals in particular – there are many, and they are often wild animals rather than the domesticated livestock of this nation of agriculture – seem to thwart the near-ubiquitous urge to shape Georgian national identity through the application or interpretation of paintings.

It isn't that one doesn't understand this urge in a nation that has tasted so few moments of independence over the past several hundred years, during which time Persian, Ottoman, Russian and Soviet administrations have ruled Georgia.

Add to that the combination of Pirosmani's realistic simplicity and our relative ignorance of the artist's inner life and intent, and the material invites a good deal of interpretative licence: is his magnificent painting of an eagle clutching a hare in an aggressor's iron grip (p. 16) an emblem of Tsarist Russia's dominance over Georgia during Pirosmani's time? It's a possibility. But an eagle and a hare are also just an eagle and a hare – and strangely enough it is the latter interpretation, the less flamboyant of the two, that means the picture lives on as more than just a historical puzzle.

Is Pirosmani's only city prospect, *The Tiflis Funicular* (p. 59) – out of a total of around 200 surviving images (from the 2,000 or so that he probably painted) – just a picture of the funicular passing from Tbilisi up to a church atop Mount Mtatsminda, or is it a religious allegory, a Jacob's ladder, a longing for heaven in the itinerant artist, who in all likelihood was familiar with church history and Persian portraiture and had seen reproductions of European art? And who furthermore sometimes felt like such a stranger among people that his exotic and utterly mistaken giraffe was taken to be a self-portrait even in his own time. It graces the back cover of this catalogue and thus forms part of this impossible parallelogram of love – what is an angel going to do with a giraffe? And yes, it is weeping – Pirosmani placed a tear in the corner of its eye.

VII In Pirosmani's world, animals have lives of their own. With the exception of the giraffe, he doesn't humanise them in a possessive sense. They are portrayed unsentimentally, but he paints them as though they were people in their own right. There's nothing in the animal portraits concerning how *we* see them – they are looking at us. And they often fill the entire surface of the image, which lends them a monumentality familiar from the churches of the late Middle Ages, with which Pirosmani was also acquainted. They are, however, never heroised; there's a strangely serene sensibility present, which here and there is also sustained by the strange light that the black canvas emits. Even level-headed German art historians this side of the millennium use the word 'magic' to describe what they see. It's rather unique.

Pirosmani's artistic approach has been compared to that of the Renaissance artist Giotto (c. 1267-1337), and now we're down in that corner of the field it's no surprise that Francis of Assisi (1182-1226) also gets mentioned as a kind of reference for his perspective on nature. These are, of course, mere tendrils sprouted with the sole intention of being able to say more about the work than the few words to which the paintings themselves seem to give rise. In the animal pictures in particular there is a wonderful equilibrium, as though they're in a world different from our own – and perhaps it's at this point that one has to give Evgenii Kriger, a contemporary critic, his due for writing of the avant-garde exhibition in 1913 – 'Pirosmani, impossible not to love'.

PIROSMANI AT LOUISIANA

I first saw Niko Pirosmani's works in Vienna, at Albertina's exhibition in 2018. I took the paintings in with the curiosity awoken when one is faced with something that's entirely new, though actually old. Since then, we at the Louisiana have had many discussions about all the things we don't know and haven't shown because they lie beyond our immediate cultural sphere.

When Sam Keller, my colleague and good friend for many years, also director of the Fondation Beyeler in Riehen just outside Basel, suddenly suggested over a year ago – in the middle of a conversation about something completely different – that Beyeler and the Louisiana should put on a Pirosmani exhibition, Louisiana jumped at the chance. And we travelled to Tbilisi, assisted by Daniel Baumann, the director of Kunsthalle Zürich, who knows Georgia and who has been involved in the curatorial collaboration between Sam Keller and myself.

The material was fantastic and it was likely that nobody or just a handful of people at these latitudes knew of this master from Georgia – so it had the potential to be an eye-opener for everyone. That sealed it, and now it's our visitors' turn.

In Tbilisi we were met with immense generosity and an exceptional commitment to the exhibition. Almost all the works come from the National Gallery of Georgia. In that regard I would like to say

THANKS TO Thea Tsulukiani, Minister of Culture, Sports and Youth of Georgia; Kakha Sikharulidze, First Deputy Minister of Culture, Sports and Youth of Georgia; Nika Akhalbedashvili, Director of the Georgian Fine Arts Museum, National Gallery and Sighnaghi Historical – Ethnographic Museum, First Deputy Director of the LEPL Georgian National Museum.

Salome Zourabichvili, President of Georgia; Konstantine Natsvlishvili, Adviser to the President of Georgia on Culture, Science and Education for facilitating our visit to Tbilisi.

Adrian Barsan, Founder, INFINITART FOUNDATION; Mahsan Tajik, Director, INFINITART FOUNDATION.

Sam Keller, Director, Fondation Beyeler, and his team: Daniel Baumann, Guest Curator, who has also contributed an interview to this catalogue; Regula Moser, Associate Curator; Markus Gross, Chief Conservator; Barbara Weber, Head of Exhibition Services; Irakliy Purtskhvanidze, Advisor, Fondation Beyeler.

Kaspar Thormod, Project Associate, Louisiana Museum of Modern Art.

The artists Thea Djordjadze, Andro Wekua, Dana Schutz, Mamma Andersson and Tal R for their participation in Louisiana Channel's film *Five Artists on Niko Pirosmani*.

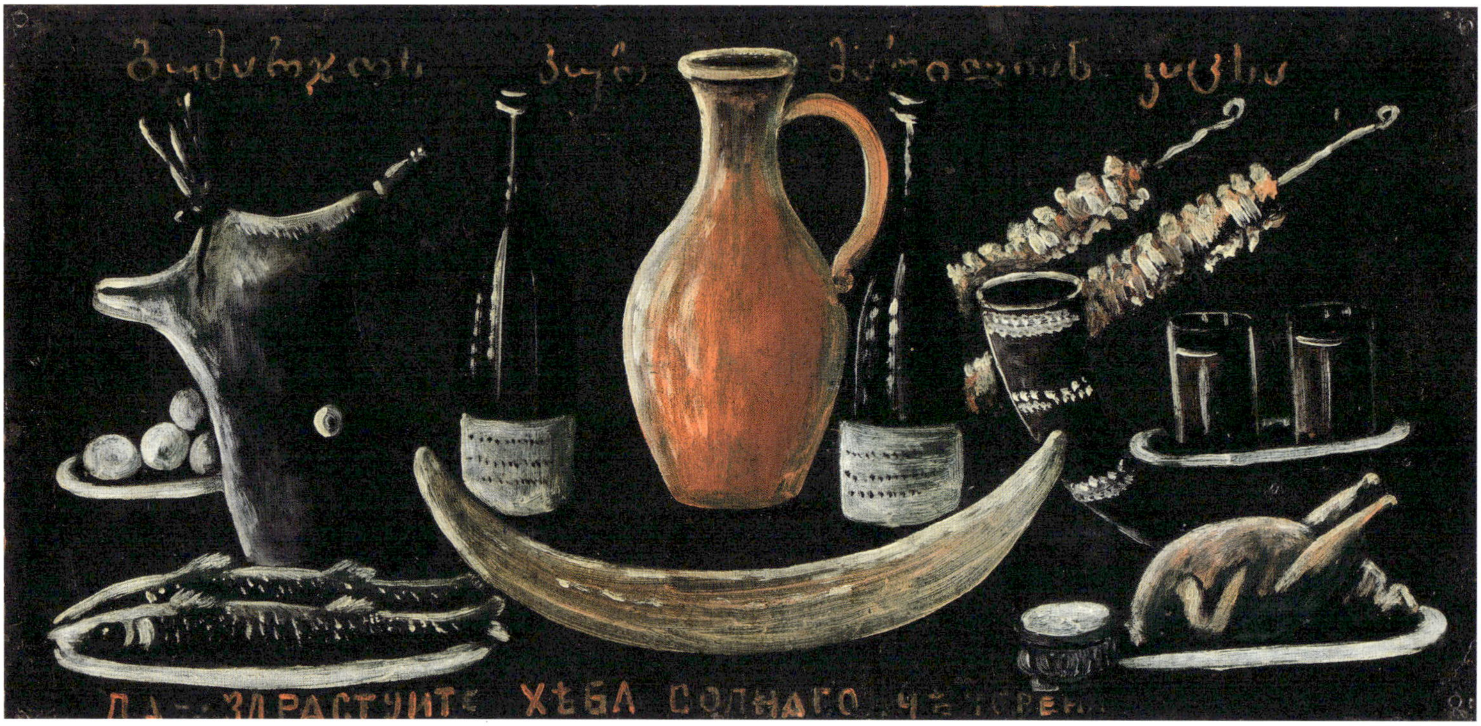

STILL LIFE
>
YELLOW LION SEJANT

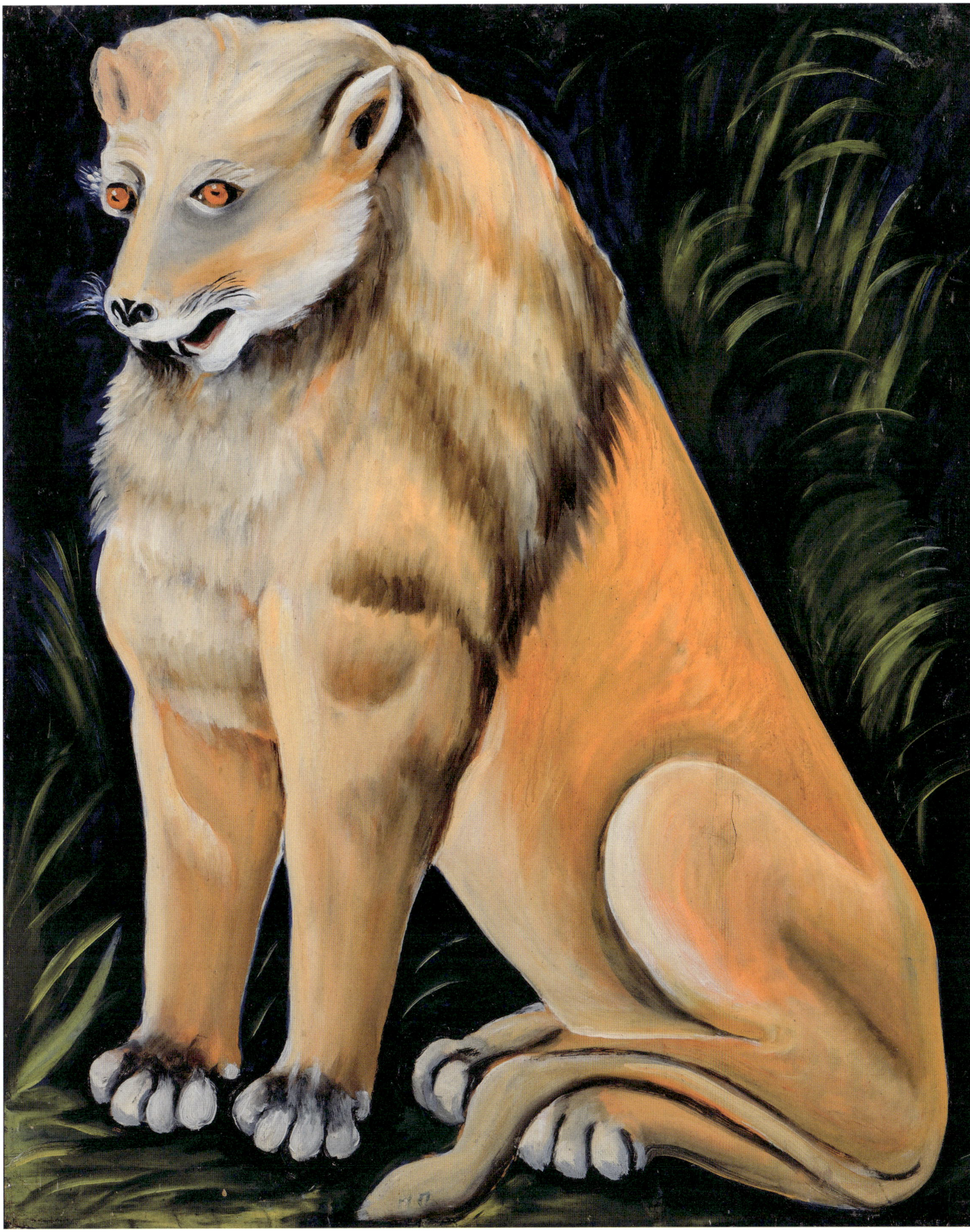

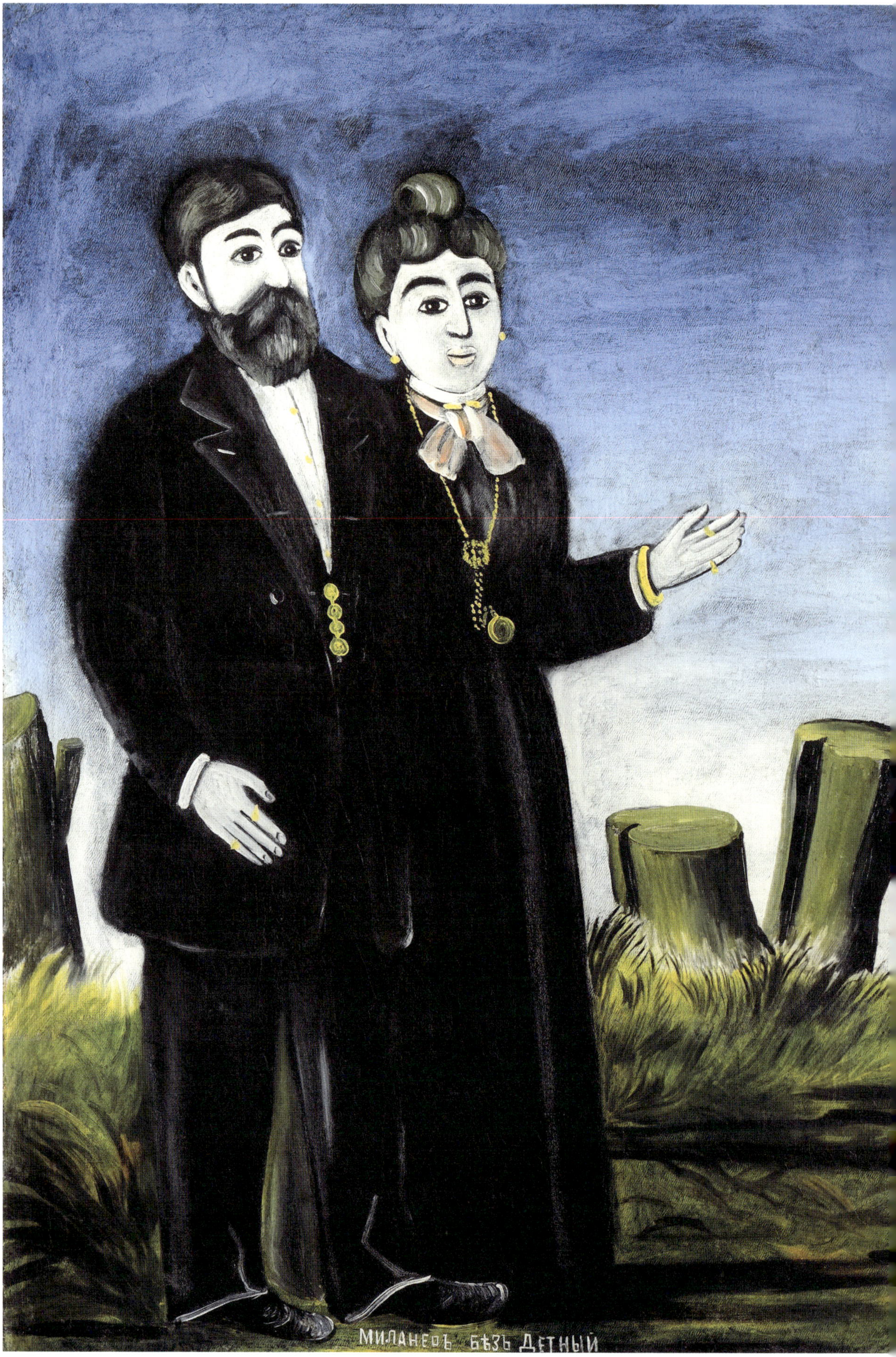

THE CHILDLESS MILLIONAIRE AND POOR WOMAN WITH HER CHILDREN

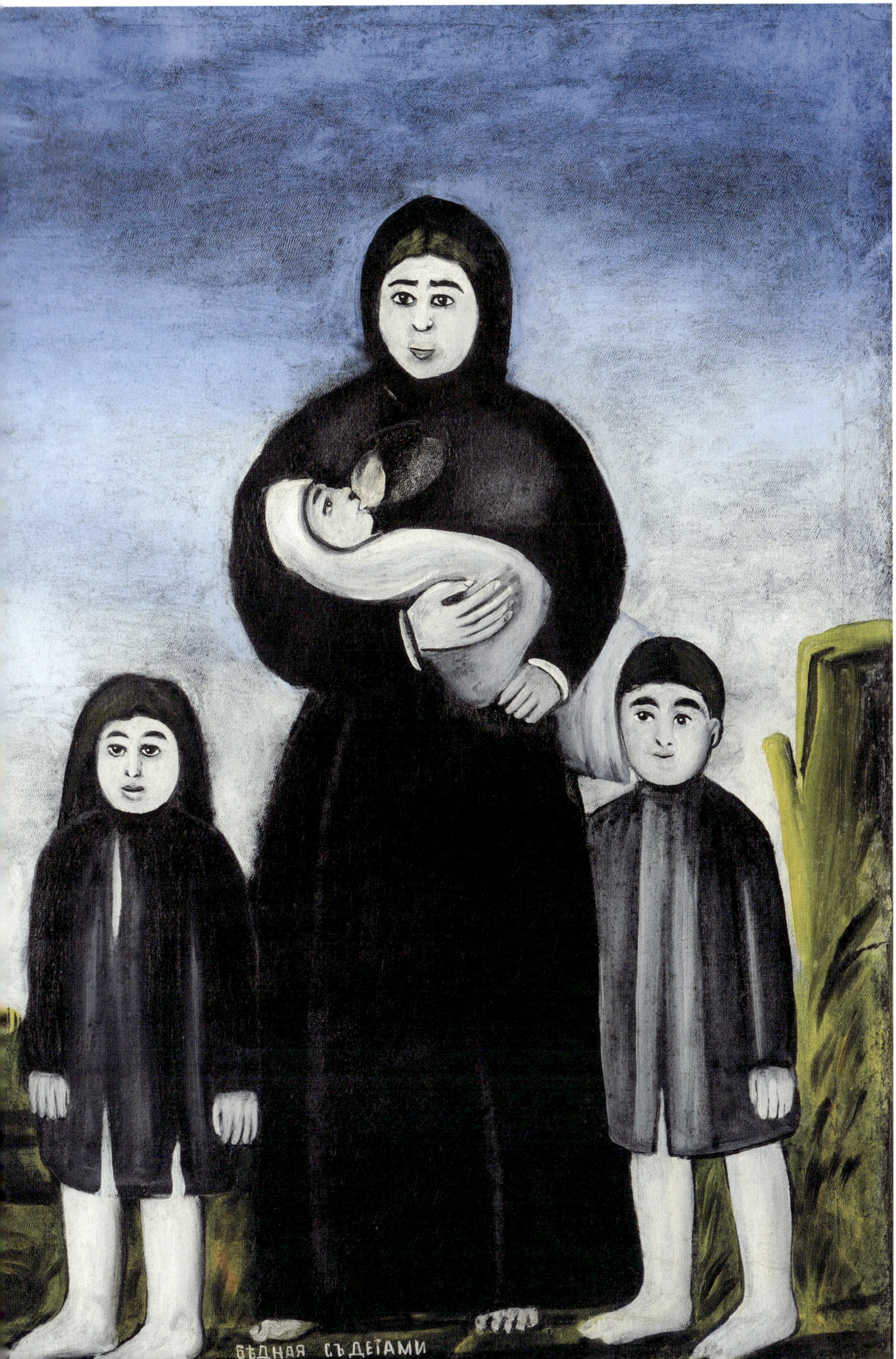
БѢДНАЯ СЪ ДЕТАМИ

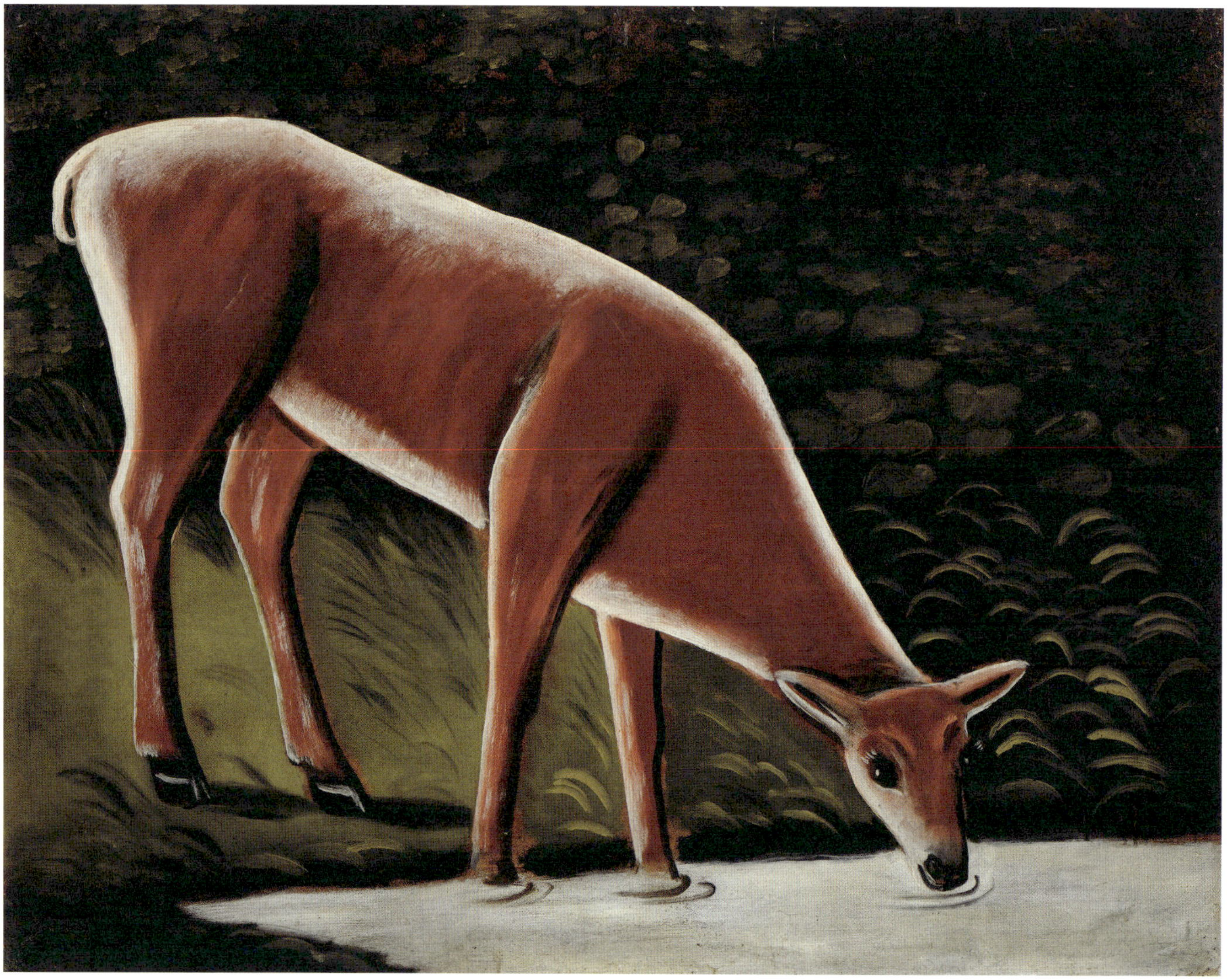

ROE DEER BY A STREAM

>

BEAR ON A MOONLIT NIGHT

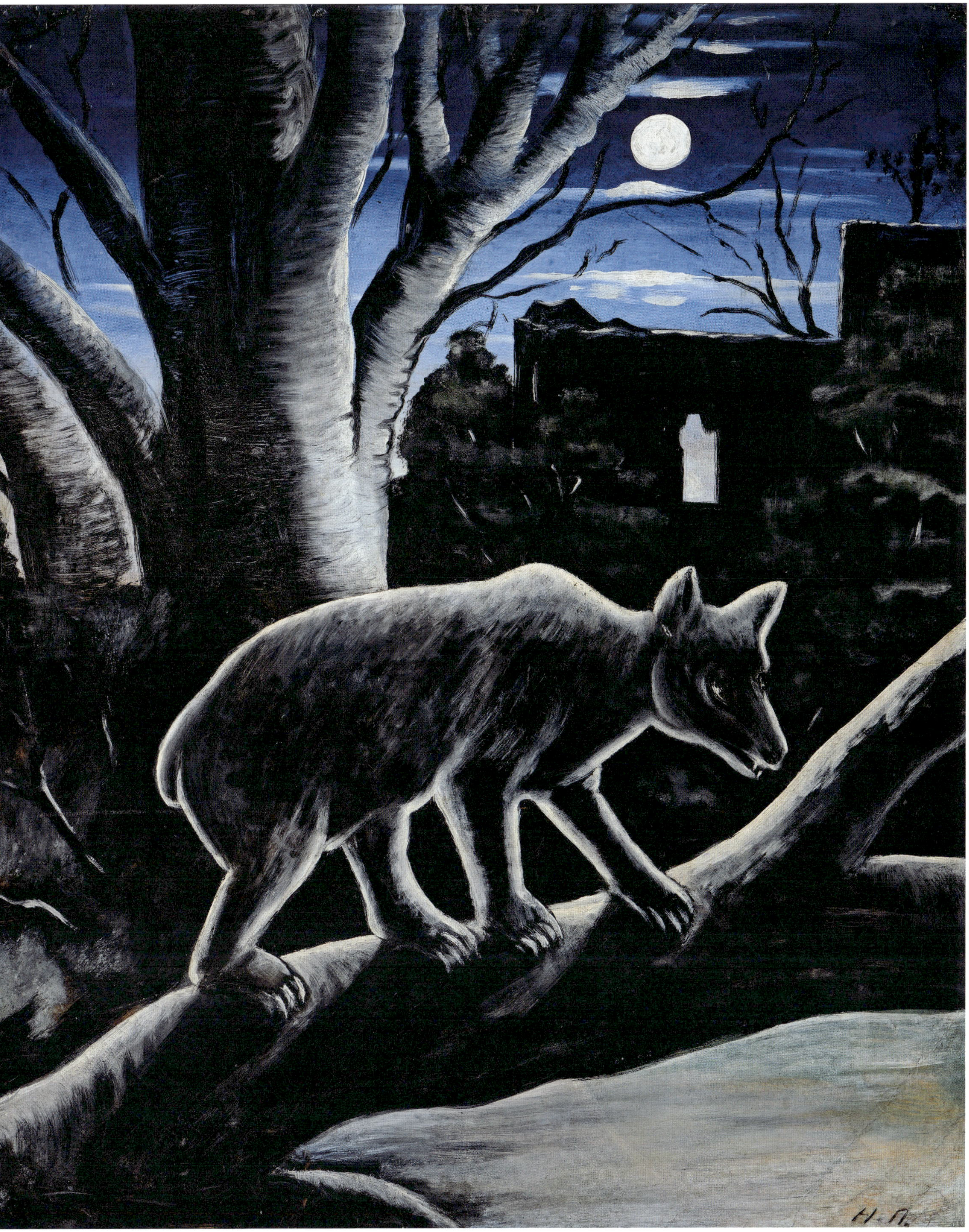
Н. П.

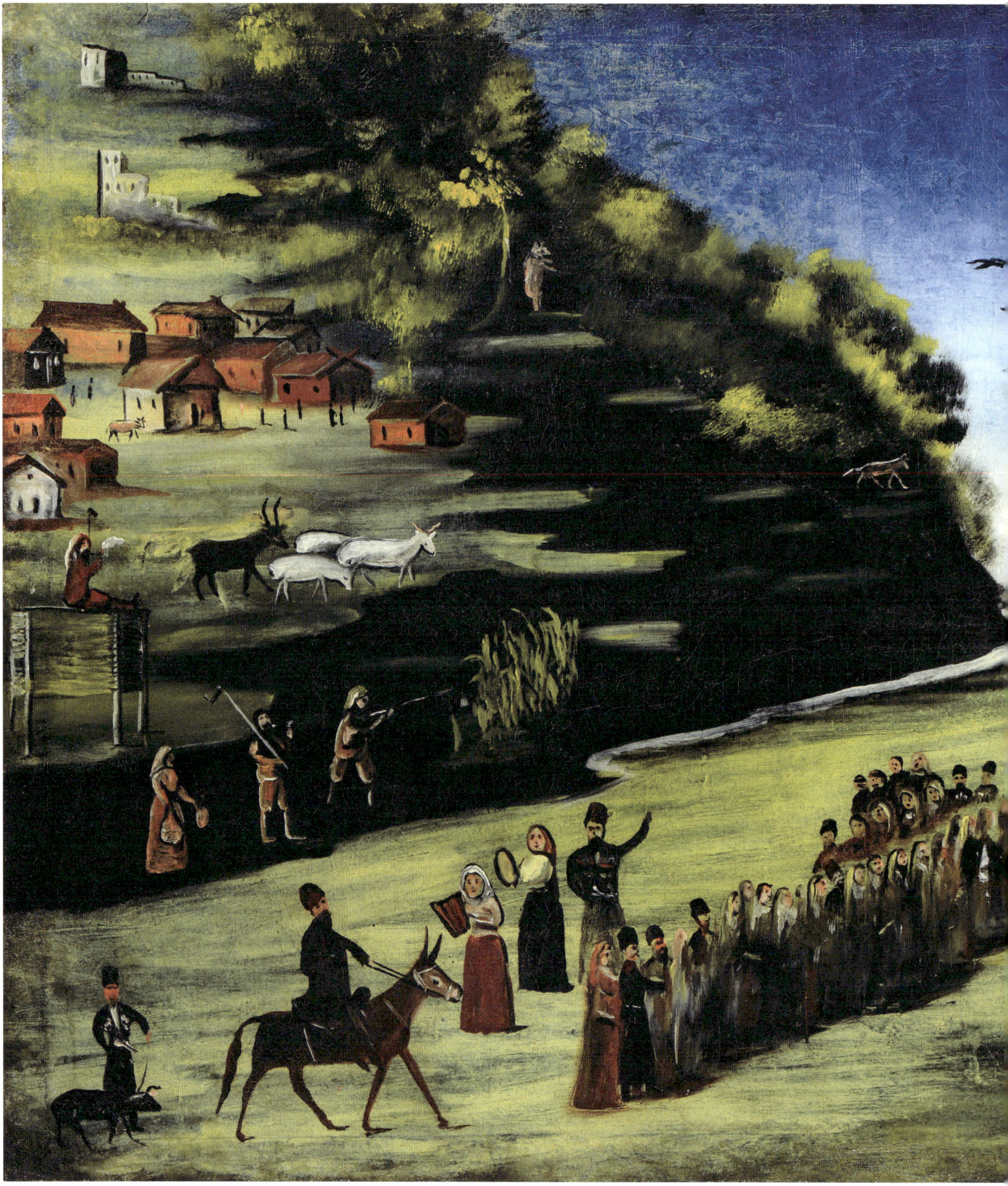

FÊTE ON THE BANK OF THE TSKHENISTSKALI RIVER

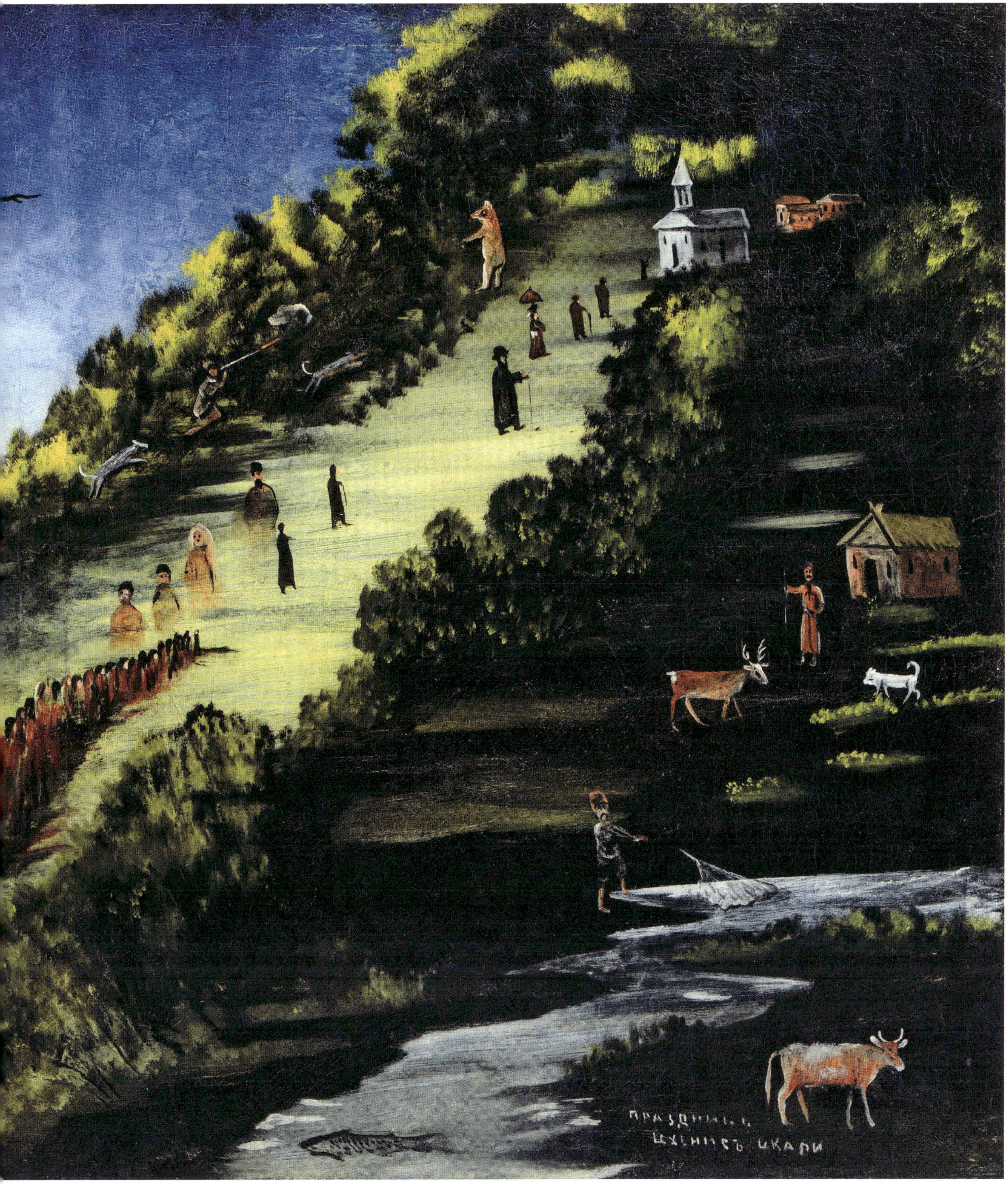
ПРАЗДНИКЪ
ЦХЕНИСЪ ЦКАЛИ

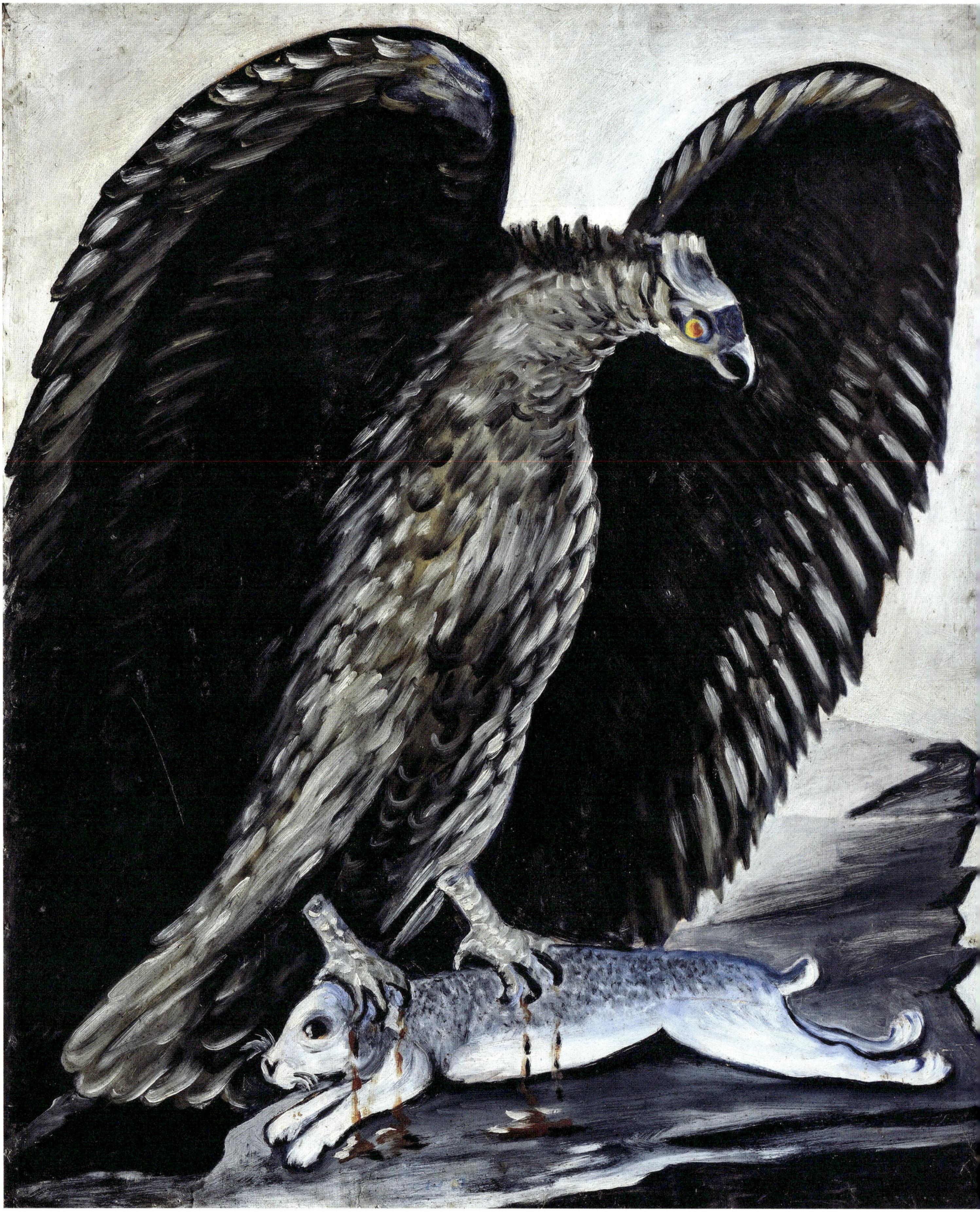

ROOSTER AND BROODER WITH CHICKS

<

EAGLE SEIZING A HARE

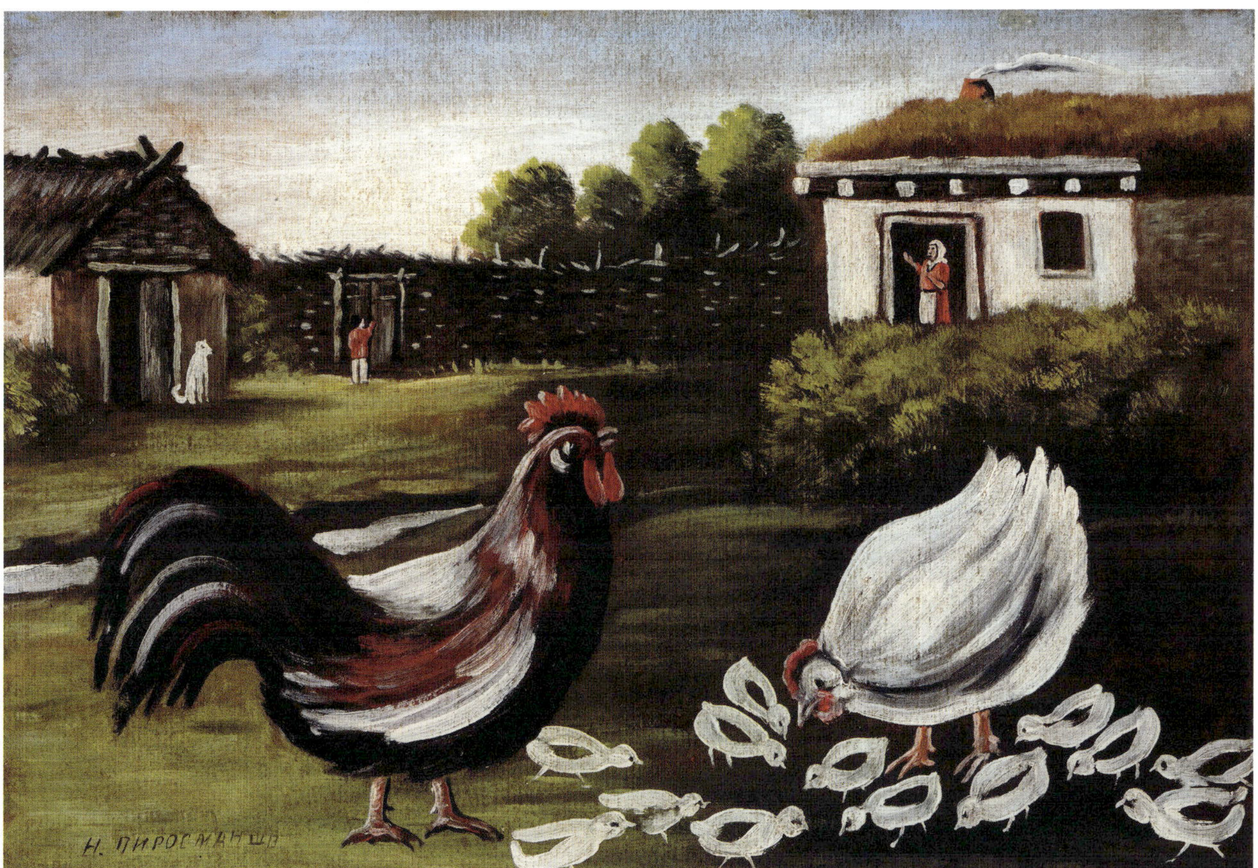

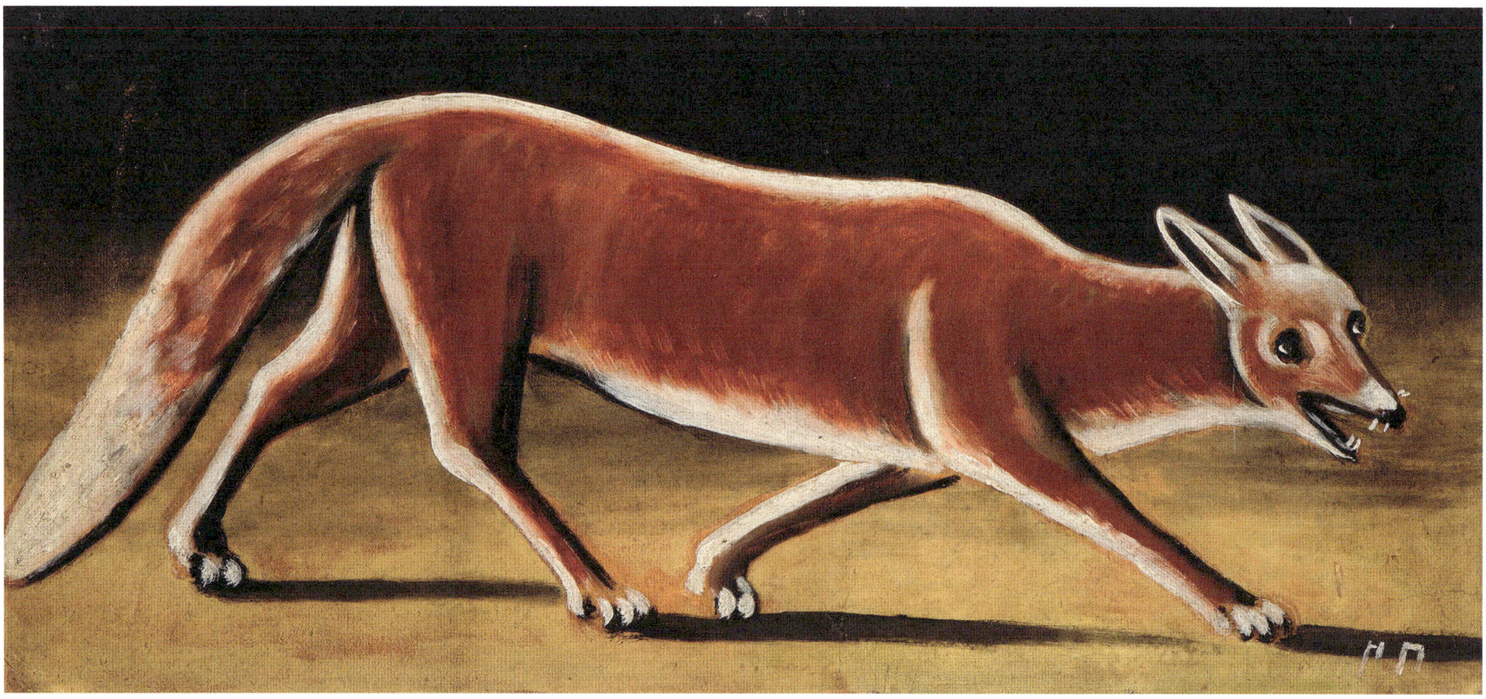

FOX
>
GIRL WITH A TOY BALLOON

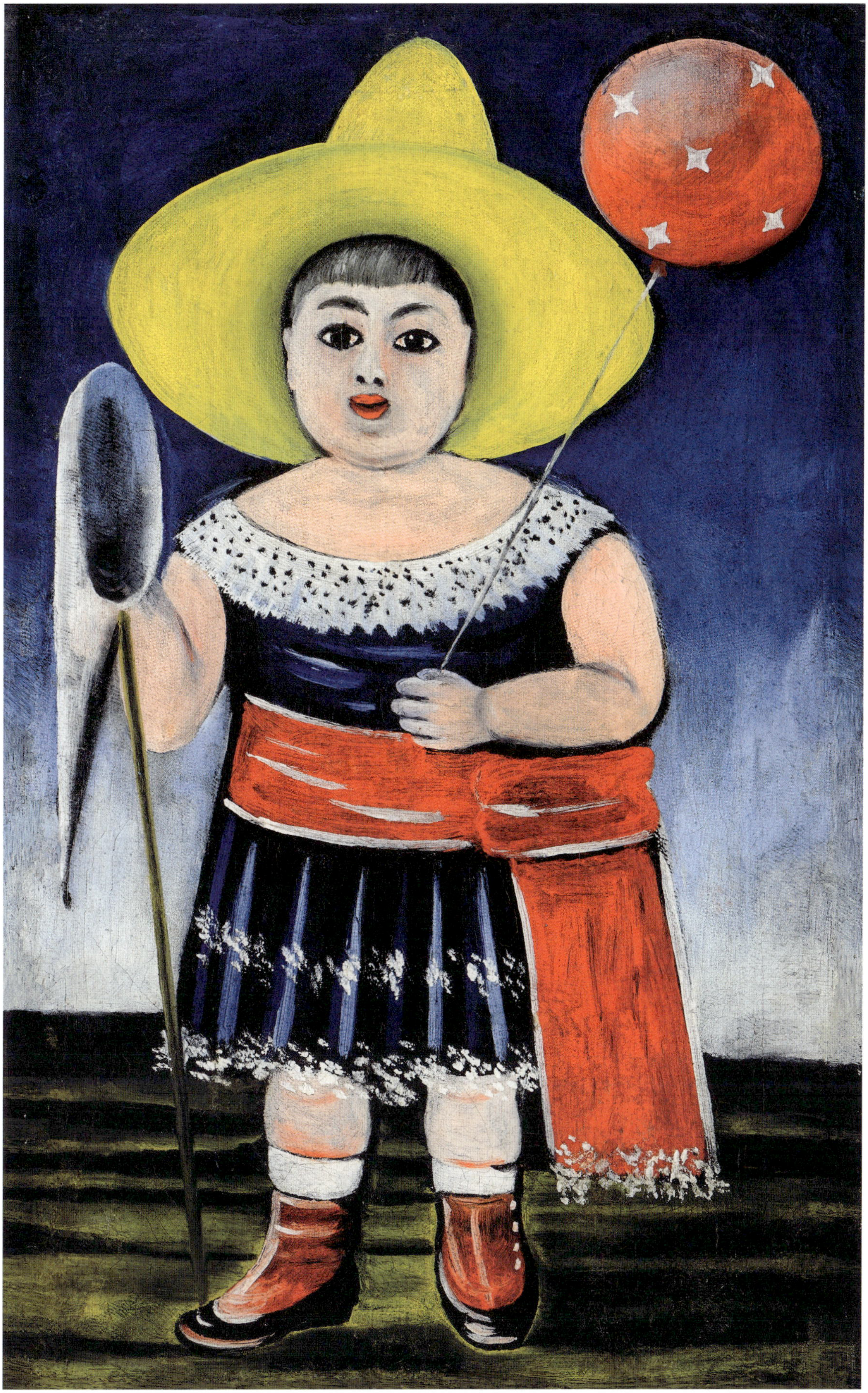

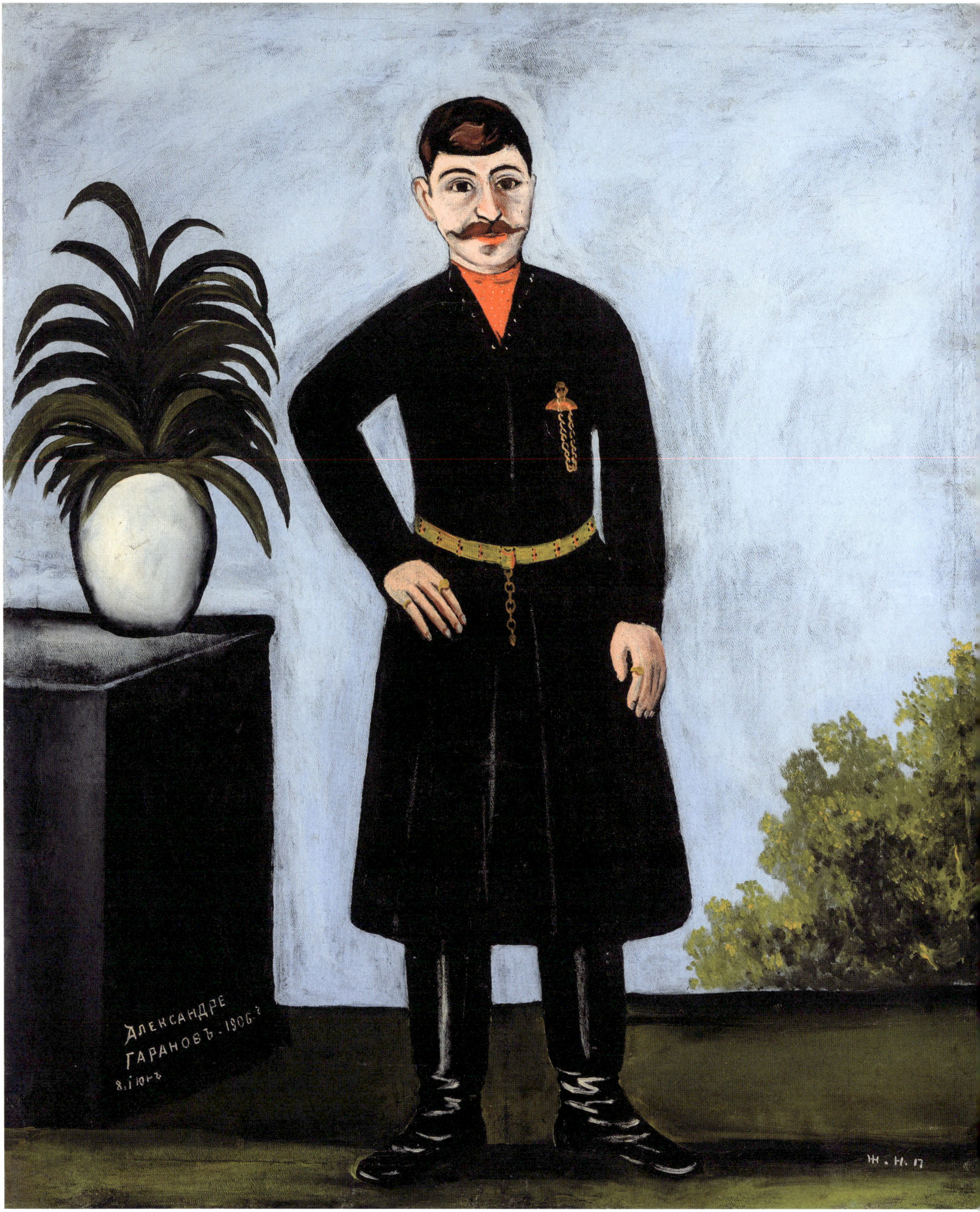
АЛЕКСАНДРЕ
ГАРАНОВЪ - 1906 г
Ж. Н. 17

WHITE SOW WITH PIGLETS

<

PORTRAIT OF ALEXANDER GARANOV. 1906

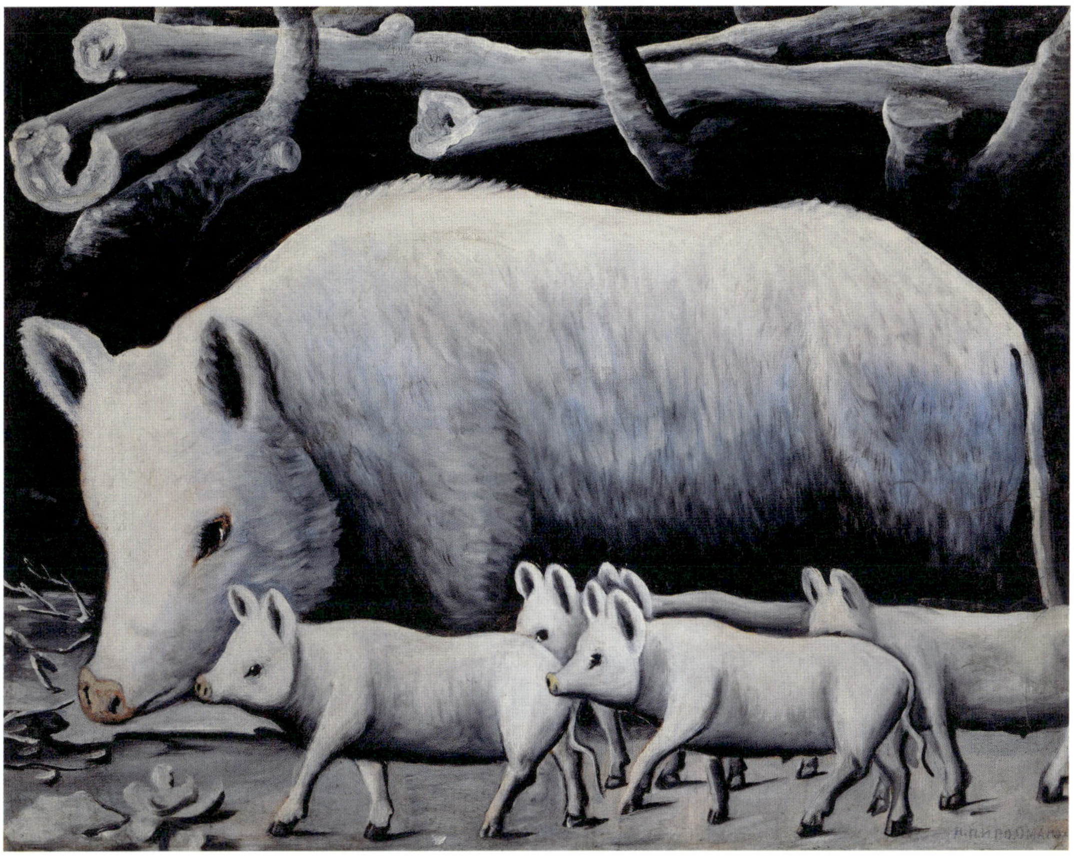

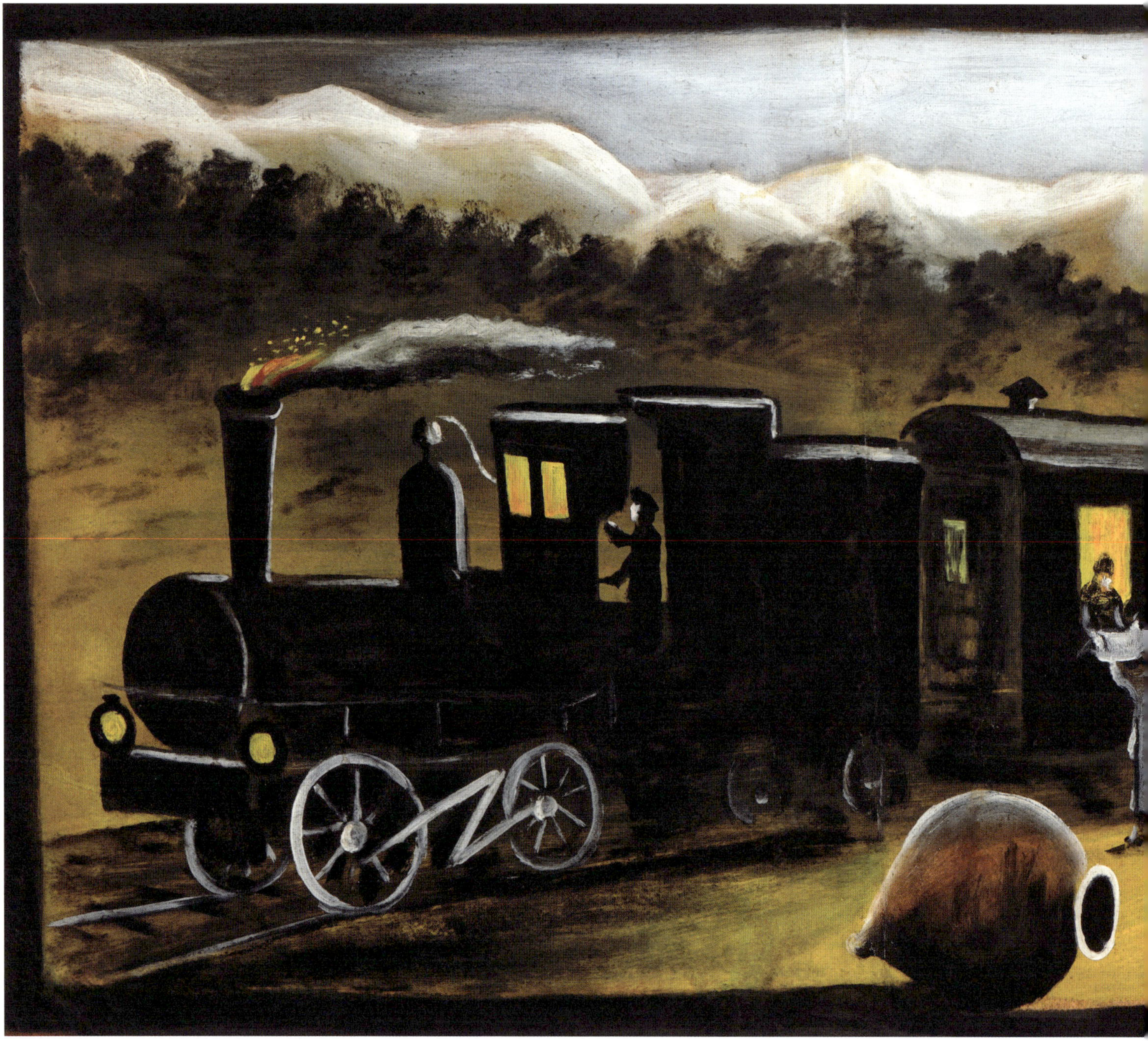

THE KAKHETIAN TRAIN

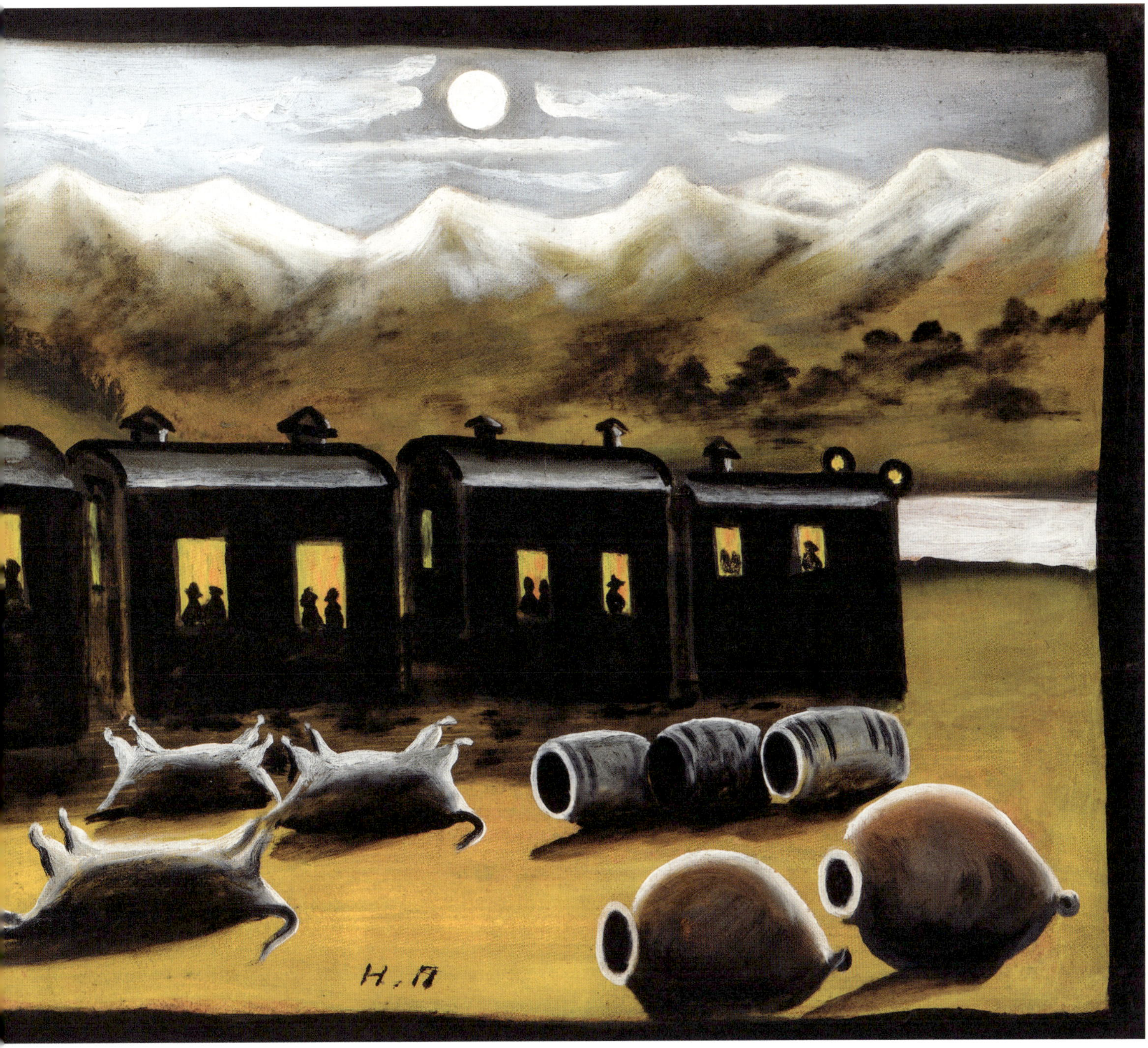
Н.П

I You have travelled through Europe, across the Aegean and the Black Sea, and now your steamer has finally arrived at the Georgian port city of Batumi. It is early summer and already warm, and although you are exhausted, you feel like one of the Argonauts finally reaching the land which, for ancient historians, was the easternmost edge of the known world, where Jason searched for the golden fleece.[1] But Batumi is not the picturesque port city of your imagination. Its buildings are modern, apart from a handful of examples from the Ottoman era, which ended a little over 30 years ago. Its streets are broad and non-cobbled. The oil industry has left its mark, especially since the pipeline from Baku was commissioned. You catch the stench of crude oil from the refineries. It is a disappointment.

On the way to your hotel you set down your luggage and watch the dock workers, known as *mushas*, hauling sacks and barrels ashore. You can't help but think that perhaps you should have taken the route from the north via Russia down through the Caucasus Mountains on the Georgian Military Highway that runs along the Terek River, after all. You have read about this road, which the Russians built and improved. The snow-decked Mount Kazbek rises over 5,000 metres above it and the landscape is said to be savage and spectacular. Knut Hamsun (1859-1952) followed this route in 1899 and wrote about it in his travelogue *In Wonderland* (1903), which you have with you. However, you have chosen the western route – it has since ancient times connected Europe to Georgia and Asia.[2] It is a romantic choice pointing the way backwards, not forwards, to present-day Georgia, which has been part of the Russian Empire since 1801.

Later, as you sit on the terrace of the Hôtel d'Europe, you can see the bustle down in the harbour. Three large steamships are moored up, surrounded by a throng of smaller vessels and skiffs. The wind has turned. You have taken this trip to Georgia because you want to experience the old world which, as so many other places, is on the verge of vanishing. But here you sit with your drink alongside other guests, who are dressed, European-style, in jackets and stiff hats. It irritates you, even if you yourself are one of them. But, you tell yourself, tomorrow begins your adventure into the unknown. Tomorrow you will take the Transcaucus Railway to Tbilisi.

The next day your train passes forested hills and later vast fertile plains with fields where oxen pull ploughs through the earth.[3] And beyond it all, the mountains, always mountains. Not far from here lies the Rioni River, which the ancient Greeks knew as Phasis and along which the Argonauts sailed up to the city of Kutaisi. Your train also stops here, and while you wait on the platform, which is decked with wide wooden planks, you watch as countless oil wagons pass by. The old and the new. This is how it is here, you think. A boy wearing a floral tunic sells fruit from a platter he carries on his head. You buy a fistful of the season's first blood-red cherries and board the train again.

In addition to the Norwegian Hamsun, you have the Russian Anton Chekhov's (1860-1904) travelogue from 1888; about his encounter with the Georgian landscape he writes: "I saw the sea in all its vastness, the Caucasian shore, mountains, mountains, mountains, eucalyptuses, tea plants, waterfalls, pigs with long pointed snouts, trees wrapped in lianas like veils, clouds spending the night on the breast of giant cliffs, dolphins, fountains of oil, subterranean fires, a fireworshippers' temple, mountains, mountains, mountains."[4]

Yes, the mountains. Georgia is defined by them: the Greater Caucasus to the north and the Lesser Caucasus a little further to the south. You have read about the country's various climates: that it is humid and hot in the west, through which you are now driving, but cooler and drier in the east. And at the middle of it all is Tbilisi, the junction of an axis between west and east and south and north – a city that has been invaded and sacked 40 times in the past 1,500 years, most recently by the Shah of Iran in 1795.[5] And yet Georgia has persisted as a Christian Orthodox country, despite coming under pressure from Islam and other religions.

You try to envision how the Byzantines, Arabs, Turks, Persians, Mongols and many others have come here and left their mark on this city split in two by the Kura River, but the images slip away like the landscape beyond the window. Instead, you pull out Hamsun's *In Wonderland* again and read: "We can now see Tbilisi far away, like a collection of dots, a world apart. Smog hovers above the city. So this is Tbilisi, which so many Russian writers have written about and where so many things in the Russian novel have taken place. For a moment I feel like a youth, looking forward in wonder and hearing my heartbeat. I have the same sensation as the first time I was to hear Georg Brandes give a lecture."[6]

II The Tbilisi in which our traveller arrives in the years after 1900 has become a multicultural, political centre of the Caucasus. But it is also a city characterised by an inherent division. As early as 1847 the Russian-language newspaper *Zakavkazsky vestnik* remarked, "Tbilisi is in some sense a Janus, with one eye looking to Asia and the other to Europe."[7]

BETWEEN THE OLD AND THE NEW

IMAGINARY JOURNEY TO TBILISI IN THE YEARS AFTER 1900

KASPAR THORMOD

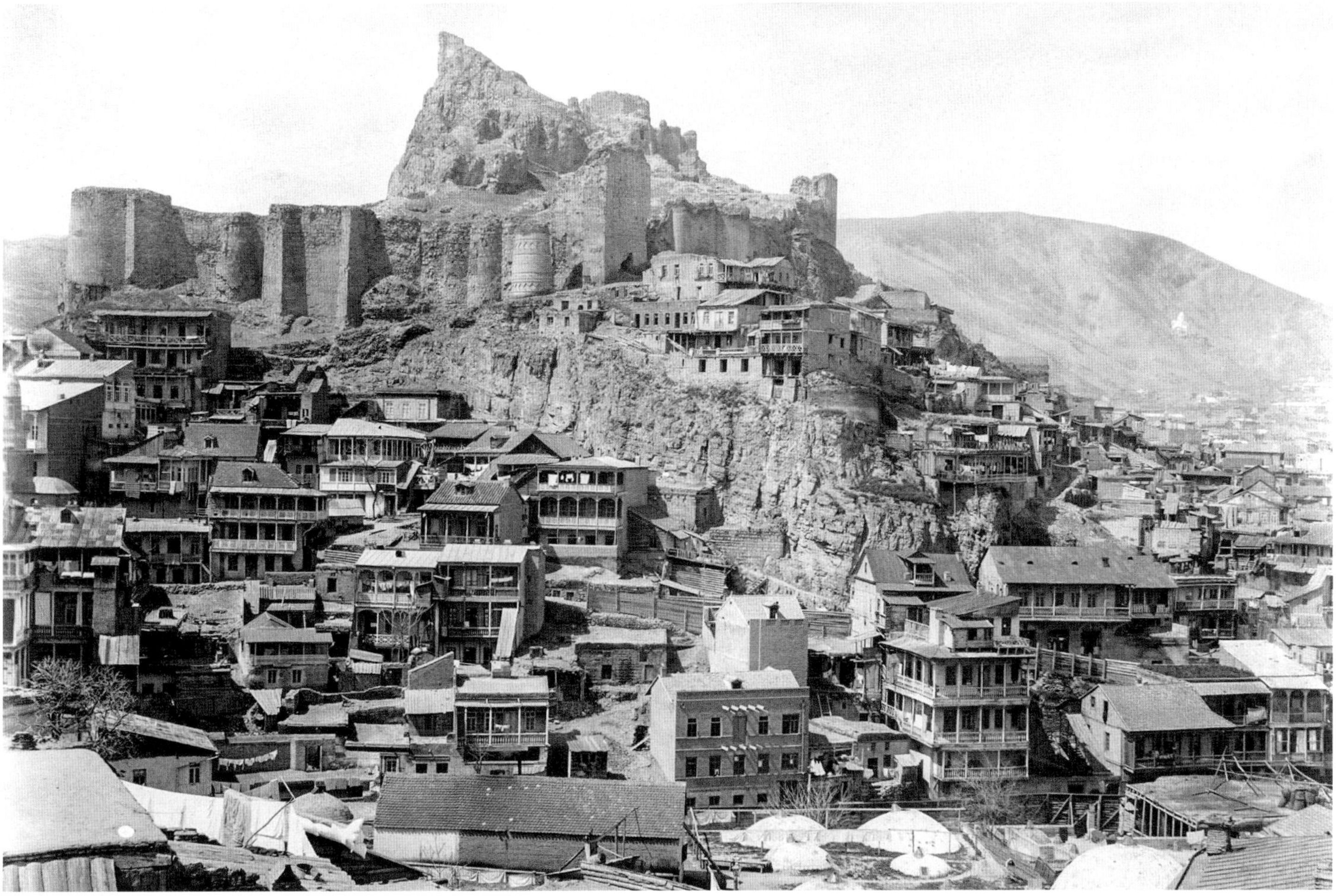

This duality was accentuated after Georgia's incorporation into the Russian Empire in 1801. In the early decades, Georgian culture was suppressed, the Russian language dominated and the Georgian Orthodox Church lost its independence. In the 1840s the Russian governor Mikhail Vorontsov (1782-1856) set out to actively Europeanise Tbilisi. While the old city centre was permitted to stand, the remains of the city walls were razed and the city expanded to the north and west.

Grand houses and villas in the style of European eclecticism were built for nobles, rich merchants and officers of the Russian administration and army. A palace with boulevards built around it was constructed for the governor, and new cultural institutions sprang up, including an opera house, which was intended not only to entertain the new and pampered Russian sector of the population with music and theatre but also to be a tool to inspire the cultural enlightenment of the Georgians and elevate Russian and European culture above what, in the Russian view, was the "semi-barbarous sounds of Persian music" which otherwise dominated the city.[8] As such, in 1853 one could for example hear Giuseppe Verdi's (1813-1901) *Rigoletto* in Tbilisi a mere two years after the opera was first performed in Venice.[9]

Some decades earlier, in the winter of 1820, the Danish linguist Rasmus Rask (1787-1832) had visited Tbilisi and reported in a letter home that he had "very little to write, as the inhabitants here (the Georgians) have little concept of literature; here there are no gymnasia, no private institutes, no libraries, no playhouses, no Protestant church".[10] Vorontsov's modern city – and the city to which our traveller comes in the years after 1900 – is radically different from the place Rask perceived.

In the second half of the 19th century the process of modernisation began in earnest to erode the Georgian way of life, although a segment of the population stubbornly persisted with the old traditions, both in the rural areas and in Tbilisi's old town. As a visitor to Tbilisi one would more often be greeted by Chopin's (1810-1849) études than by the ashugh troubadours' poetry performances in Georgian, Armenian, Azerbaijani, Turkish or Persian.[11] But as a by-product of Europeanisation, a new national self-awareness also emerged, nourished by critical ideas about, for instance, national liberalism, anti-imperialism, socialism and Marxism.[12]

THE NARIKALA FORTRESS ABOVE TBILISI'S OLD TOWN.

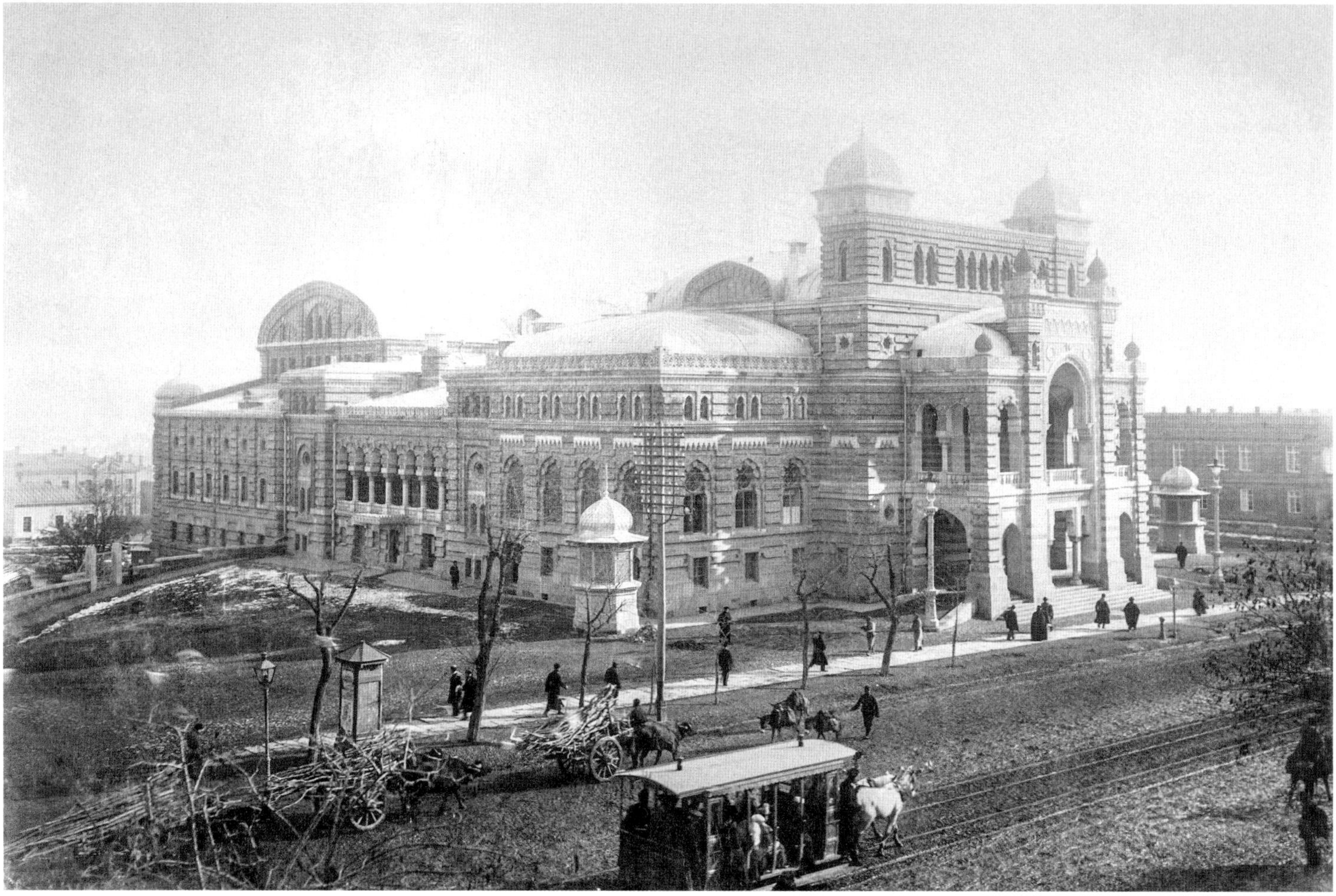

Georgian intellectuals were educated at the universities of Saint Petersburg and Moscow and returned home with new patriotic ideas about the Georgian nation and folk culture, and at the same time urbanisation meant that a new Georgian working class rapidly emerged and became preoccupied with the novel ideas of the age.

All this meant that in Tbilisi there arose a resistance to being part of the Russian Empire. This opposition grew further in 1905, when a workers' march in Saint Petersburg was brutally suppressed, sparking the First Russian Revolution, which also saw strikes, demonstrations and bombings in Georgia.[13] Here, the social struggle was also a national struggle, one that only bore fruit in the period 1918-1921, when Georgia briefly gained independence.

The city through which our traveller will be adventuring has thus undergone rapid development and is in a period of flux. Tbilisi remains a distinctive multi-ethnic population made up of Georgians, Turks, Persians, Indians, Tatars, Jews, Germans, British, mountain people, Kurds, Armenians, Russians and other peoples. Among the city's 159,000 inhabitants in 1897, the largest population group was Armenian, at 38 percent, while Georgians made up just 26.3 percent and Russians 24.7 percent.[14] Throughout the 19th century Armenian merchants had controlled a large proportion of the trade in Tbilisi, and around the year 1900 they and the Russians own virtually all major businesses. Georgians have limited access to positions of economic or political power, although the fact that they are Orthodox Christians means that they are regarded further up the hierarchy than, for example, Muslims or Jews.[15]

But the great influx from the countryside to the city continues, meaning that Georgians are beginning to become the largest population group, and by 1910 the population will have risen to 286,000.[16] Tbilisi is now a city where Western modernity and Eastern folk culture meet – a place where the old has not yet disappeared, even if the new has taken over.

III You have slept poorly. The night was hot and humid and you woke up bathed in sweat. But even if you are weary, you spend the whole morning walking around the modern district where your hotel is located. In the Mushthaid Garden you take a seat at a place with outdoor tables and begin to watch people. It seems as though the intellectual, European-leaning portion of the population frequents this place.[17] This establishment, you imagine, could just as well be in a Parisian park. Ladies and gentlemen, young and old, they are all dressed in modern dress and jackets.

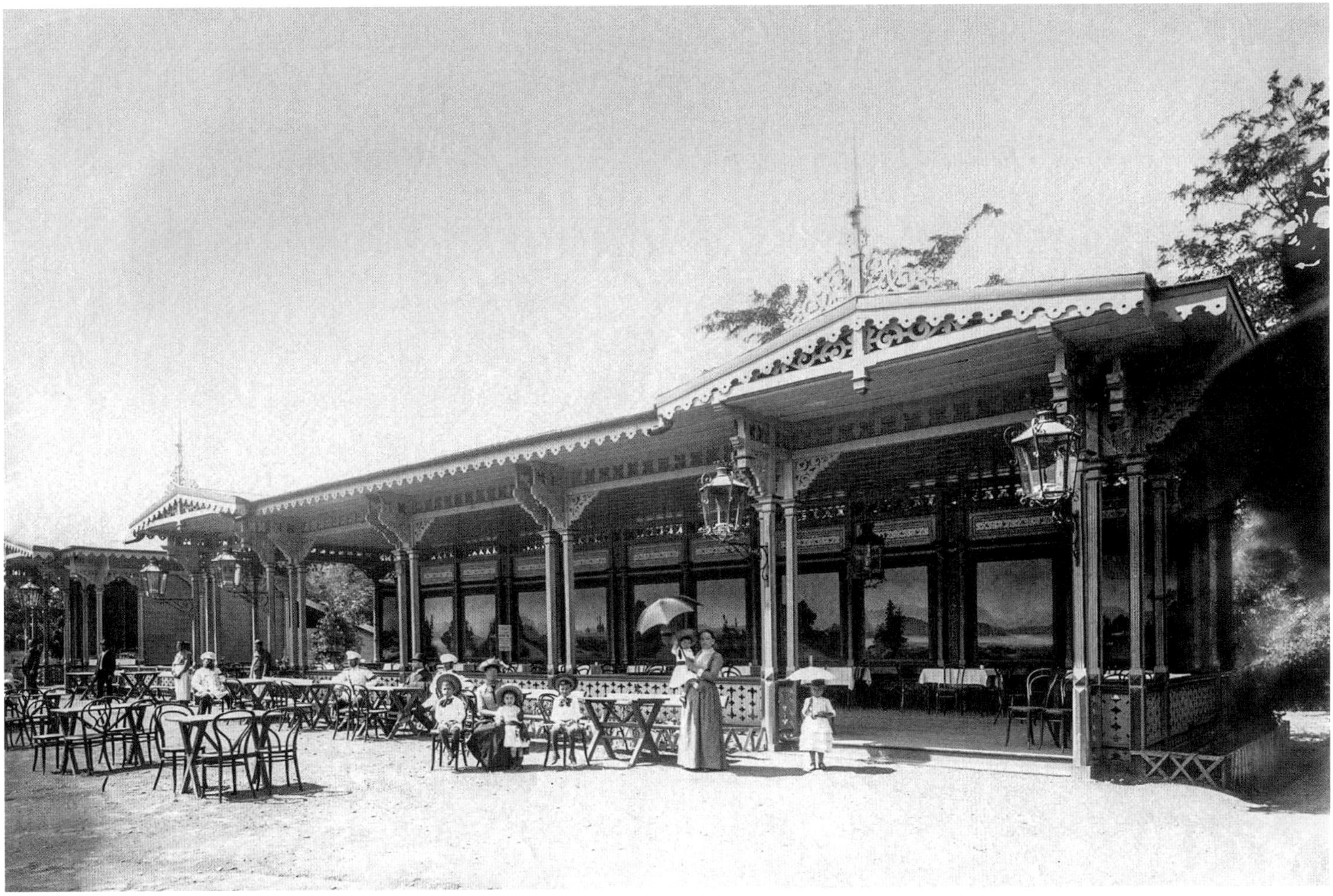

The same is true on the boulevards, which are distinguished by luxury and elegance. It almost resembles a miniature version of London's Regent Street.[18] You pass a cinema and stop in front of some large window panes. In their reflection, the houses and the street are visible behind you, through you. You watch the electric tram glide by.[19] You straighten your jacket. No one notices you here. As a European, you fit in perfectly, but this thought makes you glum – there's no difference any more.

The houses are two or three stories high, created in a blend of Renaissance, Baroque, Russian neoclassical architecture and Moorish style. In the distance you can see the recently opened funicular – the steepest in the world – that leads from the city up to the top of Mount Mtatsminda. On the way back to the hotel, you pass the opera, not the one that Vorontsov commissioned, which burned down in the 1870s, but the new opera inspired by Richard Wagner's (1813-1883) opera house in Bayreuth (built 1876), which has had numerous elements from Islamic architecture added to it.[20]

After a rest, the afternoon light is dimmer and more tangible. You lie on your bed and wonder why you came here. It's clear that you have no interest in the new part of Tbilisi, which resembles so much else in Europe. You haven't travelled this far to see Italian operas but because you have an ethnographic interest in experiencing local life in the old world – everything that is on the brink of disappearing, which you have read about in the many travelogues of the great writers from Tbilisi's Asian side – texts by Hamsun, Alexandre Dumas (1802-1870) and Alexander Pushkin (1799-1837).

The diplomat and writer Vicomte Eugène-Melchior de Vogüé (1848-1910) has also been here and in 1890 described Tbilisi as a "hybrid town, half Russian and half Oriental. In the centre of it the victors have built a palace, a museum, barracks, boulevards lined with hotels and shops, which vie with those of Moscow." And then he adds: "The moment you return to the faubourgs you find yourself in the East again."[21] Like De Vogüé, you will see the small open workshops of jewellers, gunsmiths, Armenian rug merchants and Persian dealers. You will observe how "(camel, ed.) drivers and passers talk back at each other in all languages", how a Circassian horseman "manages with graceful ease his thorough-bred Kabarda", or how a Tatar "going to the bath-house mounted on his donkey [...] fingers his chaplet and amber beads as he passes near a pope, who is bargaining for a silver-gilt icon in front of a goldsmith's window."[22]

RESTAURANT IN THE MUSHTHAID GARDEN WITH PARISIAN INSPIRED OUTDOOR SERVING.

<

TBILISI'S NEW OPERA HOUSE. DESIGNED IN THE 1880S BY THE RUSSIAN-GERMAN ARCHITECT VIKTOR SCHRÖTER (1839-1901), FINISHED IN 1896.

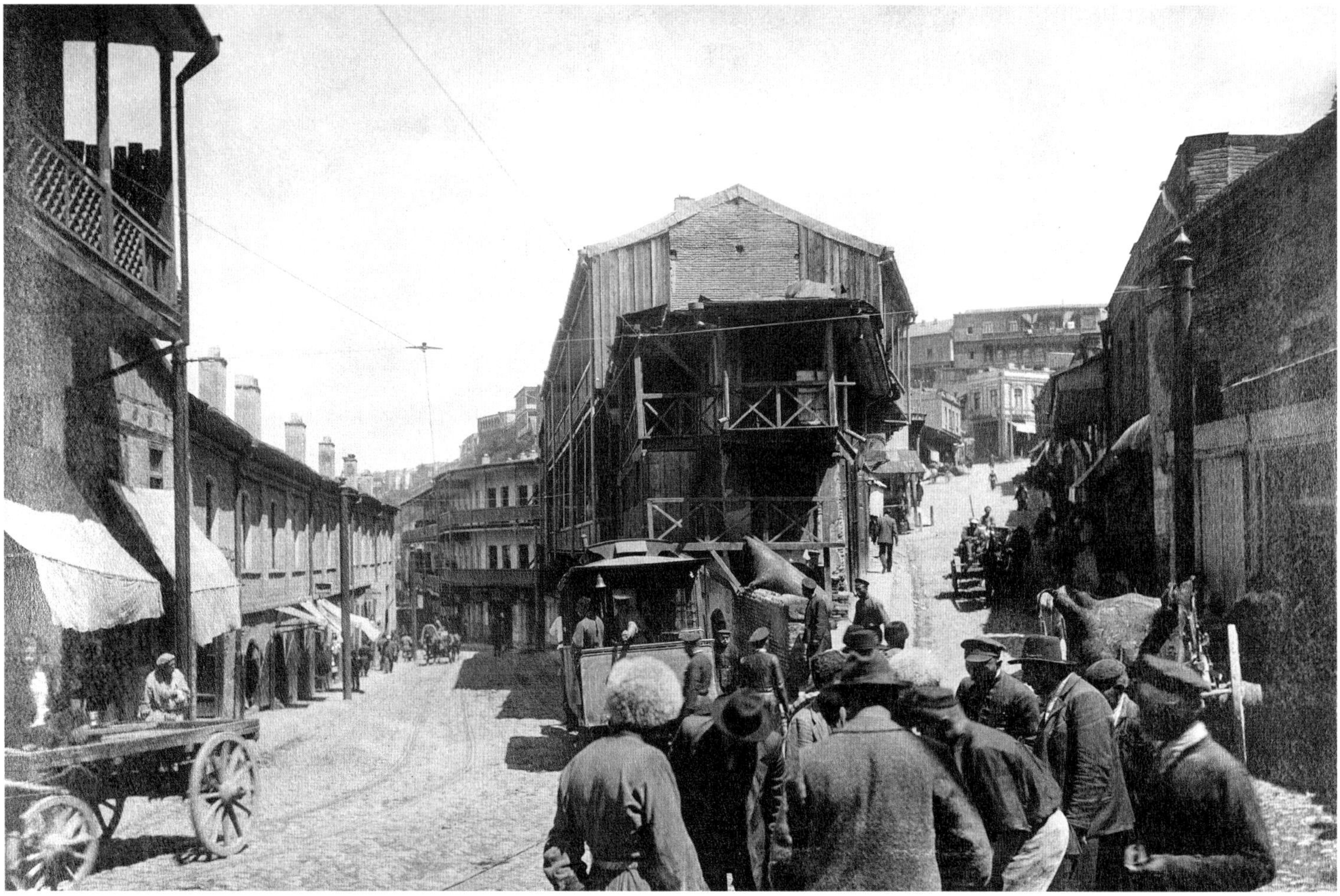

As you gather your things and get ready to go out, you consider whether people from Asia are as fascinated by the European modernity of Tbilisi as you are by its Asian street life. Are we always seeking the other, that to which we do not belong and do not fully understand?

As you enter the old town, you notice how it's not just people's clothing and language that changes. Beyond the boulevards the sounds also bristle in a different way. The fug of donkey dung and dog excrement hangs in the air. A uniformed Russian officer buttoned up in a green jacket elbows his way up the steep street through the crowd of water vendors, men in turbans, long tunics and leather boots. In one place a Muslim woman stands beneath a sign of two frothing tankards of beer that reads "Deutsches Bier!"[23] Tbilisi has a German-speaking diaspora – farmers from Prussia, Austria and Switzerland who came here in the early 19th century and brought their beer halls and beer gardens with them.[24]

The old wooden Georgian houses everywhere have covered balconies overhanging the streets. You can see people eating or sleeping out on them. Barely any of the buildings stem from before 1800, since the Shah laid the city so emphatically to waste in 1795, but the layout of the medieval city has remained unaltered.[25] You wander up a narrow alley, which ends in some stairs that give you access to the next street via a balcony. It's as though these balconies aren't private spaces, you think. These are public places where people meet and their lives open up.[26]

Different religions and peoples have lived alongside one another in the old town for centuries. Within a few streets you pass Georgian and Armenian churches, a mosque and a synagogue, but dare not look inside even if you want to. In the side streets you see Persians, Tatars, Lezgins and many other groups that you are unable to identify.

You have heard it said that the various peoples behave differently in Tbilisi than when they are in their homelands. Here parts of the Muslim minority are known to have a relaxed relationship with food and clothing so that some Muslim women do not wear veils, while the men drink alcohol and eat slaughtered meat that isn't halal.[27]

Among the Georgians, you recognise two distinct types, both belonging to the lower classes. In a workshop sits a *karachokheli* wearing a black tunic and a hat made from the fur of a Karakul sheep. He is a member of a guild and is the epitome of virtue and honour. The most important thing for a karachokheli is fellowship with others in his group, which is often marked by celebrations around the table. Out on the street, the other type moves quickly between people, and you take a step to the side and observe him. This is the *kinto,* whose light clothing is a kind of caricature of the karachokheli's, lacking the latter's dignity and gravitas.

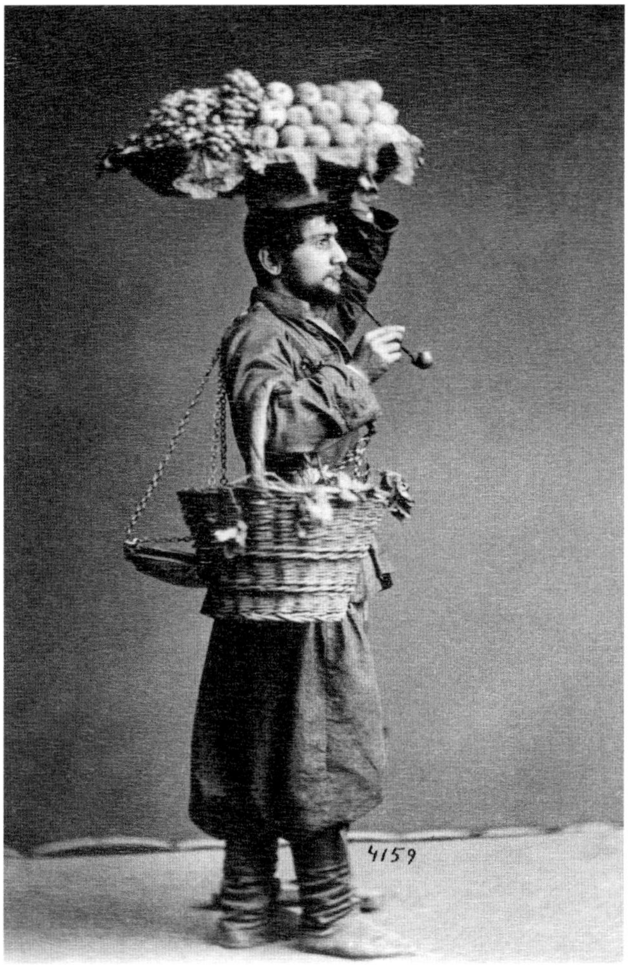

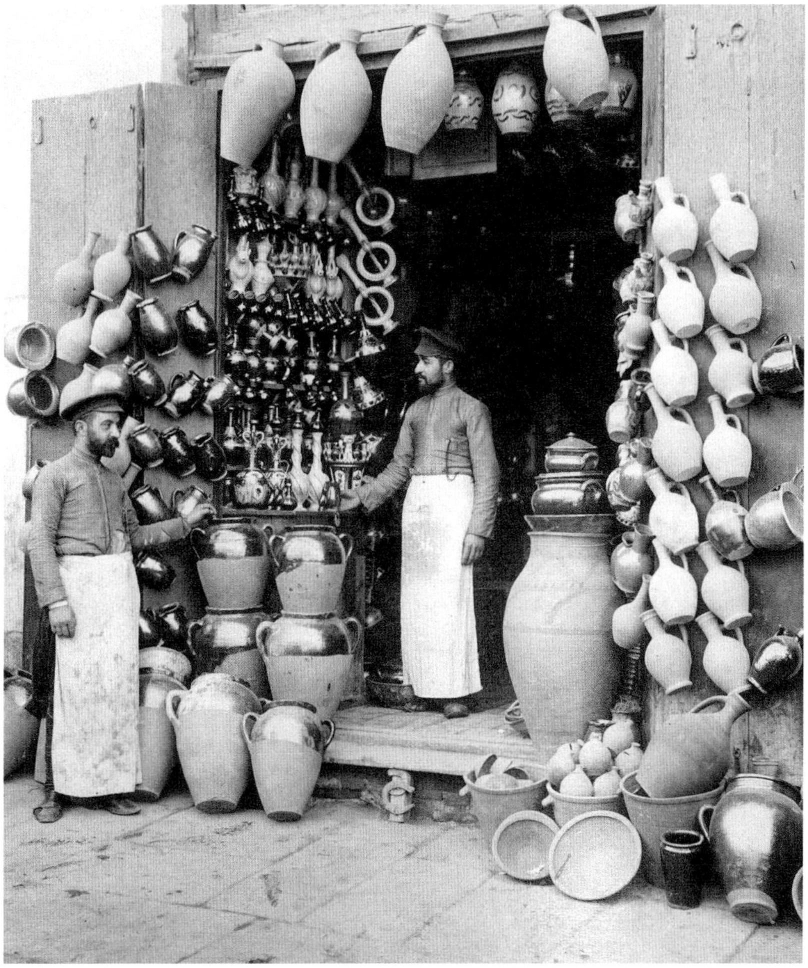

A kinto performs odd jobs: he often peddles fish, fruit or other goods on the street. He is a cheeky and jocular character who speaks the language of the street, often a mixture of Georgian, Russian, Armenian, Turkish and Persian.[28] You can't help but smile and tip your hat as you continue past workshops where craftsmen hammer iron on anvils, make jewellery, belts, weapons or pottery, or sew long robes.[29]

At one place a Russian gentleman in a light jacket, bowler hat and cane is selecting a carpet from an Azerbaijani rug merchant. Dogs lie sleeping all about, and a little further on you almost trip over one of them. There is a calmness in the streets, in spite of the crowds. Traders do not try to attract customers by shouting, as you have seen in other cultures. You do however notice a number of distinctive signs outside shops, bakeries, greengrocers, butchers and places to eat: images of fish, bread, meat skewers, wine and fruit presented against black backgrounds.

The street resembles a little gallery, you realise all of a sudden.[30] All the local restaurants – known as *dukhan*'s – also have signs of this type, featuring figures raising glasses or pouring orange wine and frothy beer. While the genteel bourgeoisie and the intellectuals come to the European-inspired cafes in the newer part of Tbilisi, a dukhan is a kind of informal wine cellar or inn where the host gladly joins his guests at their table. These places are typical of the old town.[31] This is where the karachokheli often hold their ritual celebrations; social life plays out here accompanied by food, wine, poetry and music.

You sense a creeping hunger and move on to the Ortachala neighbourhood, where you will eat dinner and learn more about Georgian fare, but first you have to make it through the crowds at the Meidani market. You stop at a greengrocer where the melons hang on strings from hooks above the door. You buy a slice of watermelon. The sweet, warm juice dribbles down your chin, so you have to use your sleeve to wipe away the moisture. At the next shop you watch how the baker takes the dough and sticks it to the inside wall of a clay oven called a *tone,* which resembles a well with a fire at its base. In Georgian, bread is called *puri,* the same as in in Hindi, because just as Georgian cuisine has elements of Mediterranean and Middle Eastern cooking in it, it also has certain connections to northern India.[32]

ONE OF THE CITY'S MANY KINTOS, WITH THE CHARM OF A STREET URCHIN, PERFORMING VARIOUS JOB FUNCTIONS. / SHOP SELLING EARTHENWARE, FROM PLATES TO AMPHORAE.

<

A CORNER IN THE OLD TOWN WITH THE CHARACTERISTIC BALCONIES AND CARRIAGES, TRANSPORTING WINE IN ANIMAL HIDES.

A haze of heat has settled over the city and in the square there is dust in the air. You rush on past waterboys and wine vendors, past stalls selling poultry, vegetables and pottery, past a group of musicians in traditional Georgian costumes playing *zurna*, *tari*, *sazi* and *daira*, which you think resembles the clarinet, banjo, lute and tambourine.[33] When you finally pass the square, you take a deep breath and sense the characteristic egg-like smell of sulphur emanating from Tbilisi's famous baths. Dumas and Pushkin have described them, and you must go down there yourself one of these days, because the Georgian word *tbili* means 'warm' and refers to the city's thermal sulphur springs.[34]

Finally, you reach the Ortachala Gardens on the banks of the Kura. These 'gardens' are to Tbilisi's Asian side what the Mushthaid Garden, where you began the day, is to the European side. People still meet here even on the hottest days, but the gardens are especially popular now, as darkness begins to fall. You see people arriving on foot, others in horse-drawn carriages. Laughter and music mingle with the roar of the Kura. The names of the gardens' traditional inns and restaurants catch your eye: Eldorado, Fantasia, Gentleman.[35] A host stands in a doorway and beckons you in. Next to him hangs a two-metre high green and white checked advertising sign of foaming flagons of beer and waiters that look like the ones you've seen on your walk through the old town. "Eldorado", it says on the sign, "A place to enjoy yourself. Proprietor Titishev. Fruit, meat skewers, wine. With barrel organ music."[36]

You sit on the restaurant's covered terrace from where you can watch the scene outside. Single women stand in the gardens' twilight as though waiting for someone. Titishev brings wine from Kakhetia and you pull out Hamsun in order to compare your own impressions of the Asian quarter with his: "Here peoples from all over the world sat in their shops and had curious things to sell. [...] here they were an assortment of Caucasian peoples, Georgians, mountain people, Ural-Altaic tribes, all kinds of Tatars, besides Indo-Europeans such as Persians, Kurds and Armenians, people from Arabia in the south to Turkestan in the north, from Palestine to Tibet. And everything went peacefully, no one was in a hurry, the people were imbued with the calm of the Orient. White and motley turbans predominated; only an occasional green or blue one was seen crowning a gorgeous long-bearded head. The belts were either of chased metal or, as among the Persians, of many-colored silk. Caucasians, Kurds and Armenians carried weapons."[37]

When you look up again you notice a painting hanging on the wall under the terrace's canopy: a strange silver-black giraffe. You stand up to take a closer look at the picture in the glow of the gaslight. The animal is presented in a barren evening landscape with the sky a deep blue at the top and white closest to the horizon. Your host, Titishev, comes out and sees you standing and looking at the picture. He takes you by the arm and draws you into the restaurant, where portraits of a white-clad chef, a supervisor and several women, standing, sitting and lying down, adorn the walls. "Niko Pirosmanashvili", says Titishev, pointing to the walls. He says something else you don't understand and then leaves again.

The portraits put you in mind of orthodox icons. They have a similar intensity. You think of the female figures in the gardens outside. Were they the painter's models? Perhaps they are some of the Georgians who have moved from the country to the city in recent decades – people whose lives had been bound up in the ritual festivities of traditional culture but who now work in industry or have had to find other ways to survive in the big city. When you come back out, you look again at the giraffe. There is something at once compelling and disquieting about it. It's painted as if it were a portrait. Human-like. Its eyes stare back at you. Does it cry? The black base colour shines through the other colours just as in the portraits inside. You sit down at your table. A gathering comes out onto the terrace. The gardens are about to come to life.

IV

Niko Pirosmani's (1862/63-1918) pictorial world, in the form both of shop signs and of paintings in restaurants, is part of the city space that our traveller is experiencing in Tbilisi. In the summer of 1910, Niko Pirosmani was hired by Eldorado's owner, Titishev, to paint pictures for the restaurant, including his famous giraffe and many portraits of people who came to the Ortachala Gardens. There would be 13 pictures in total.[38] The motifs in these images are easily recognisable, but they also exhibit an otherness that cannot be reduced or explained by reference to the surrounding society. This is what catches our traveller's attention: the black base colour shining through; the curious colours and gaze of the giraffe; the iconic way in which the people portrayed appear to step out of the images. Somewhere between the icon and the advertising sign. But even if Pirosmani is in many ways entirely his own person, his work contributes to the plurality of literary and artistic currents that characterised Tbilisi during these years, and which it is important to understand if the city's many dimensions are to emerge.

Over the centuries, Georgian literature has grown out of the encounter between a myriad of different traditions, taking in Byzantine, Caucasian, Turkish, Persian and Arabic influences.[39] By virtue of being an Orthodox Christian country in the Caucasus, Georgia has acted as a nexus, first between the Hellenistic and Byzantine traditions and the Islamic/Persian world, and then between the Western Christian and humanist traditions and the Orient.[40] Especially in the period from the 11th to the 13th century, Georgia experienced a golden age from which perhaps the most important work of Georgian literature originates, namely Shota Rustaveli's (c. 1160-after 1220) epic poem *The Knight in the Panther's Skin* (c. 1220), which unites a number of cultural influences and forms a bridge between the Middle Ages and the modern world.

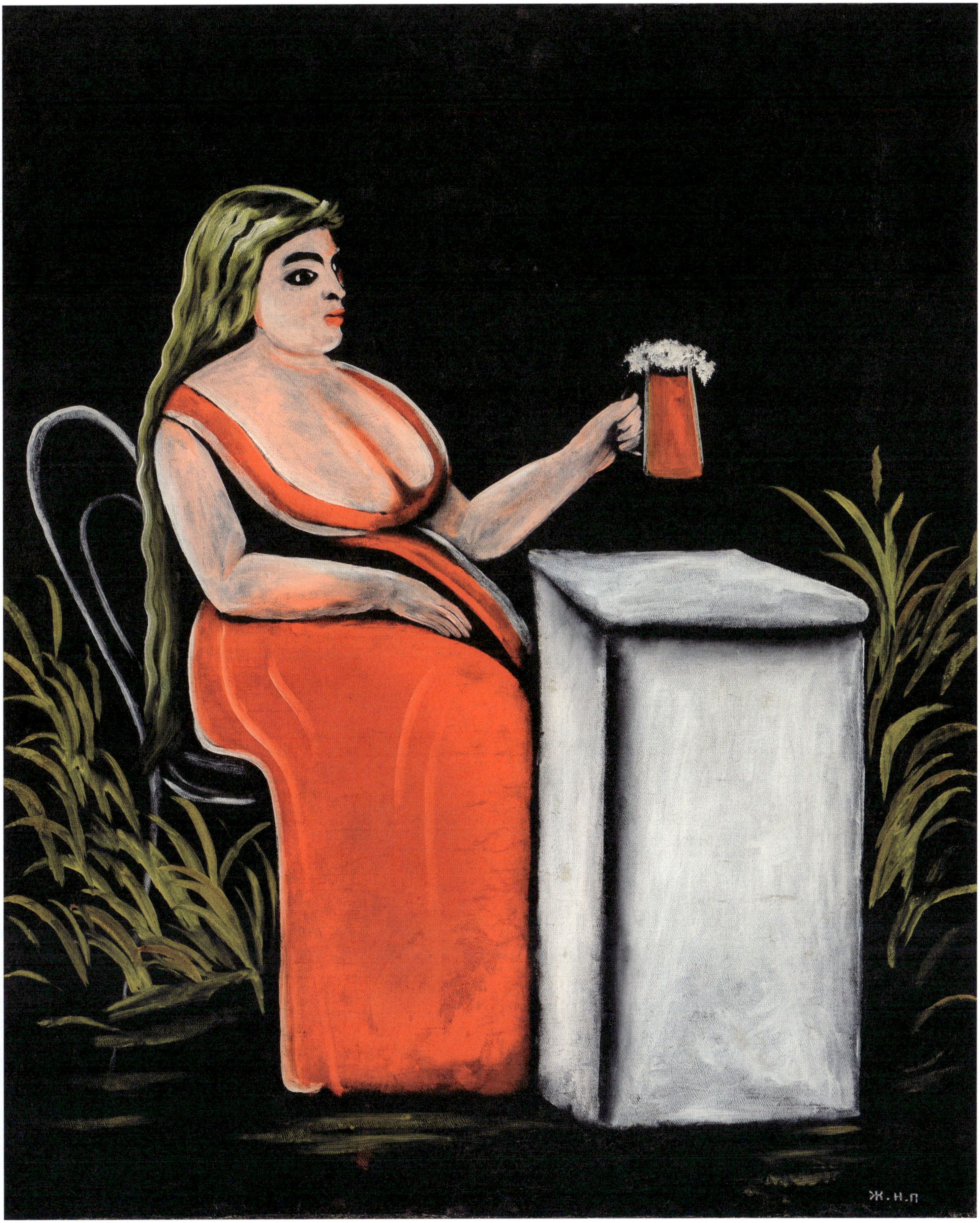
Ж.Н.П

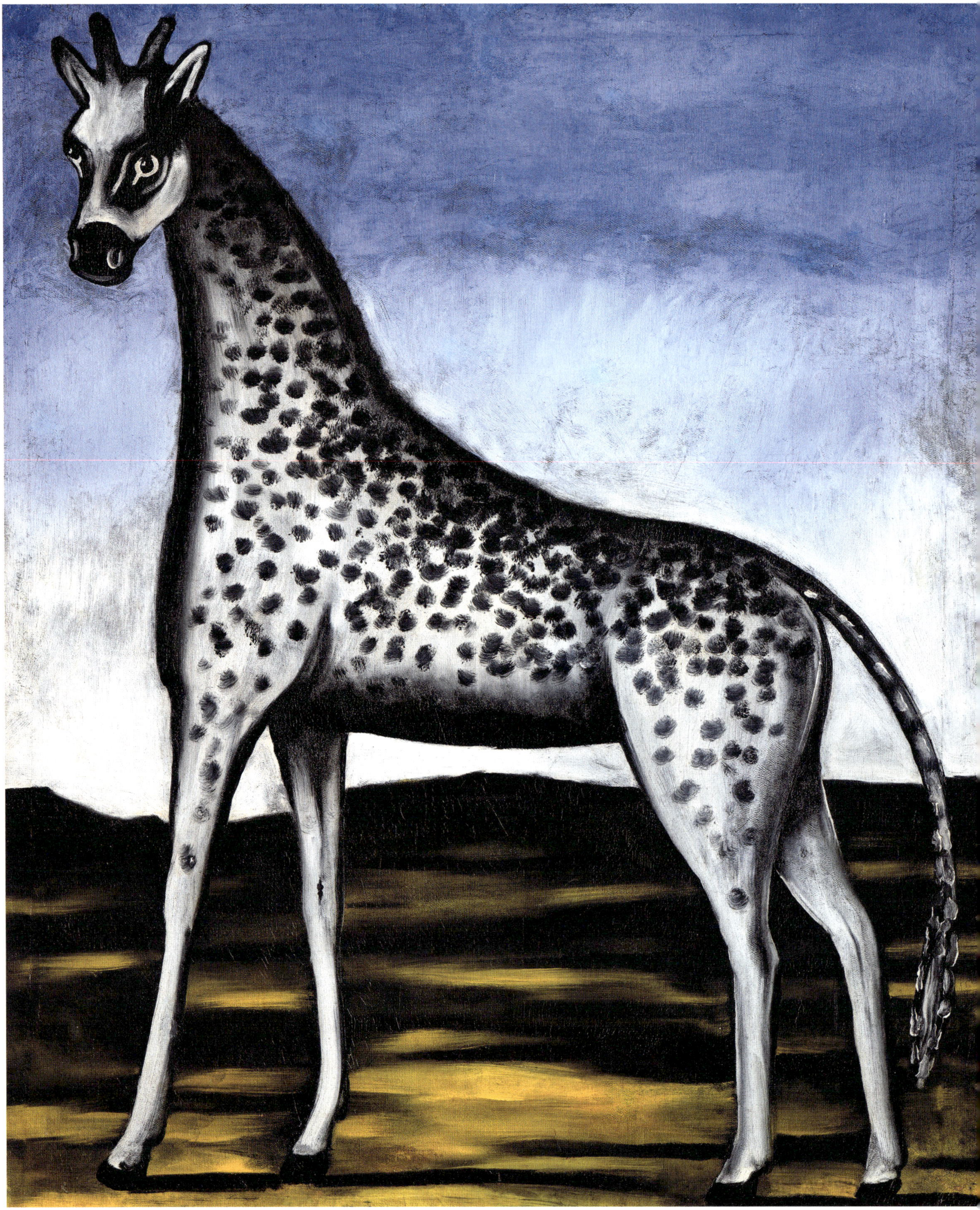

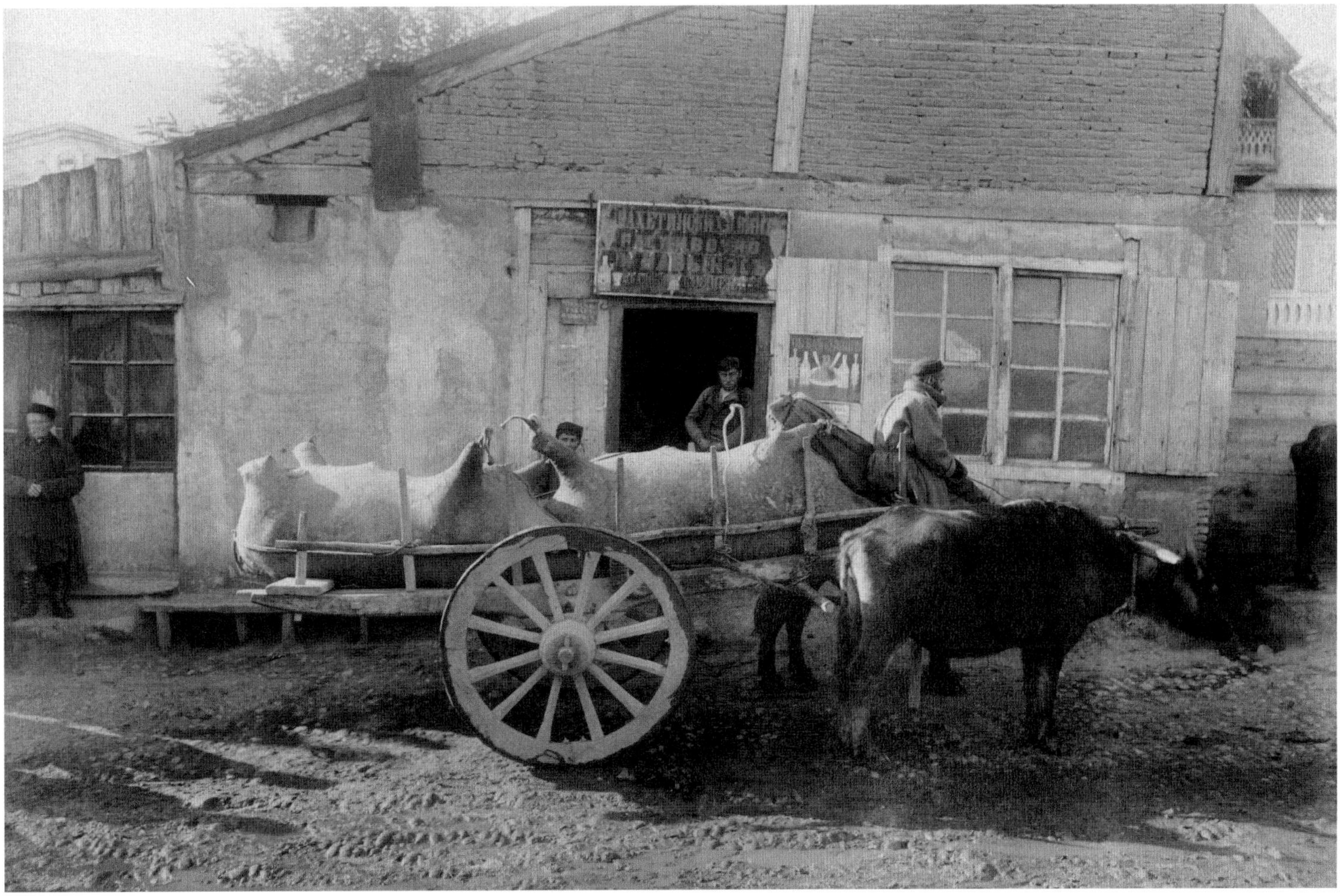

Virtually nothing is known about Rustaveli himself, but his work has become as vital to the Georgian culture and language as Shakespeare (1564-1616) is to the British and Dante (1265-1321) is to the Italians.[41] The poem is reminiscent of the chivaldric romances that we know from European medieval literature. However, Rustaveli juxtaposes Hellenistic, pagan-Caucasian and Christian values in a virtuosic way, which has lent the poem a particular universality and unifying function for the Georgian people.[42] A great deal of Georgian grammar and vocabulary have their origins in Rustaveli's text, and through the centuries when Georgia was invaded by foreign powers, the poem about the friendship between the knights Avtandil and Tariel has defined Georgianness, and was something to be learned by heart.[43] At the end of the 19th century, Rustaveli's poem again became a symbol of the Georgian nation and thus part of its efforts to secede from Russian domination.[44] It is also telling of Rustaveli's importance that although Pirosmani does not often portray historical figures or themes, he has done precisely that for Rustaveli and Queen Tamar (1160-1213), to whom *The Knight in the Panther Skin* is dedicated.

While Georgian literature was restricted by Russian censorship in the first half of the 19th century, Governor Vorontsov's reforms in the middle of the century opened up for the emergence of greater numbers of readers and writers.[45] The writer Ilia Chavchavadze (1837-1907) became the leader of a new influential group of Russian-educated Georgian intellectuals referred to as the *tergdaleulni*, meaning 'those who have drunk from the Terek', i.e. the river that marks the border between Georgia and Russia.[46] Chavchavadze was inspired by European notions of liberalism and believed that literature should be used to bring about political change.[47] He actively worked to protect Georgian culture and language from Russification, thus becoming a major figure in the national movement. In 1888, Chavchavadze also helped to cement Rustaveli's *The Knight in the Panther Skin* as a national icon.[48]

Gradually, the international influence of Georgian literature intensifies, and the years after 1900 see the rise of two distinct movements in particular: some pursue realism and view literature as an instrument of revolution; others cultivate symbolism and *l'art pour l'art*.[49]

DUKHAN IN TBILISI WITH SIGNBOARDS.

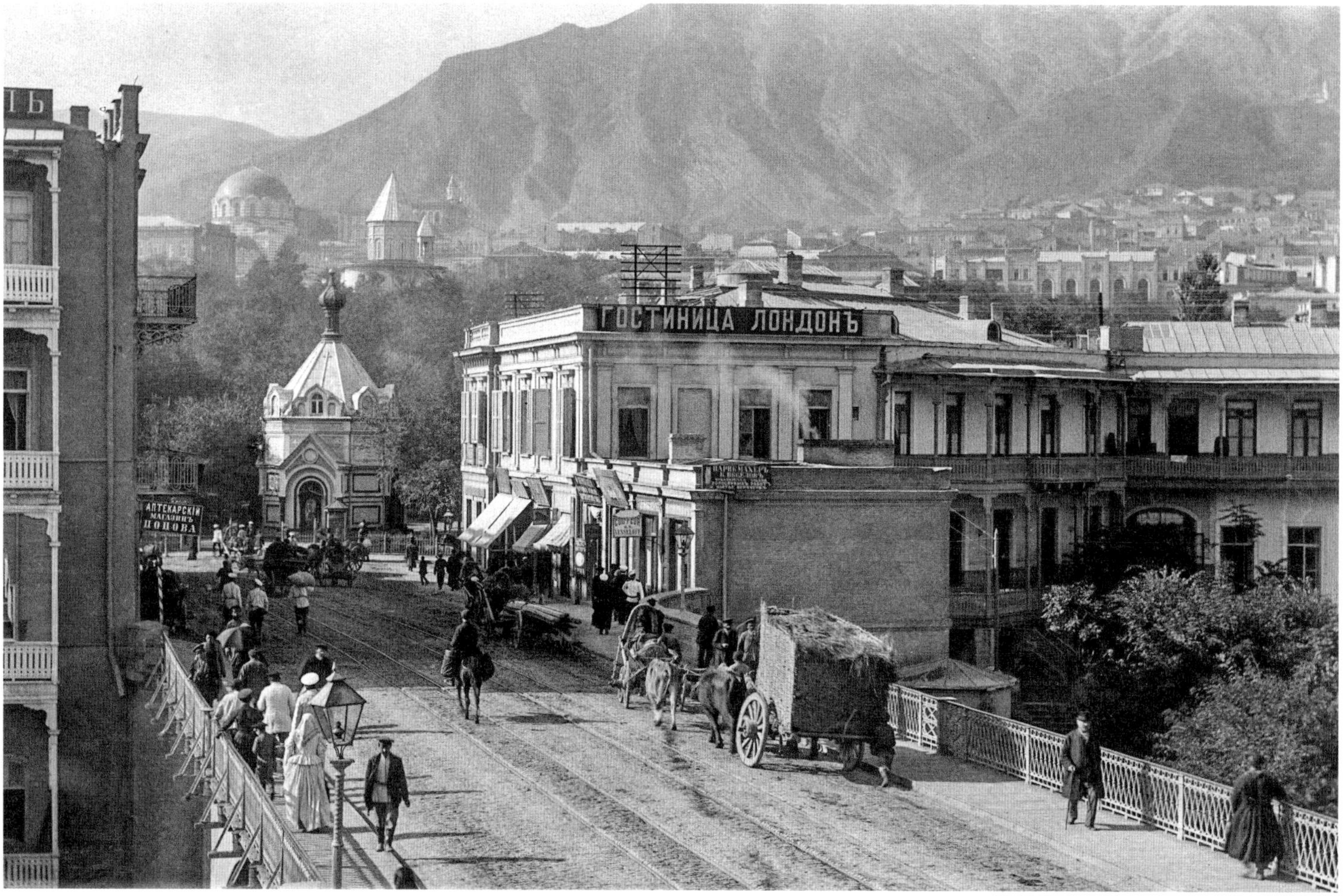

But a third trend, which is particularly interesting in relation to Pirosmani, is the turn towards Caucasian folk culture and folk poetry, which can be found with the poet Vazha-Pshavela (1861-1915), who had an enormous influence on later generations.

Vazha-Pshavela, whose real name was Luka Razikashvilis, was Pirosmani's favourite author. The two met in 1914.[50] Vazha-Pshavela came from the mountains north of Tbilisi and had studied briefly in Saint Petersburg before being forced to withdraw due to impoverishment and return home. He had an ethnological interest in the folk poetry of the mountain dwellers, which he collected because these traditions were about to disappear. His own poetry draws on the pre-Christian folk poetry traditions, on the Greek tragedies, and on local dialects from the mountain regions of north-eastern Georgia, which he in turn fuses with elements from German romanticism, Shakespeare and the Bible.[51] His poetry is imbued with pessimism, rage, forlornness and a love of nature (devoid of people), and his heroes are often outsiders who are on the periphery of the social community.

The lack of edification and his use of dialects that diverged from the official language made it difficult for contemporaries to incorporate Vazha-Pshavela into the national struggle for independence. Even so, over time he came to be acknowledged as one of the greatest poets who, in a way, stood beyond time and constituted a bridge to the half-pagan, half-Christian world of folk poetry.[52] He also wrote short stories for children in which the world is experienced through the eyes of animals, for example *A Roe-Deer Fawn's Story* (1883), which is an early version of the Bambi tale.[53] Here we experience how the little roe deer witnesses its mother being killed and dismembered by a hunter. One also finds precisely this emphasis on folk culture and the distinctive personification of animals with Pirosmani.

If in literature the Georgians have Rustaveli's *The Knight in the Panther Skin* as a national icon that transcends the time and space of the Middle Ages, Georgian visual art in this period developed with a post-Byzantine figurative language and a variety of features from folk culture and the East. Any direct influence from European art arrived only in the 17th and 18th centuries, when missionary Catholic monks brought with them new painting techniques.[54] European currents were also being conveyed through Russian art during this period. However, it is not until the first half of the 19th century that a secular and distinct Georgian portrait art, in the form of the 'Tbilisi portrait school', emerged. These portraits of nobles and upper class are characterised by a strong influence from Byzantine murals mixed with features from Iranian art and miniatures as well as European portraiture, resulting in

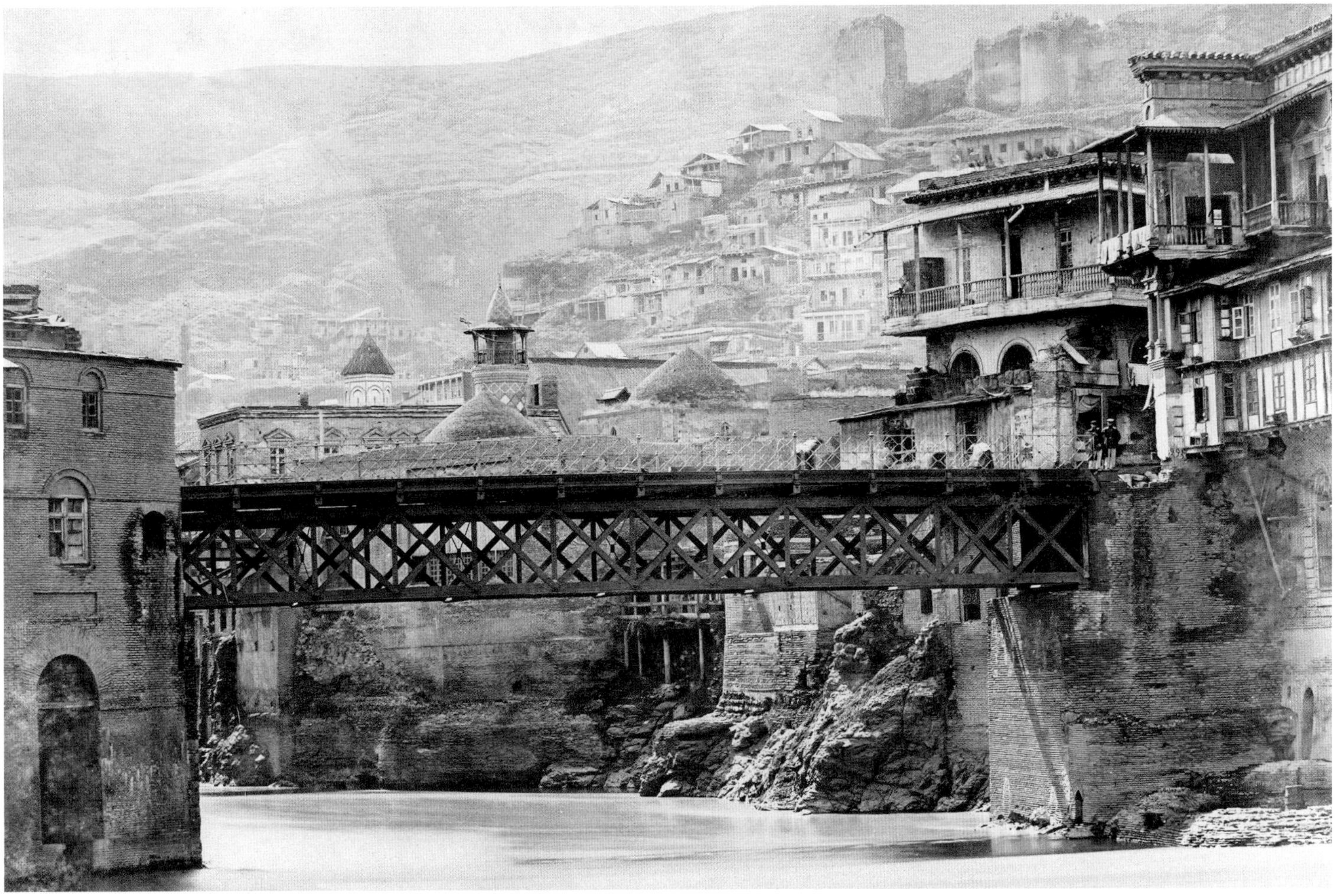

a uniquely Georgian style of linear, static and flatly represented portraits.[55]

As in literature, the art scene in the second half of the 19th century was dominated by Georgian artists educated in Saint Petersburg and Moscow. Realism began to gain ground in painting, just as it did in Russian and European art. Georgian everyday life and landscapes became principal motifs.[56] An artist like Gigo Gabashvili (1862-1936), possibly born in the same year as Pirosmani, portrayed figures from Tbilisi's different social classes. Like Pirosmani, Gabashvili did not individualise his portraits but instead accentuated general features – types – which resulted in a general monumentalisation of those being portrayed.[57]

At the same time that realism was gaining ground in painting, photography was also beginning to play an increasingly important role. One of the most prominent Tbilisian photographers was Dimitri Ermakov (1846-1916), whose parentage reflects the city's ethnic complexity: his father was an Italian immigrant; his mother was of German-Austrian origin.[58] Ermakov was deeply interested in ethnographic photography and, from the end of the 1860s onwards, documented, for instance, landscapes and folk life in Transcaucasia and the Middle East.[59] In 1870 he opened a photography studio in Tbilisi, where he sold his pictures. Ermakov also became one of the most important portrayers of Tbilisi's old town, where he, for example, photographed the work of craftsmen as they carried on old traditions that gave the city its unique character.[60] In this way, his pictures captured the development that the city was undergoing up to the year 1900.

Gradually, and also under the influence of the Russian artists group Peredvishniki, realism in Georgian art took an increasingly critical stance to social and ethnic inequality. This criticism particularly concerns the Russian Empire's dominance over the South Caucasus.[61] But this new critical awareness could be read not only in the motifs of Georgian painting, but also in the satirical journal *Molla Nasreddin*, printed in runs of 25,000 copies and published in Tbilisi in the period 1906-1917. Written in Azerbaijani and dominated by caricatures, the journal reached Muslim readers in India, the Caucasus, the Middle East and North Africa. Political and religious satire was at its heart, explicitly criticising among other things the dominant form of Islam in Iran (Shiism), leading to fatwas being issued against the publication, which was smuggled into Iran nevertheless.[62]

AVLABARI BRIDGE ABOVE THE KURA RIVER.
<
HOTEL LONDON AND GRAND HOTEL WITH, AMONG OTHER THINGS, THE TOWER OF ST. GEORGE'S CHURCH IN THE BACKGROUND.

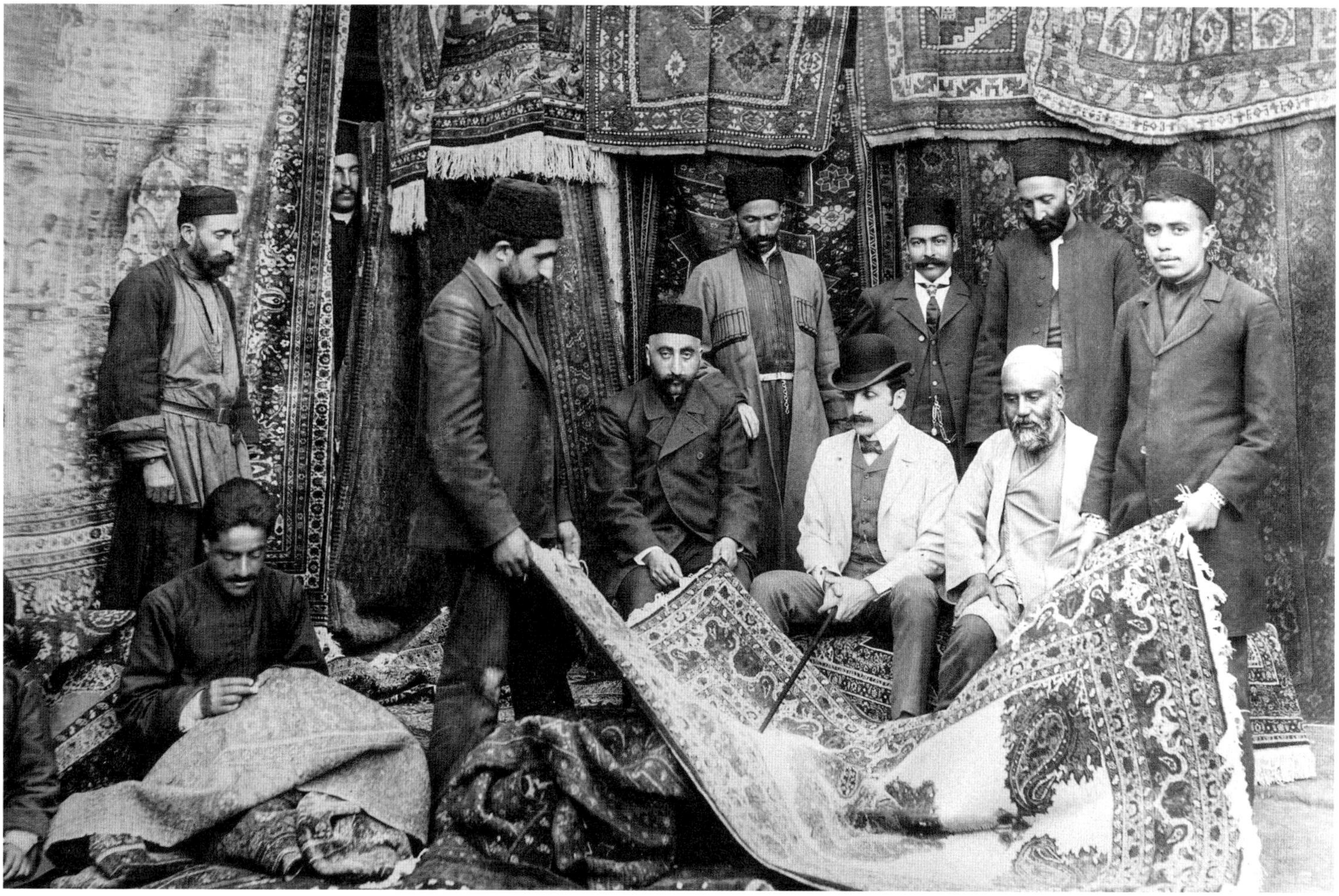

The artists and writers working for *Molla Nasreddin* came from a transnational environment and were clearly inspired by European artistic traditions but were at the same time critical of European cultural dominance and Russian colonialism.[63] Thus, the journal is an example of how, in Tbilisi, there was freedom – when one did not write in Russian or Georgian – to create a platform with a progressive democratic focus through which topics such as gender, sexuality and religious oppression were discussed.

In this way, in the years after 1900, Tbilisi was dominated by a burgeoning national self-awareness that was also expressed in elements of art and literature critical of Russian hegemony. It was in this time of turmoil that Pirosmani painted his distinctive signs, animals and images of a Georgian folk culture that were about to vanish. And, not knowing any of this, it is here our traveller finds himself.

V You look around at the others in the gathering. They have raised their glasses, and you raise yours too. They saw you sitting there alone and invited you over to their table beneath Pirosmani's giraffe. Their faces are cheerful. There is something noble about their plain black tunics, their full beards and sheep's wool hats. The host, Titishev, brings *shashlik*, puri, cheese and more wine. At the end of the table sits the toastmaster, the *tamada*, who is in charge of the ritual toasts.[64] Unlike the others, his beard is long and white. He stands up and speaks for a long time, as though telling a story, and you see the others eating and nodding and listening, and suddenly the whole party breaks into song, and you don't understand a thing, but afterwards your neighbour, the only one in the company who speaks a little German, speaks to you: "Here, wine can be without women, but never without song," he says.[65] The tamada raises his glass again, and even though you feel the alcohol thrumming through your body, you do the same. This is how it continues. You will be caught up in the atmosphere and experience how Georgians use the meal to build and affirm feelings of kinship and national traditions. It is a kind of enchantment of everyday life which, via the ancient codes of celebration, connects them with the past in a social community. "Sakartvelos gaumardzhos!" says the man with the white beard. "A toast to Georgia," your neighbour whispers, serving your plate with more grilled meat.

And while our traveller sits at the Eldorado in the Ortachala Gardens and witnesses how the feast and the wine bring the social community and the Georgian past to life, time and space begin to merge. Here, Tbilisi is both West and East, centre and periphery, epic and exotic.[66] What no one around the table knows is that in the next

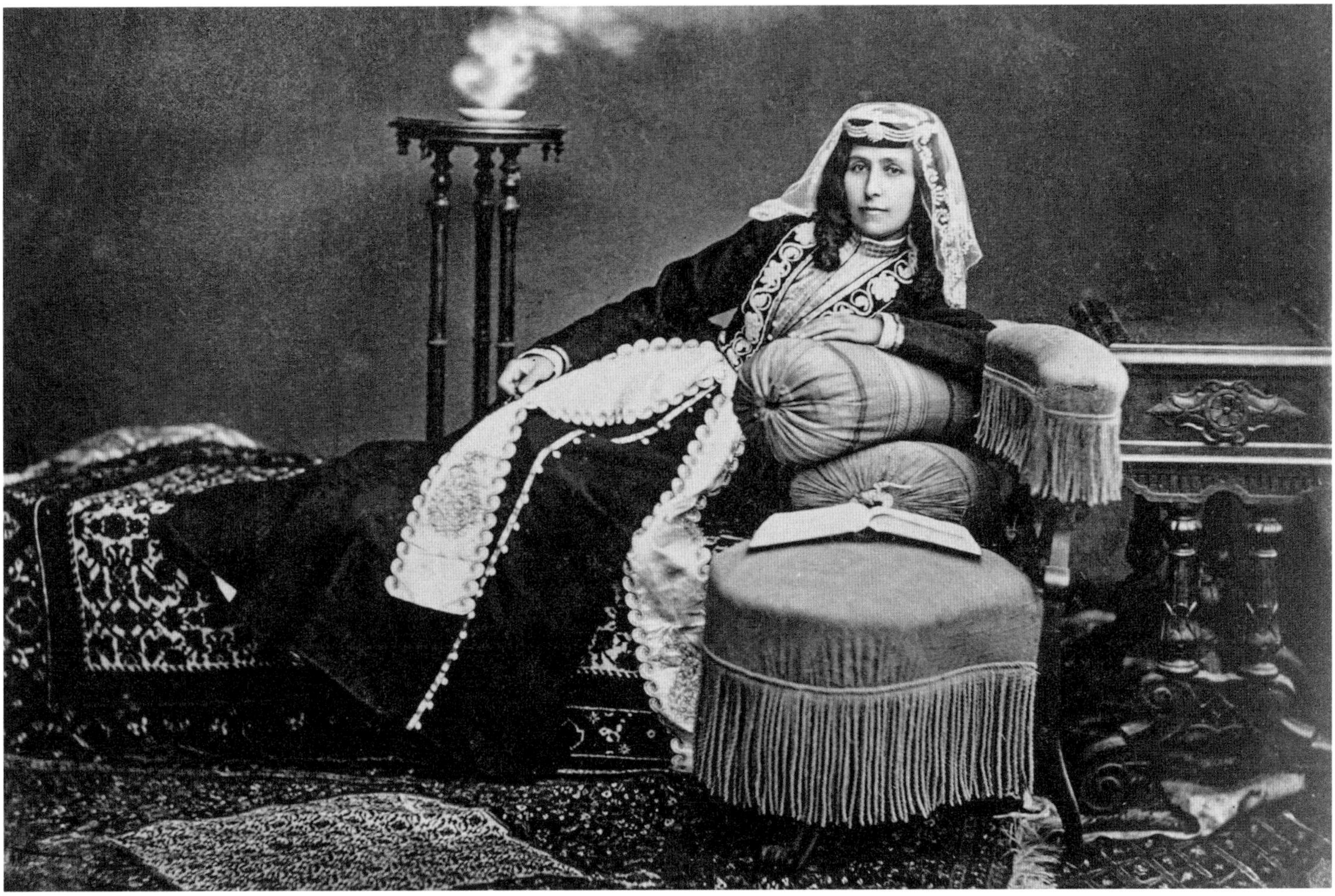

few years there will be a world war, the Russian Empire will collapse, and Georgia will be free. In the summer of 1912, Pirosmani will be discovered by the two Georgian brothers Kirill and Ilia Zdanevich (respectively 1892-1969 and 1894-1975) and the Russian artist Mikhail Le Dentu (1891-1917), yet he will die destitute and alone in the spring of 1918. One month later, Georgia will gain independence and Tbilisi will briefly be transformed into a centre of avant-garde art and literature, attracting European and Russian artists and poets.[67] Symbolists, expressionists, Dadaists, acmeists, futurists, cubists ... A modern world will emerge, and despite the fact that this world has very little to do with Georgia's past, Pirosmani's art will be called a link between folk culture and this new age. A bridge between the old and the new. But in 1921, the Bolsheviks will invade Georgia and soon the new artist cafes will disappear again. The poet Grigol Robakidze (1880-1962) from the symbolist group the Blue Horns would later write about the period that "all around everything was crumbling, and Tbilisi remained the only city that greeted this destruction with a song".[68] It would be 70 years before a traveller could visit a free Georgia again.

Notes

1 Nikoloz Aleksidze, *Georgia: A Cultural Journey through the Wardrop Collection* (Oxford: Bodleian Library, University of Oxford, 2018), 9-10. **2** Aleksidze, 11. **3** Oliver Wardrop, *The Kingdom of Georgia: Notes of Travel in a Land of Women, Wine and Song* (London: S. Low, Marston, Searle and Rivington, 1888), 5. **4** Quoted in Darra Goldstein, *The Georgian Feast: The Vibrant Culture and Savory Food of the Republic of Georgia* (Berkeley, California: University of California Press, 2013), 8. **5** Goldstein, 10. **6** Knut Hamsun, *In Wonderland*, trans. Sverre Lyngstad (Brooklyn: Ig Publishing, 2003), 120. **7** Quoted in Nicholas V. Iljine, ed., *Memories of Tiflis* (Frankfurt am Main: Fachhochschulverlag, der Verlag für angewandte Wissenschaften, 2018), 76. **8** Ronald Grigor Suny, *The Making of the Georgian Nation* (Bloomington: Indiana University Press, 1994), 93. **9** Iljine, *Memories of Tiflis,* 240. **10** Quoted in Hans Scherfig, *Morgenrødens Land: Literær rejse i Grusien* (København: Gyldendal, 1971), 138. **11** Aleksidze, *Georgia,* 15; Suny, *The Making of the Georgian Nation,* 115. **12** Janet Afary and Kamran Afary, *Molla Nasreddin: The Making of a Modern Trickster, 1906-1911* (Edinburgh: Edinburgh University Press, 2022), 30. **13** Aleksidze, *Georgia,* 106, 119; Afary and Afary, *Molla Nasreddin,* 56–57; Suny, *Making of the Georgian Nation,* 168-71. **14** Suny, 116. **15** Afary and Afary, *Molla Nasreddin,* 24. **16** Iljine, *Memories of Tiflis,* 98. **17** Aleksidze, *Georgia,* 18. **18** Aleksidze, 19-20. **19** Iljine, *Memories of Tiflis,* 118. **20** Iljine, 308. **21** Quoted in Goldstein, *Georgian Feast,* 23. **22** Goldstein, 23. **23** Aleksidze, *Georgia,* 15. **24** Afary and Afary, *Molla Nasreddin,* 121. **25** Iljine, *Memories of Tiflis,* 72. **26** Goldstein, *Georgian Feast,* 29.

WOMAN FROM THE GEORGIAN NOBILITY RECLINING ON A DIVAN WITH AN OPEN BOOK AND A CENSER.

<

A RUG MERCHANT FROM AZERBAIJAN DISPLAYS HIS COMMODITIES.

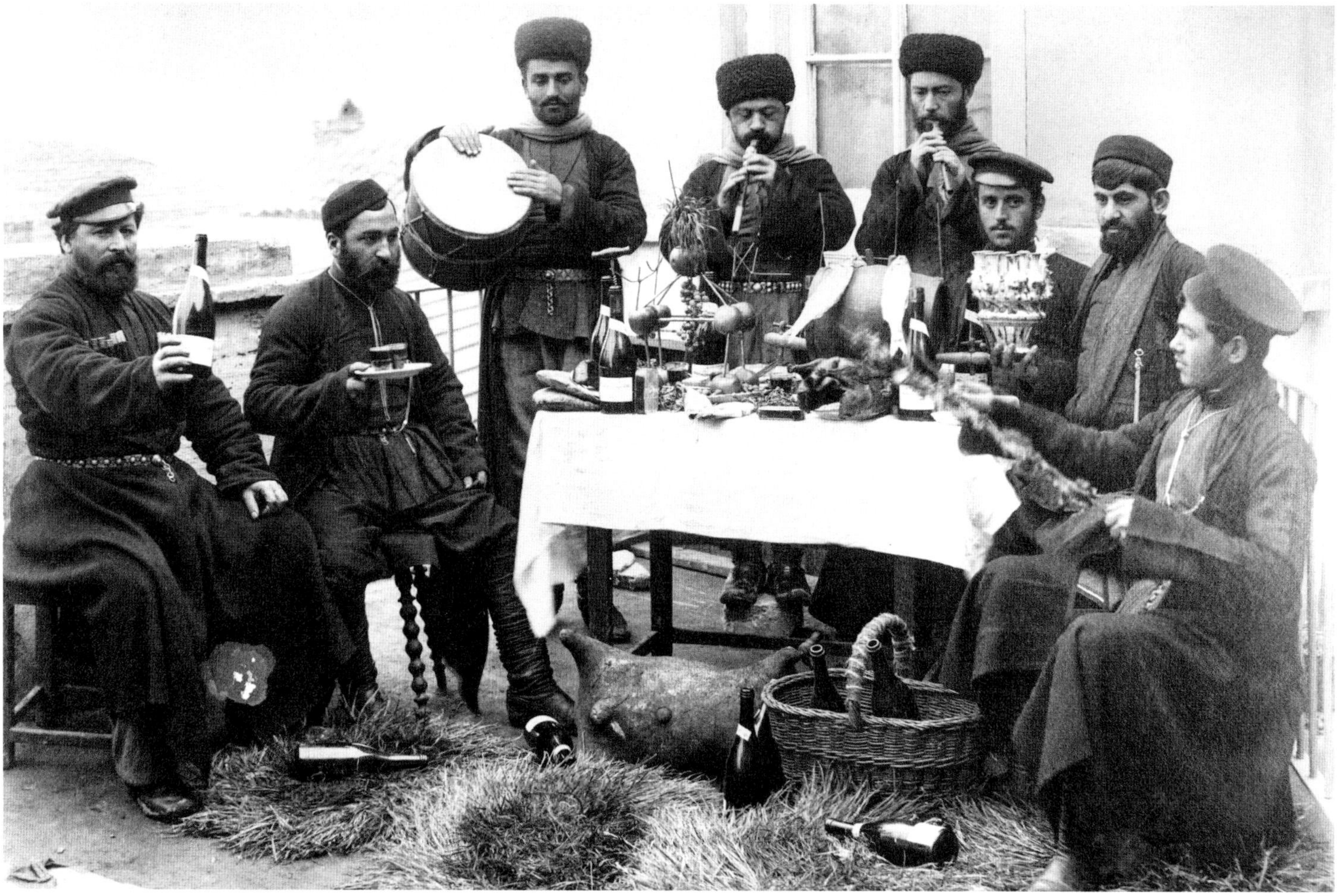

27 Afary and Afary, *Molla Nasreddin,* 119. **28** Iljine, *Memories of Tiflis,* 42, 271. **29** Hamsun, *In Wonderland*. **30** Erast Kuznetsov, *Niko Pirosman: 1862-1918* (Leningrad: Aurora, 1983), 14. **31** Klaus Albrecht Schröder, Bice Curiger and Adrian Ciprian Barsan, *Niko Pirosmani: Wanderer between Worlds* (Berlin: Hatje Cantz, 2018), 100. **32** Goldstein, *Georgian Feast,* 45. **33** Goldstein, 37; Iljine, *Memories of Tiflis,* 251. **34** Goldstein, *Georgian Feast,* 26-27. **35** Goldstein, 28. **36** Nino Müntnich, *Niko Pirosmani: Naive Malerei Georgiens* (Köln: Walther König, 2022), 35. **37** Hamsun, *In Wonderland,* 132. **38** Müntnich, *Niko Pirosmani: Naive Malerei Georgiens,* 34-35. **39** Aleksidze, *Georgia,* 55. **40** Donald Rayfield, *The Literature of Georgia: A History* (London: Garnett Press, 2013), 285-92, Kindle. **41** Iljine, *Memories of Tiflis,* 330. **42** Iljine, 332; Aleksidze, *Georgia,* 41. **43** Aleksidze, 42. **44** Aleksidze, 50. **45** Rayfield, *Literature of Georgia*, 5080-5088, Kindle. **46** Suny, *Making of the Georgian Nation,* 125-126; Aleksidze, *Georgia,* 17. **47** Rayfield, *Literature of Georgia,* 5491, Kindle. **48** Aleksidze, *Georgia,* 50. **49** Rayfield, *Literature of Georgia,* 6433-6438, Kindle. **50** Schröder, Curiger and Barsan, *Niko Pirosmani,* 47, 178. **51** Iljine, *Memories of Tiflis,* 337; Rayfield, *Literature of Georgia,* 6442-6444, Kindle. **52** Rayfield, 6441, Kindle. **53** Rayfield, 6673, Kindle. **54** Irina Vladimirovna Arsenishvili, *Georgian Easel Painting: Second Half of the 18th Century to the 1920's* (New York: Nova Science, 2009), 5. **55** Arsenishvili, 11; Yaroslava Bilinkina, "Tiflis Portrait School. On the Mutual Influence of Cultures in the Georgian Art", in *International Interdisciplinary Conference: Pirosmani and Georgian Culture* (Tbilisi, 2013), 33-34; Iljine, *Memories of Tiflis,* 171. **56** Nina Taylor-Terlecka, "Image and Text: A Literary Approach to the Paintings of Pirosmanashvili", in *International Interdisciplinary Conference: Pirosmani and Georgian Culture* (Tbilisi, 2013), 181. **57** Arsenishvili, *Georgian Easel Painting,* 31. **58** Afary and Afary, *Molla Nasreddin,* 159. **59** Herman Maes and Lika Mamatsaschvili, *Masters of 19th Century Photography: Dimitri Ermakov, Photographer and Collector* (Tbilisi: Georgian National Museum, 2014), 32. **60** Maes and Mamatsaschvili, 36. **61** Afary and Afary, *Molla Nasreddin,* 12. **62** Afary and Afary, 3. **63** Afary and Afary, 12. **64** Goldstein, *Georgian Feast,* 35. **65** Taylor-Terlecka, "Image and Text: A Literary Approach to the Paintings of Pirosmanashvili", 195. **66** Iljine, *Memories of Tiflis,* 129. **67** Iljine, 139; Nana Kipiani, "The Great Experiment", Artforum 51, no. 8 (April 2013), https://www.thefreelibrary.com/The+great+experiment%3A+Nana+Kipiani+on+Georgian+modernism-a0325892834. **68** Goldstein, *Georgian Feast,* 9.

Kaspar Thormod (born 1984), Ph.D., author and art writer, Denmark. He has written the books *Artistic Reconfigurations of Rome: An Alternative Guide to the Eternal City, 1989–2014* (Brill: Leiden & Boston, 2018) and *Rom falder* (C&K Forlag, 2012).

GEORGIAN MUSICIANS BY A TABLE SET WITH EVERYTHING FROM SHISH KEBAB TO TEA AND WINE.

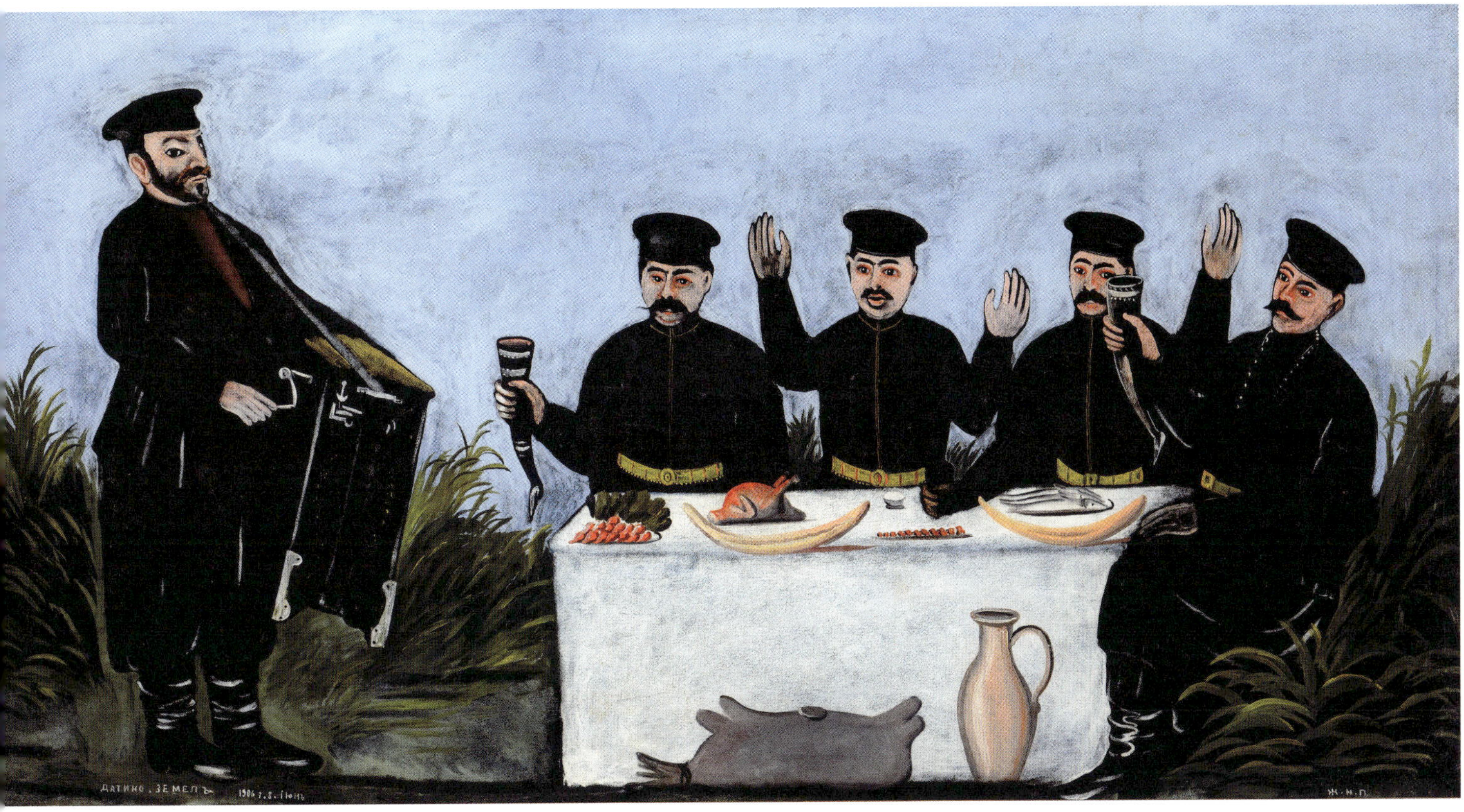

CAROUSAL WITH DATIKO ZEMEL, THE ORGAN GRINDER. 1906

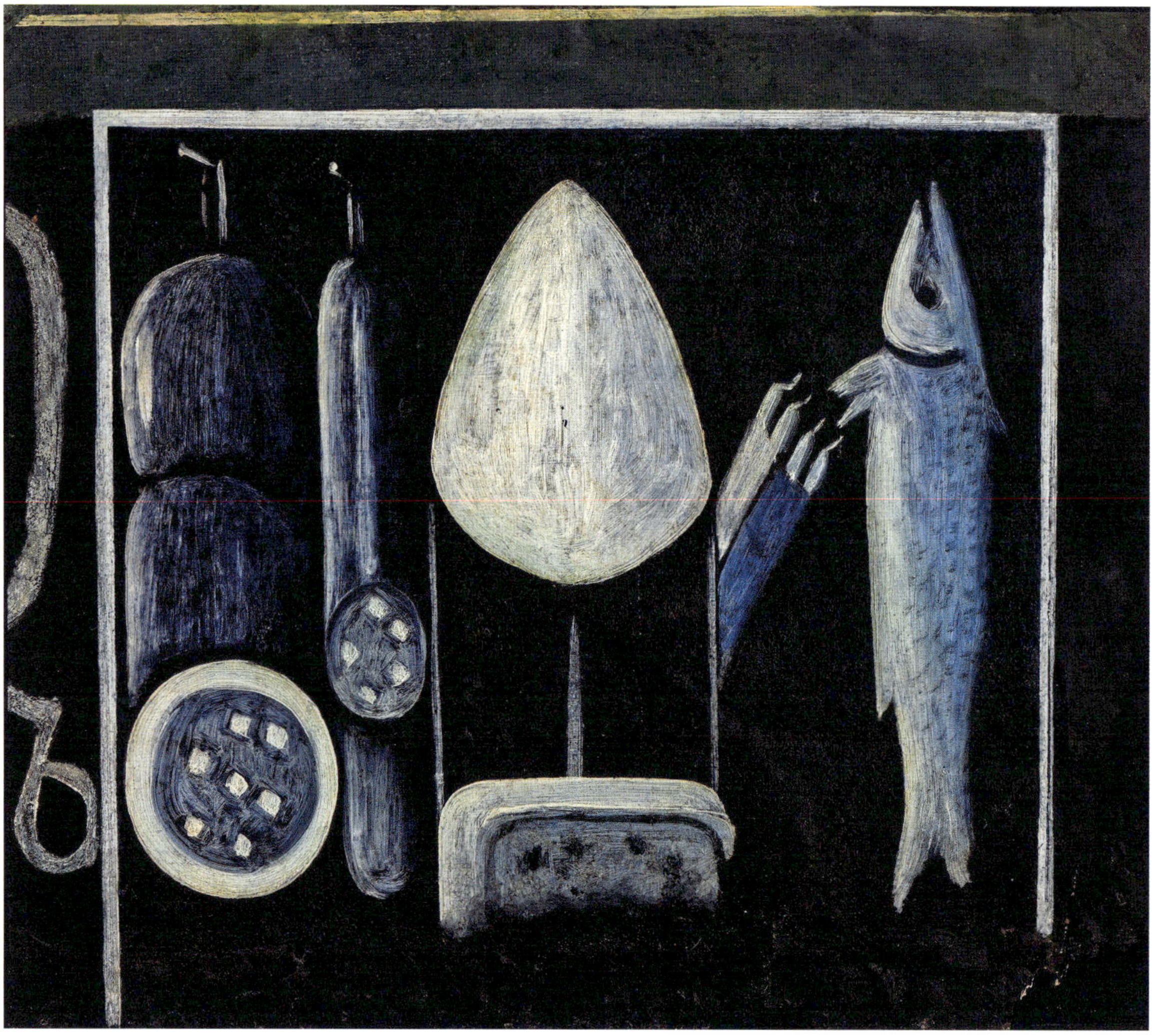

STILL LIFE WITH A LOAF OF SUGAR
(FRAGMENT OF SIGNBOARD FOR A WINESHOP IN DIDUBE)
>
WOMAN WITH FLOWERS AND PARASOL

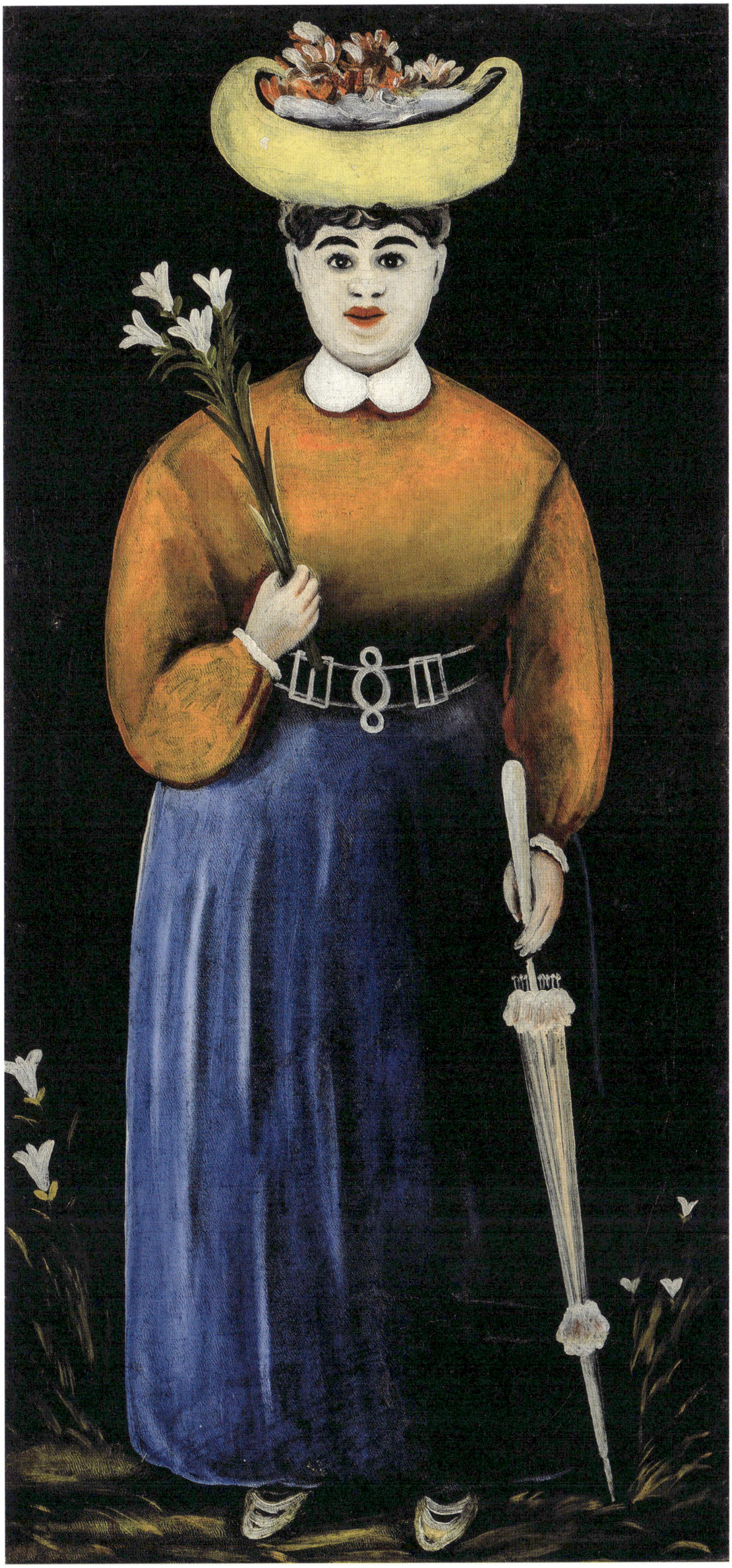

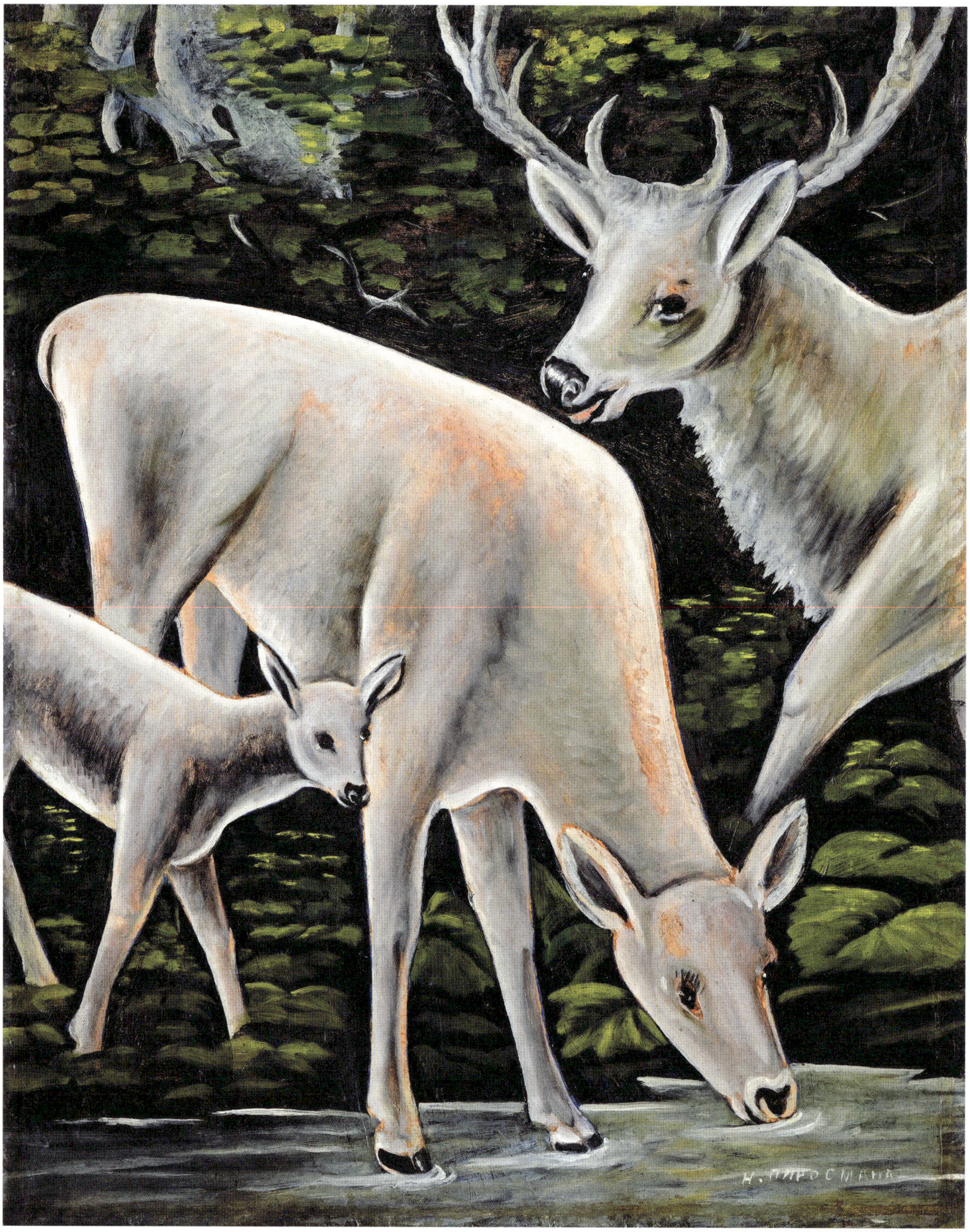

THREE DEER BY A STREAM

>

AMBLING HIND

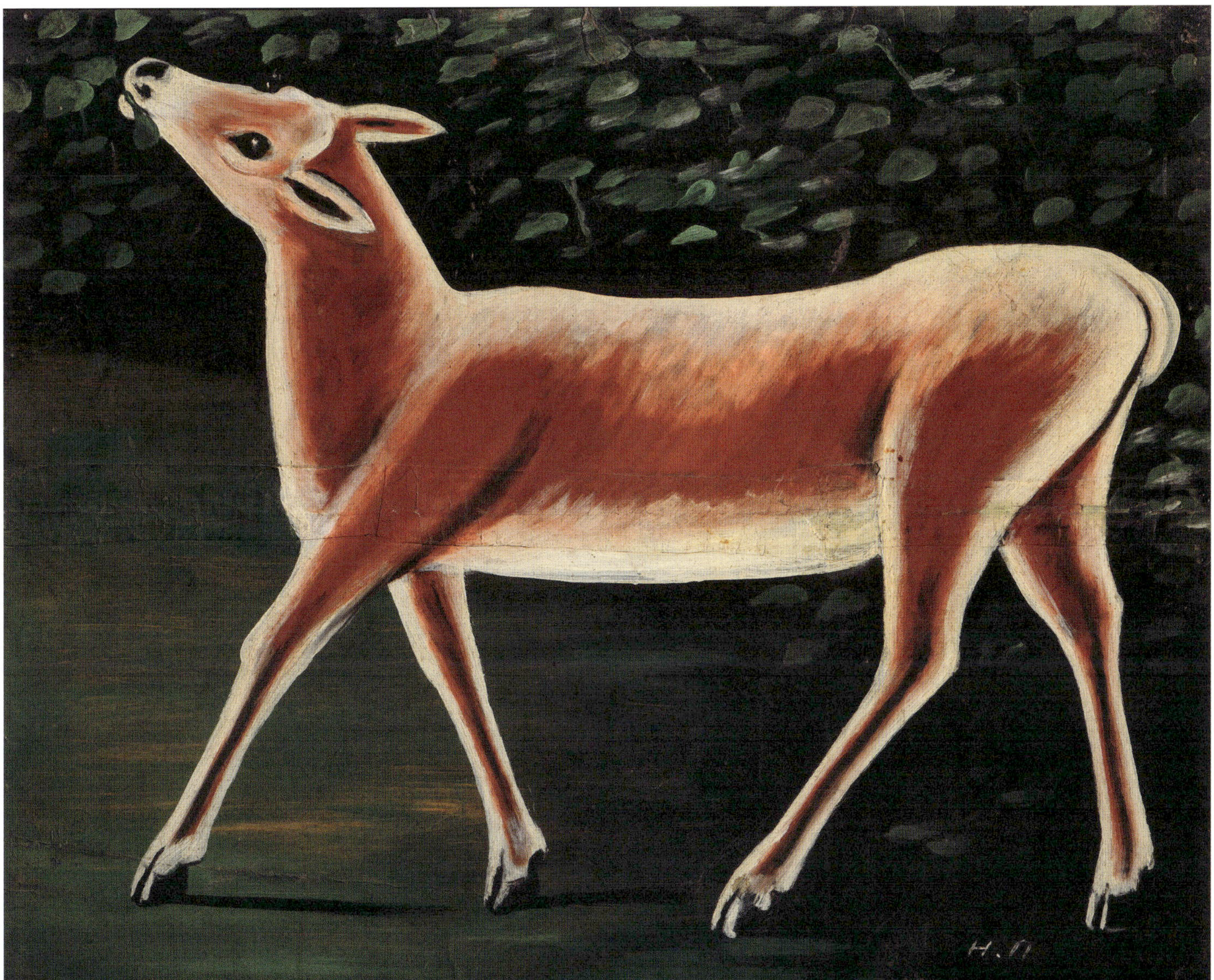
Н.П

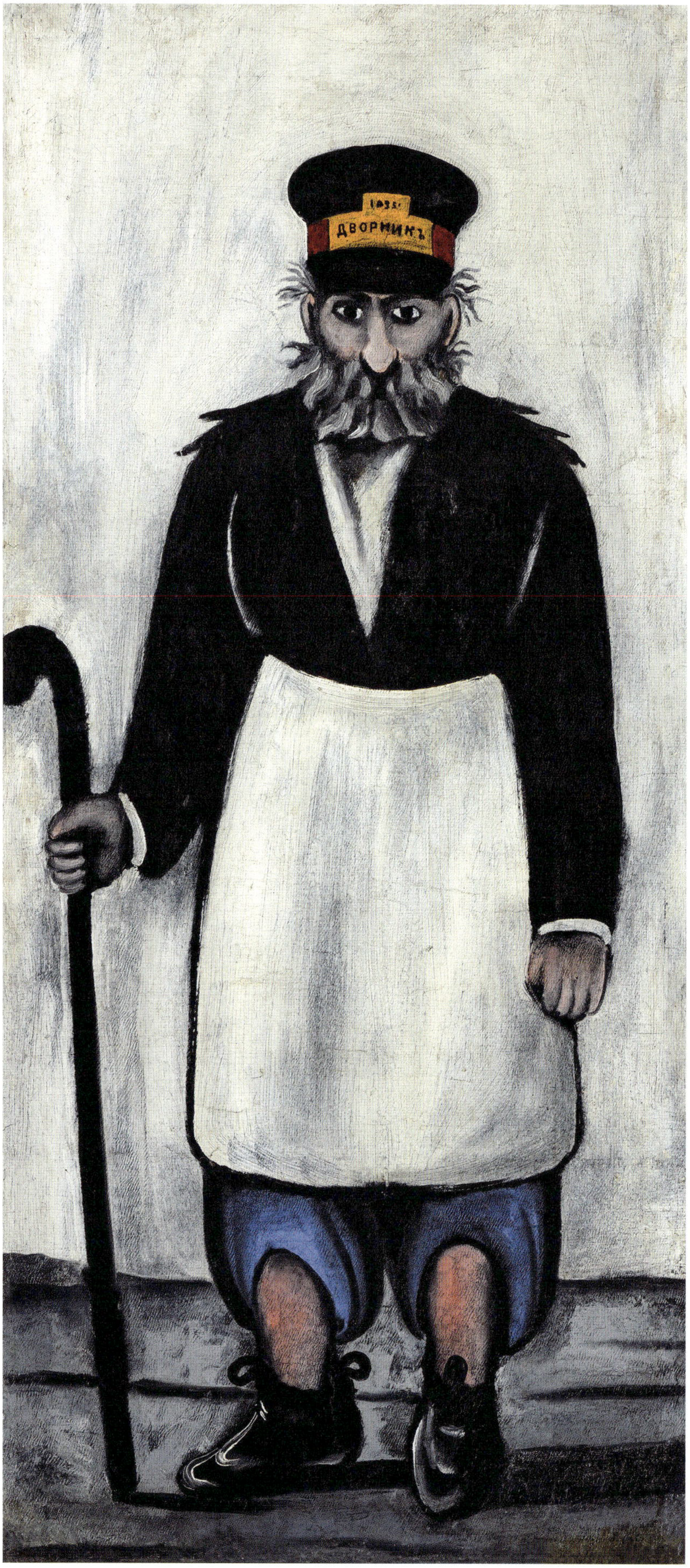

JANITOR

>

BOY FIREWOOD VENDOR

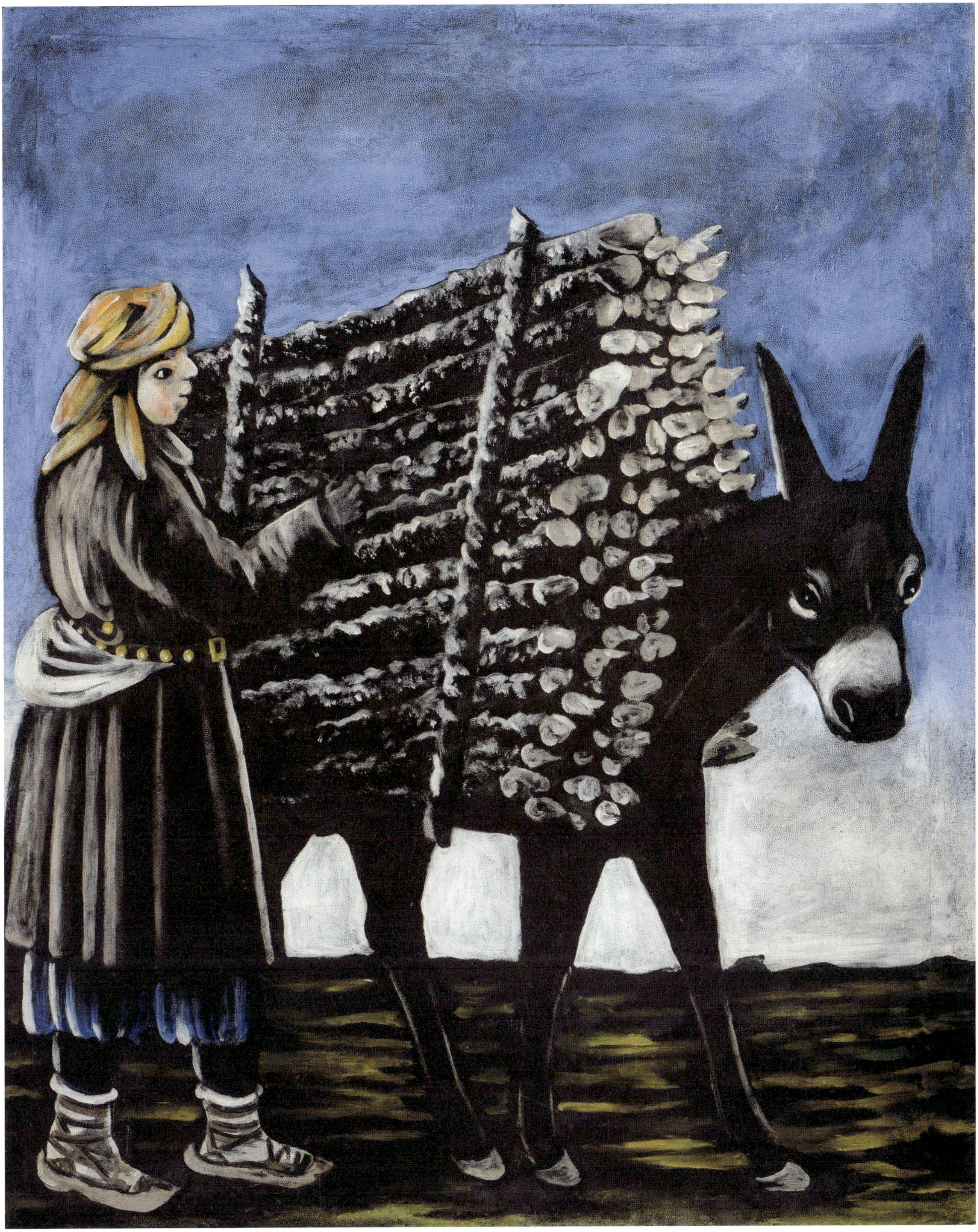

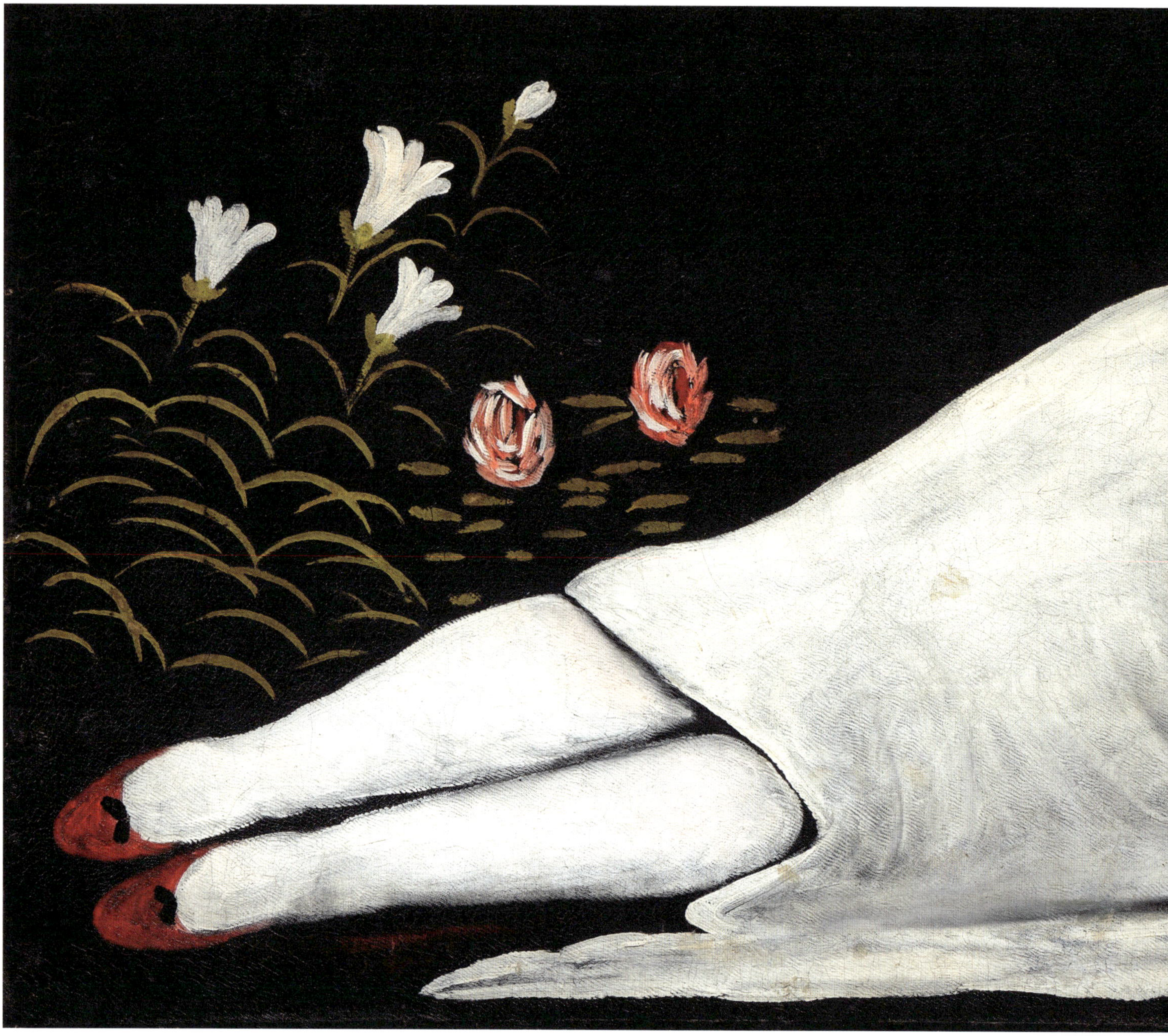

ORTACHALA BELLE (HALF OF DIPTYCH)

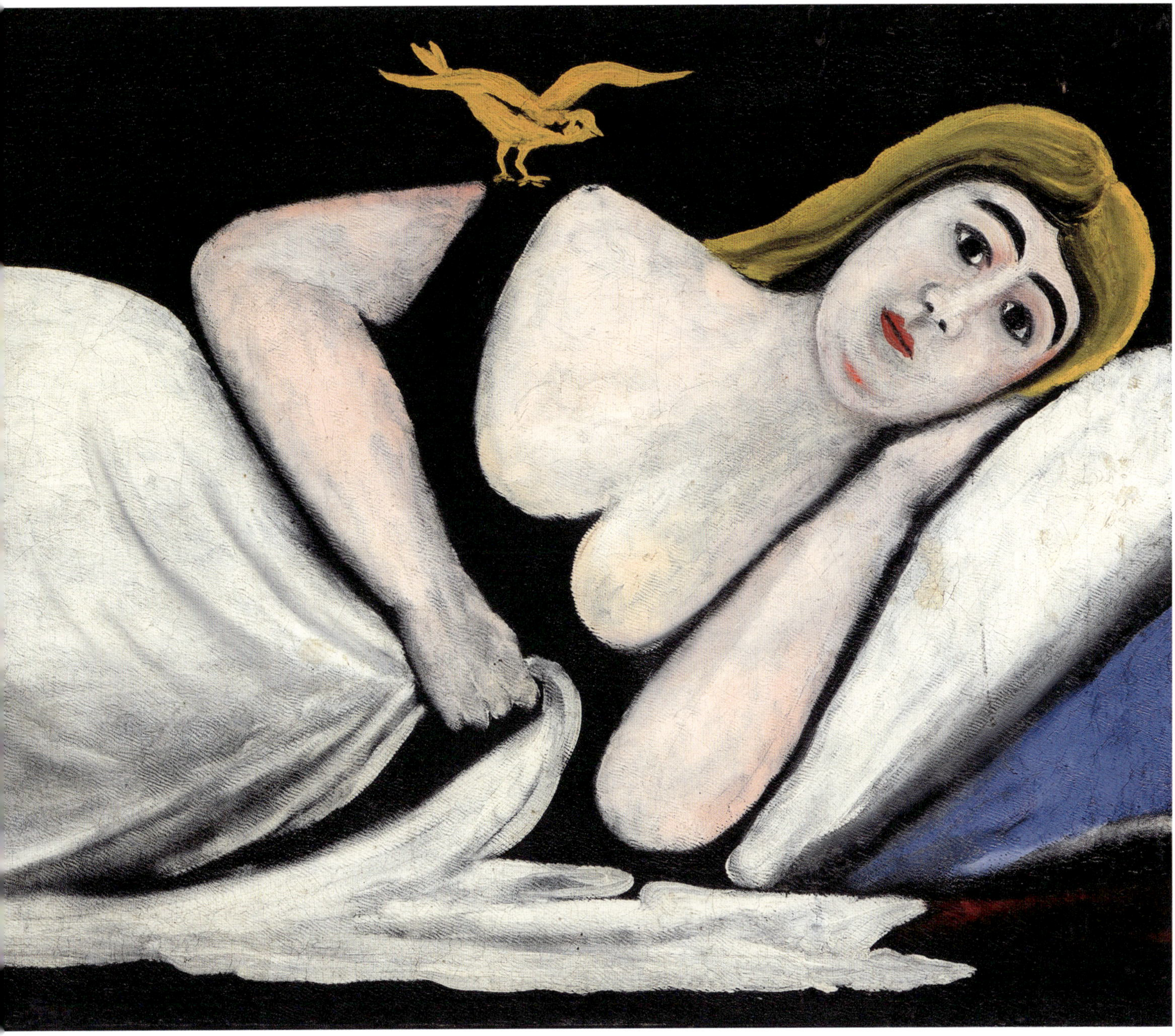

I asked myself when I first saw Pirosmani's paintings, and I could not remember. I do know that I've always been very fond of his pictures. He's been there since my childhood. I also can't remember whether I first saw a Pirosmani in the flesh in a museum, or if I saw his works in illustrations. His presence was a constant. But the admiration has never ceased. There is a kind of strength that permeates his paintings.

It's not that easy for me to sum up what constituted my fascination for Pirosmani. To me his paintings always had an aura, an inner strength. I liked to draw as a child and as a teen I started taking painting courses. At that point I was even more in awe of Pirosmani's pictures. But I think it was the directness of the paintings that touched me most. The fact that he takes life *as it comes*. That he neither criticises nor admires it, he just depicts it. In his paintings, Pirosmani was able to grasp life in its fullness, but at the same time, pictorially, he reduced it to the essential. He realised this with minimal brushstrokes that to me translate as direct, honest and strong. I've always been impressed by Pirosmani's vision, by his reduced compositions.

Looking back at the artistic circles contemporary to Pirosmani, you realise how modern he was. Pirosmani was born in the 19th century. He only lived 18 more years after the turn of the century. But his vision clearly surpassed the century he was born in. What sets Pirosmani apart is his reductionist style applied to figurative painting. He was a self-taught artist, but you can tell that formally he was finding ways to convey the world in a pure, direct manner in his paintings.

There is a seed of modernity in his work that is surprising, considering his background, the life he led. And speaking of his life, the artistic and intellectual circles of the time knew little to nothing about him until approximately six years before his death.

But, honestly, for a long time I didn't know much about his life either. There's something like a myth of Pirosmani that the public shares, and which, of course, is not very nuanced. The reasons for this are complicated, but, in part Pirosmani's reception after his death and the myth that he became at one point have something to do with Georgia's political past. By Soviet standards, culture must be national in form and socialist in content. From being seen as avant-garde, Pirosmani was reinvented as a personification of 'simple, rural, merry Georgian folk'. This being in opposition to what the Soviets wished to eradicate: which was Georgian intellectuals and intellectuality. It worked. The myth of the naive, popular painter was created. Surely this helped popularise Pirosmani greatly, but for a long time his image was mythologised and sentimentalised.

The fact that Pirosmani was a self-taught painter was of no great social advantage to him during his lifetime. But on the other hand, this shows even more the kind of artist that he was. He worked completely outside of what was officially considered serious art. At least until the Zdanevich brothers (Kirill (1892-1969) and Ilia (1894-1975)) discovered his work. But, there are stories of Pirosmani painting in the midst of a crowd. So, at least within his community which was made up of working-class people, he did receive recognition. And this is what's so interesting about him: his paintings spoke both to the working class and to the avant-garde.

His paintings and his subject matter can be read as simple, but the avant-garde saw beauty and refinement precisely in this simplicity and in the reduction of the shapes, and in his bright colours. Pirosmani was looking for the essence of things in his representations.

In Pirosmani's paintings there are sometimes costumes or objects that can be identified as belonging to Georgian culture. But when I look at his pictures, I think they are much more universal than they're often being perceived. What strikes me is the love that beams from his painting. It's not antipathy for a certain class or favouritism for another, it's just love for life in its diversity. I think that's what attracts me – in combination with the amazing colours. Pirosmani's use of colour is very particular. He painted on black waxed tablecloths or oilcloths which gave his colour more vibrancy. He also applied the paint in a very direct manner; he probably wasn't mixing the colours that much.

Some of the paintings he made were commissions from patrons who paid for his food and drinks. There are many anecdotes about this. For instance, when people would commission a painting, they would have very specific requests about what they wished Pirosmani to paint them. Once Pirosmani complained to Ilia Zdanevich about one of the commissions: "Look at this picture, this is a rabbit. Why a rabbit? Why is it necessary? But the patron asks me insistently: 'Do it for my sake.' What should I do? I paint it, I don't want them to complain. That's how they destroy my paintings." He's really complaining.

THEA DJORDJADZE:

» LOVE BEAMS FROM HIS PAINTING «

TOLD TO ROXANNE BAGHESHIRIN LÆRKESEN

So you wonder how many of Pirosmani's works were such commissions, and how many his own choices. He portrayed the working class – which he knew – in many instances. And sometimes he painted exotic animals, like the *Giraffe* (p. 32), perhaps after photographs, and that resulted in a black and white giraffe. One could really say that he was portraying life as he saw and experienced it. But it's also just one of the many anecdotes that helped create the myth of Pirosmani. We don't know why he painted. Did he really complain about the commissioned work or was it his inspiration? Maybe he saw some animals and was wildly inspired. We have no idea, we can just keep adding to the narrative.

Pirosmani's presence, all the way, has formed my perception of art, sometimes without me knowing it. Recently I remembered that for one of my early exhibitions, a group show at Kunstverein Düsseldorf in 2001, I made an homage to Pirosmani. Thinking of his little milk and grocery shop I made a kiosk with fresh fruit and vegetables that reminded me of his *Fruit Stall* painting. But I had completely forgotten again that it was an homage to Pirosmani. I think Pirosmani is such a big part of my life that sometimes I don't even realise how much of an impact he has had on my art and on my way of seeing things and bringing things into a space.

This exhibition at the Louisiana Museum of Modern Art is a manifestation of the fact that he is still relevant today. The work carries its strength through the centuries; it feels so fresh and so young and so unique that it carries itself through the years.

Thea Djordjadze (born 1971) is a Georgian contemporary artist who lives in Berlin. Her objects and installations investigate the idiosyncrasies of particular exhibition conditions and the transitory experience of space. In 2023 she shows among other places at Wiels, Brussels.

The interview was originally made for Louisiana Channel and later adapted for print by Malou Wedel Bruun. Discover the interview with the artist at channel.louisiana.dk

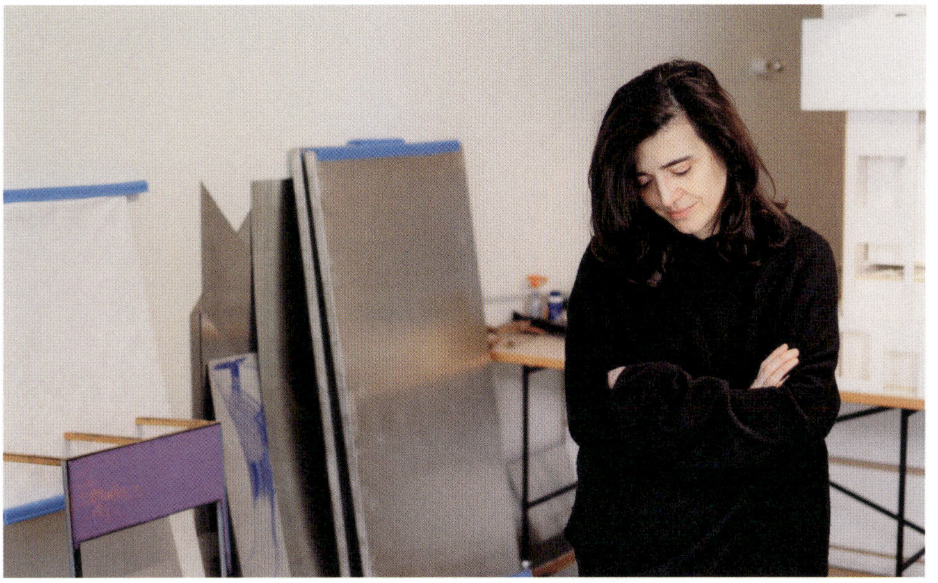

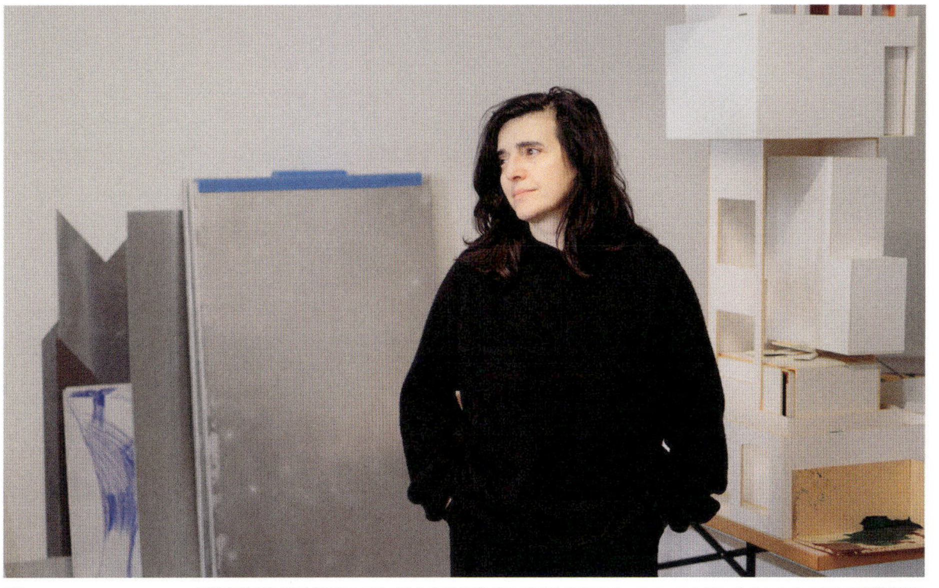

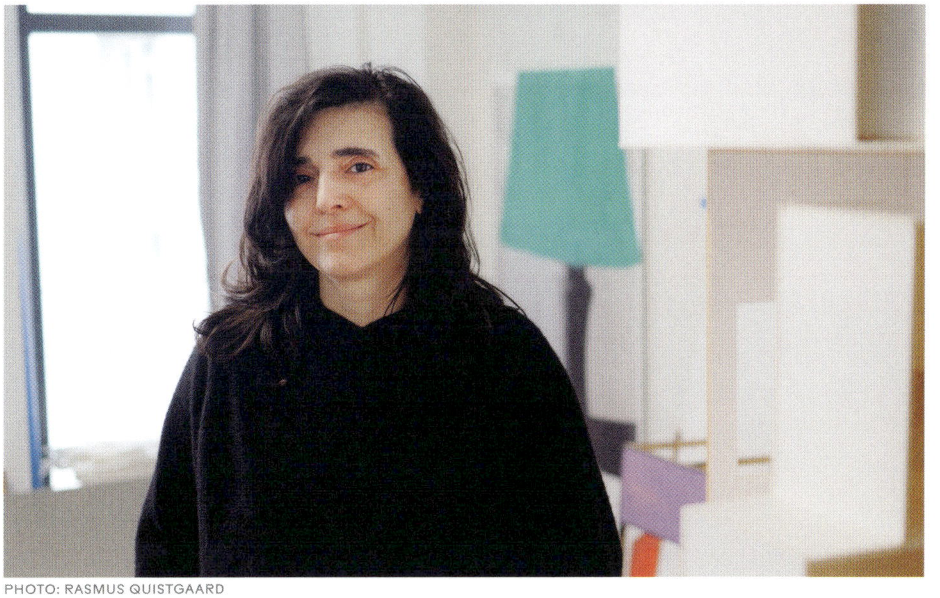

PHOTO: RASMUS QUISTGAARD

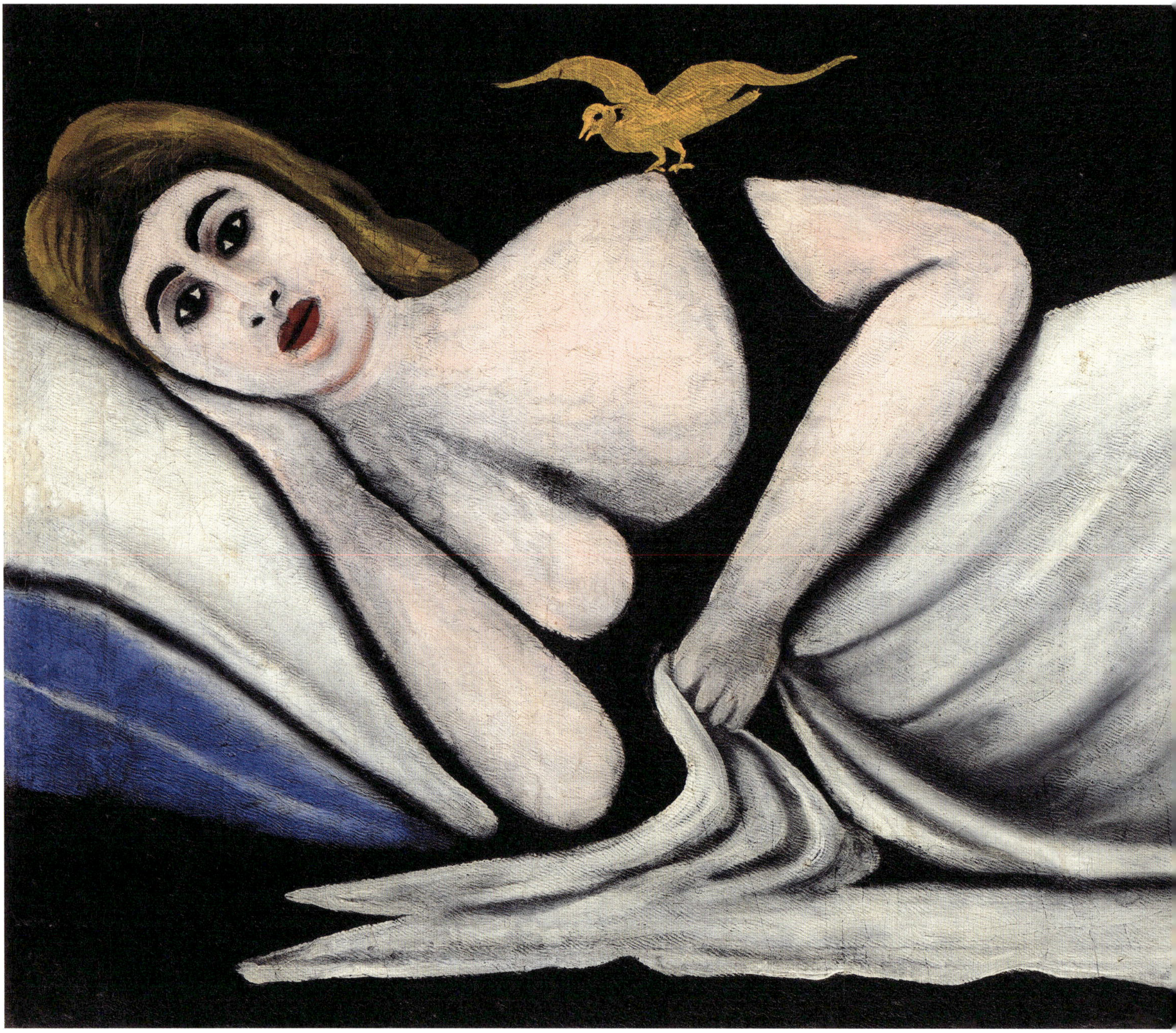

ORTACHALA BELLE (HALF OF DIPTYCH)

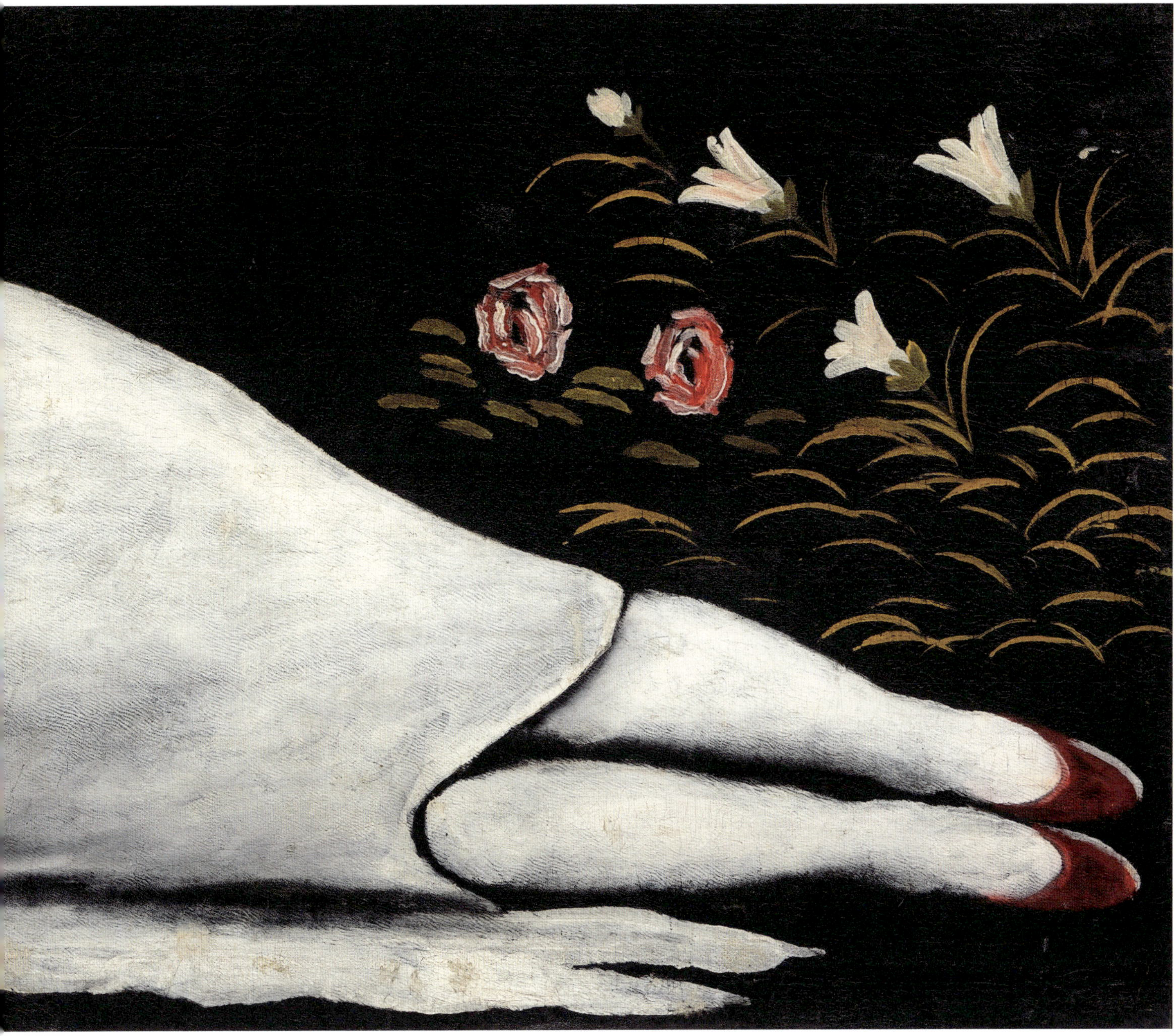

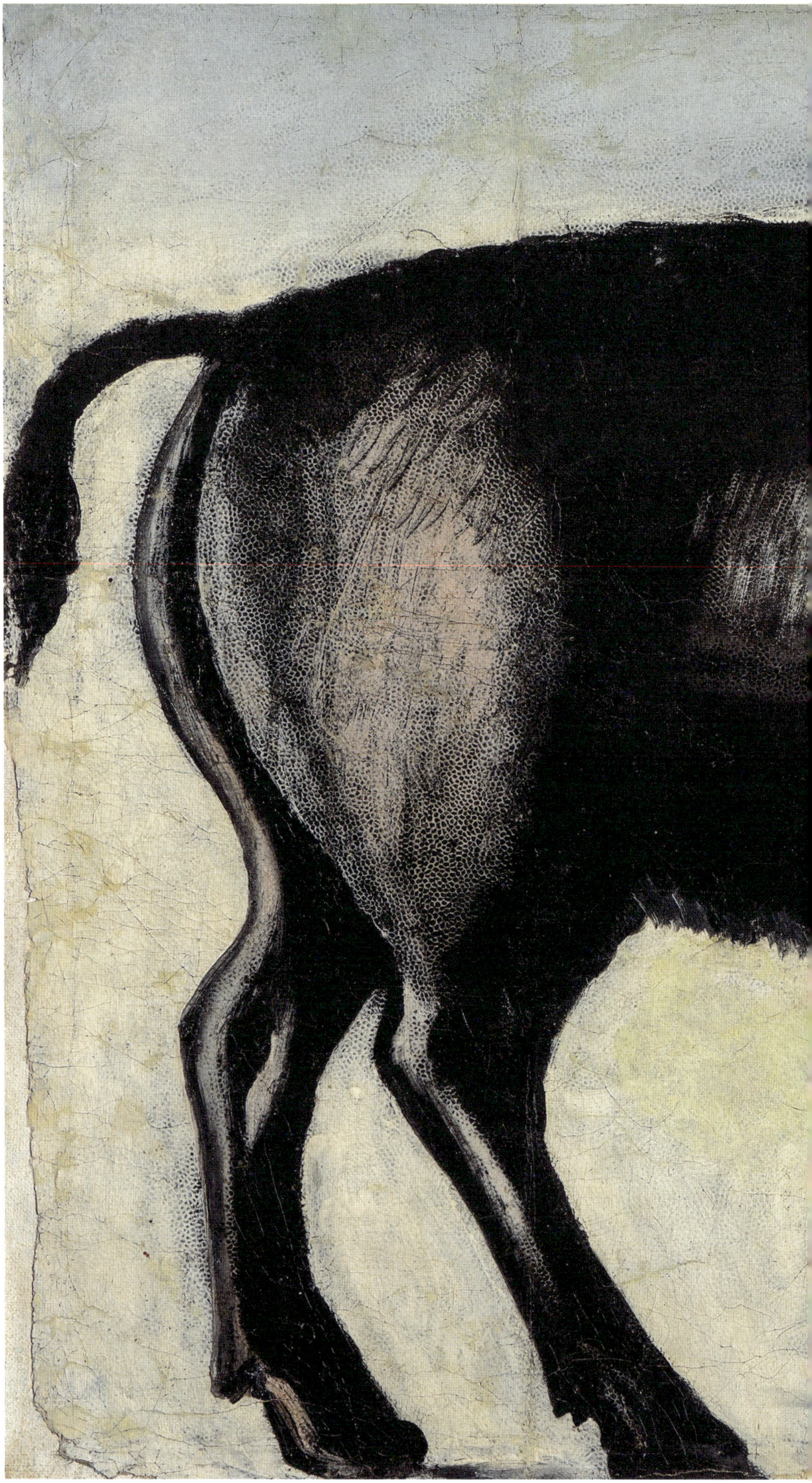

BOAR

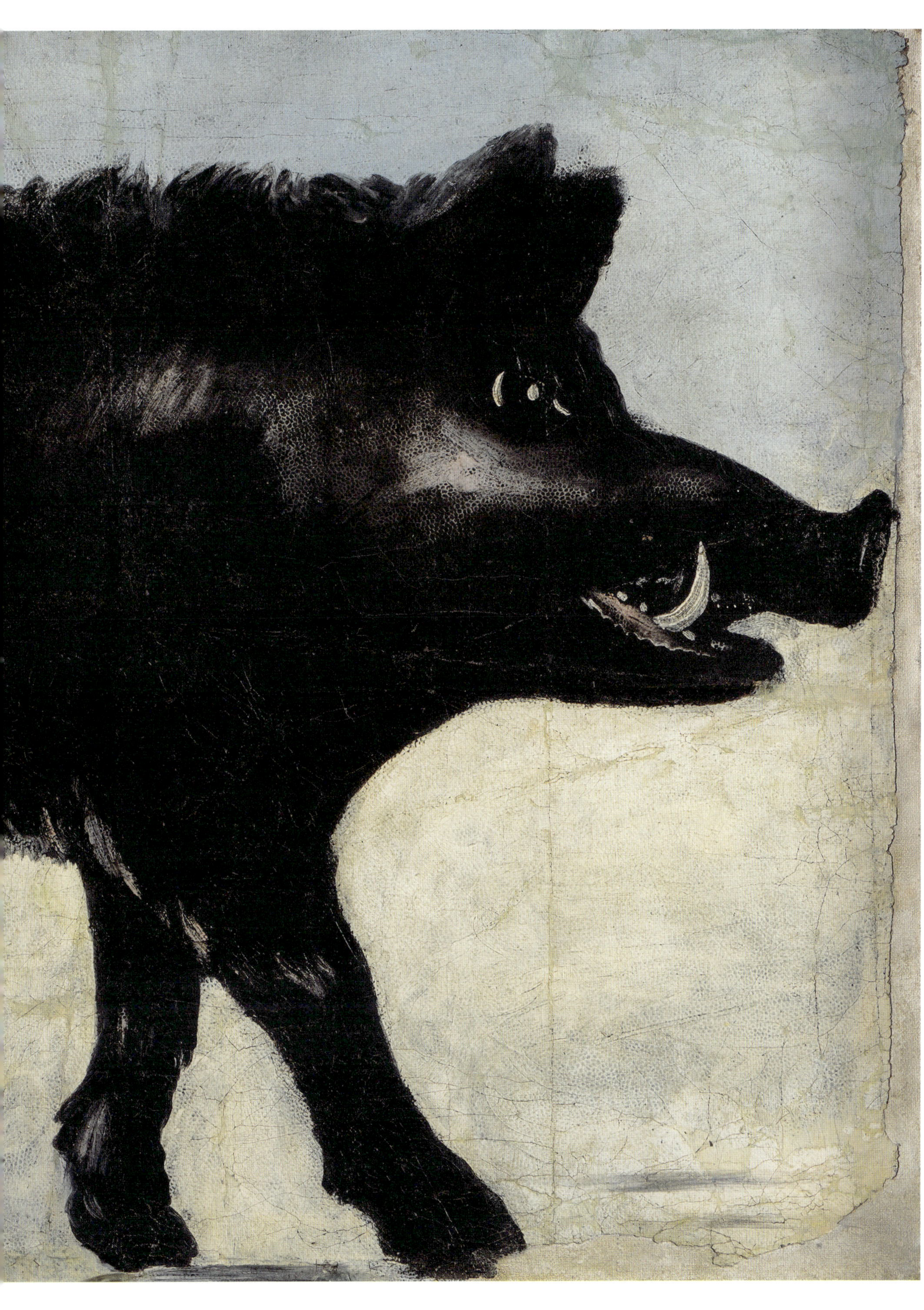

FRESCOES FOR A CHURCH WITHOUT RELIGION

A CONVERSATION WITH NANA KIPIANI AND LEVAN CHOGOSHVILI

DANIEL BAUMANN

How did I meet Nana and Levan? It all started at the end of the 1990s when I found an email by the Georgian art historian Nana Kipiani in my inbox. She had heard from curator Peter Pakesch, a mutual friend, that I was doing informal film evenings and wanted to invite me to come to Tbilisi in order to stage such an evening. In the end it did not materialise for various reasons. In 2003, I met Mzia Chikhradze, another Georgian art historian, in Basel and the idea of an exhibition of young contemporary artists in Tbilisi came up. Long story short: I called Pro Helvetia Swiss Arts Council to see if they would support such an initiative and they did, annually from 2004 to 2009.

These exhibitions involved many different people, but always Nana Kipiani, the artist Levan Chogoshvili (her husband) and Gela Patashuri, another artist. While in Tbilisi, Nana introduced me to modernism in Georgia (I didn't know anything about it) and of course to the work of Nikolaj Pirosmanashvili, now known as Niko Pirosmani (1862/63-1918). I had majored in history of art and didn't know anything about this chapter of European modernism – nor did anybody else I knew. I was scandalised. And so we decided to set about correcting it in 2009 with the exhibition *The Fantastic Tavern: The Tbilisi Avant-Garde* at Casey Kaplan Gallery in New York (curated in collaboration with Nana Kipiani, Levan Chogoshvili, Tea Tabadaze and Mzia Chikhradze) and in 2018, *Georgische Modernismus: Die Fantastische Taverne* (Georgian Modernism: The Fantastic Tavern) at Kunsthalle Zürich (curated in collaboration with Nana Kipiani, Levan Chogoshvili and Tea Tabadaze).

Throughout the years, I have met Nana and Levan again and again, often in their apartment. It dawned on me that Nana was not only a specialist on modernism in Georgia and on Pirosmani, but a doyenne of Georgian art history. I love how precise and unconventional her and Levan's thinking is and I admire them for the way they keep their integrity throughout most difficult times. They are the great intellectuals we miss so much. Therefore, the following conversation is as much about Pirosmani and Georgia as it is a tribute to two amazing people – and a friendship. *Daniel Baumann*

A MODERNIST DARLING REDUCED TO A SHOVEL

Daniel Baumann: You got to know Niko Pirosmani during the Soviet time in the 1960s and 1970s. Was he a known artist back then?

Nana Kipiani: You know, Pirosmani was a known artist from the middle of the 1910s. He was talked about in many texts, in journals, literature, in experimental texts, even in caricature. Eminent writers and artists like Ilia (1894-1975) and Kirill Zdanevich (1892-1969) and Grigol Robakidze (1880-1962) wrote about him and discussed his art, but also about what kind of artistic person he was.

In the 1910s quite serious texts mainly in newspapers were written. In 1922 the neo-symbolist group Blue Horns published a number of texts by different authors in their periodical newspaper *Bahtrioni*. In 1926 an important catalogue with other texts by writers and artists was published. In 1927 the filmmaker Leo Esakia (1890-1969) published the book *New Art and Niko Pirosmanashvili*. Beno Gordeziani (1894-1975), the member of the avant-garde group H_2SO_4, published several remarkable articles too. It's important to highlight that they all wrote about his art and life and not about his social status.

In the 1930s the communist press takes him over by obviously stressing a different point of view: now, he is presented as a poor artist who drank a lot while being unique and talented, a standout figure, even a genius. This started and established the still prevailing but wrong idea of 'Pirosmani the primitive artist'.

Of course, they never placed him and his oeuvre in the context of modernism in Georgia where he truly belongs, even though he was not a modernist. Instead he was branded as the example of the craftsman and the man who works on trains as opposed to the bourgeois artist of the independent social-democratic Georgia from 1918 to the mid-1920s. This new reading started to surface in 1928 with Stalin (1878/79-1953) getting into power, followed by his purges that killed most of the Georgian intelligentsia orpushed them out of the country.

By the 1940s, Pirosmani was totally forgotten, and he only resurfaced in the mid-1960s again. It was the Soviet film *Pirosmani* by the Georgian filmmaker Giorgi Shengelaia (1937-2020) that brought Pirosmani back in 1969. The film has quite some qualities, but it reiterates the cliche of the poor and tragic drunkard and became the image for the so-called Soviet bohemians in the 1960. This became one of the bases for Pirosmani's new popularity until today, but it is highly questionable.

DB: How was it possible for Pirosmani to have a comeback in the 1960s?

NK: One important reason was him being the perfect illustration for the all-pervasive Soviet cultural policy expressed by the Stalinist formulation "socialist in content, national in form". By this slogan and ideology, the differences of the many regions and nations could by subsumed and channelled into one big nation while giving them the impression of their own identity. By the 1960s everybody had nearly forgotten about the very short period of independent Georgia from 1918 to 1921; it was erased from the Georgian history, from teaching at schools and the universities. The new Soviet generation knew nothing about modernism and the avant-garde – it had been totally banned, and for decades the works were hidden away in different museum storages.

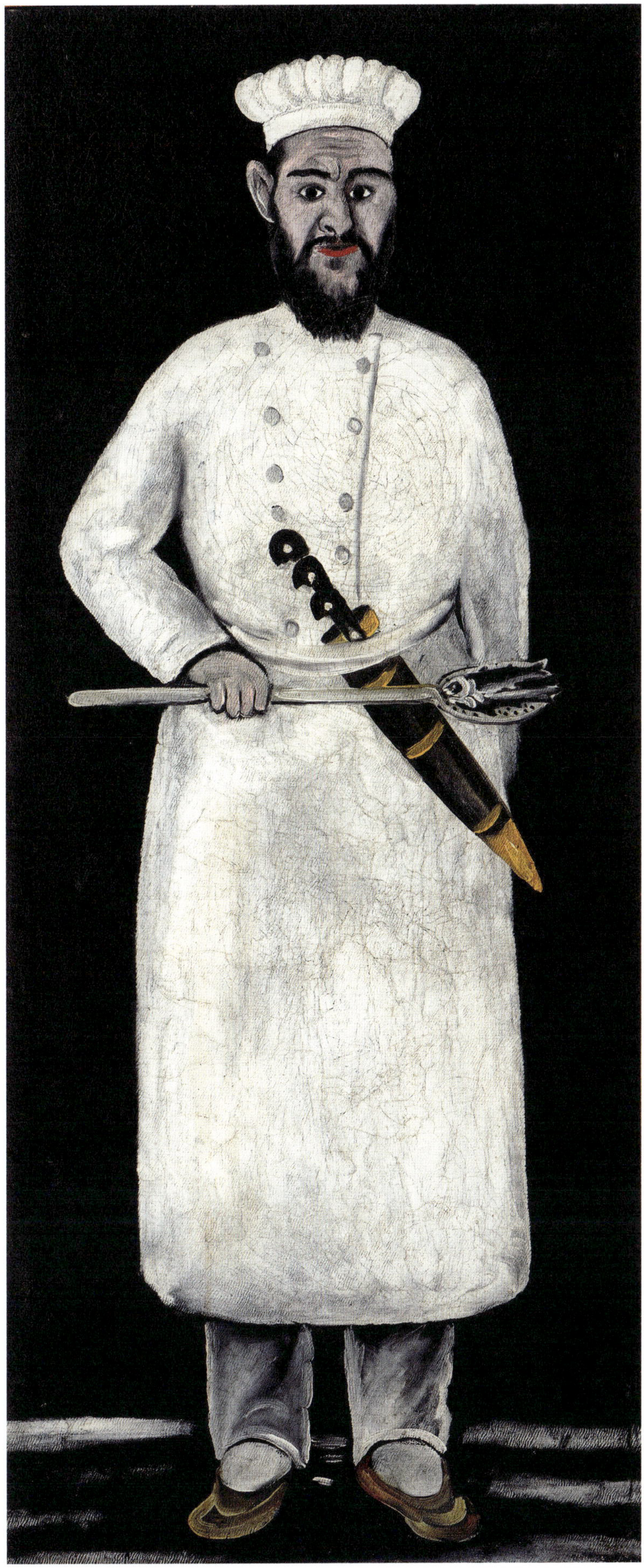

COOK

Georgian modernism was rediscovered only in the middle of 1990s. So, officials gave Pirosmani one additional function – and I think it is really very tragic to obscure an entire generation of modernists and avant-gardists between the 1910s and 1920s. He became 'the lonely genius with folk roots', which was important for propaganda. Beside him, only some realist and semi-realist artists of that period were allowed to be seen.

Levan Chogoshvili: So, Pirosmani was 'national in form', meaning Georgia, and the content of his work was interpreted as socialist; for instance, the poor people with children as opposed to the rich and bourgeois without children as you can see in his painting *The Childless Millionaire and Poor Woman with her Children* (pp. 10-11).

NK: But this is not what Pirosmani was painting, he was never interested in social problems or conflicts. It's a much more universal theme and message, showing the diversity of life as it is. The poor and the rich as it is thematised by the Bible as an allegory, even a *memento mori*.

LC: I have to tell you a story, as it shows yet another reality. In the 1960s, Pirosmani wasn't the very famous artist he is now; it was a very different time. A relative of mine, Papuna Tsereteli (1904-1985), was a collector, something rather uncommon for the Soviet Union. He collected everything – art, photography, furniture and so on – and he also owned two paintings by Pirosmani. I was a young man then and one day he told me that he was walking down the streets of Tbilisi in the late 1950s and saw a Kurdish woman in her traditional clothes cleaning the pavement. At that time, almost all street cleaners were Kurdish, as for instance Armenian people were mostly shoemakers. So, he sees the Kurdish women with a broom in one hand and an improvised shovel in the other. When he got closer, he saw that the shovel was actually a painting by Pirosmani.

DB: You mean a copy or a print?

LC: No no, a real original painting by Pirosmani. There was no technique to print in colour at that time in the USSR. So, he asked the woman to give him the painting, but she refused because she needed it to do her work. In the end, he gave her a sum of money of the value of two bottles of wine or so and he got the painting by Pirosmani. He was very proud of it, but could not sell it, because there was no market, nobody wanted to pay for Pirosmani nor for a very important modernist painter like David Kakabadze (1889-1952). My father tried to buy some of the abstract but forbidden paintings by Kakabadze because he, as a mathematician, was interested in abstraction. But it was absolutely impossible even though he knew Kakabadze's wife. My father said half-ironically that maybe if he asked her, if he could buy an abstract painting by her husband, she would think he was crazy. So were the times. You know, in the mid-1940s, the professors at the Art Academy in Tbilisi had to sign a petition demanding Kakabadze be shot as an 'enemy of the people'. He was fired from the Academy, and tried to teach math or French instead but was forbidden to do so. He ended up painting signs and posters for shops, like Pirosmani.

DB: Did he get killed by Stalin?

LC: No, but that's another long story.

THE FRENCH CONNECTION

NK: So back to Pirosmani and the 1960s. When years later I first saw the film *Pirosmani*, I didn't like it. Maybe it is a good film.

LC: I have seen it many times. They really wanted to make a good film, not just propaganda. As Nana said, Giorgi Shengelaia was the director. And he pretended to be an unofficial filmmaker, which he was not exactly. Erlom Akhvlediani (1933-2012) was commissioned to write the scenario, he was a quite good novelist and scriptwriter. And the main role was played by the artist Avto Varazi (1926-1977), maybe the most talented Georgian artist of the 1950s and 1960s. Varazi was an unofficial artist, an intellectual coming from a renowned scientist's family, he was popular among other artists and among non-conformists in Moscow and he was actually doing pop art. He was a heavy drinker, and they chose him for the part, saying that he was like Pirosmani. You see how the cliche of the poor drinking artist was perpetuated even on that level too, but the film was well received in Europe and won some prizes.

DB: Together with the exhibition at the Musée des Arts Décoratifs in 1969, this relaunched Pirosmani's career.

NK: The exhibition in Paris goes back to Ilia Zdanevich, who discovered Pirosmani together with his brother Kirill and the artist Mikhail Le Dentu (1891-1917) in 1912 in Tbilisi. Ilia Zdanevich owned many paintings by Pirosmani (in 1930, his brother, Kirill, was forced to sell them to the National Gallery of Georgia. It was a newly established museum by modernist artist Dimitri Shevardnadze (1885-1937), who was responsible for nearly all collections which now are owned by the National Museum of Georgia, ed.).

As for Ilia Zdanevich, he moved to France in 1920 and got involved with the Paris avant-garde scene, organised lectures, artistic balls and designed and produced fabrics for Coco Chanel (1883-1971). He befriended Max Ernst (1891-1976), Joan Miró (1893-1983) and Pablo Picasso (1881-1973) – the latter made an etching portraying Pirosmani in 1972. So, there was fertile ground in Paris for Pirosmani already. However, Zdanevich was not even invited to the opening in Paris, as he was *persona non grata* to the Soviets.

LC: You know, in Stalin's time you could get arrested just for having relatives abroad. That was enough reason. It happened to people in my family and most families.

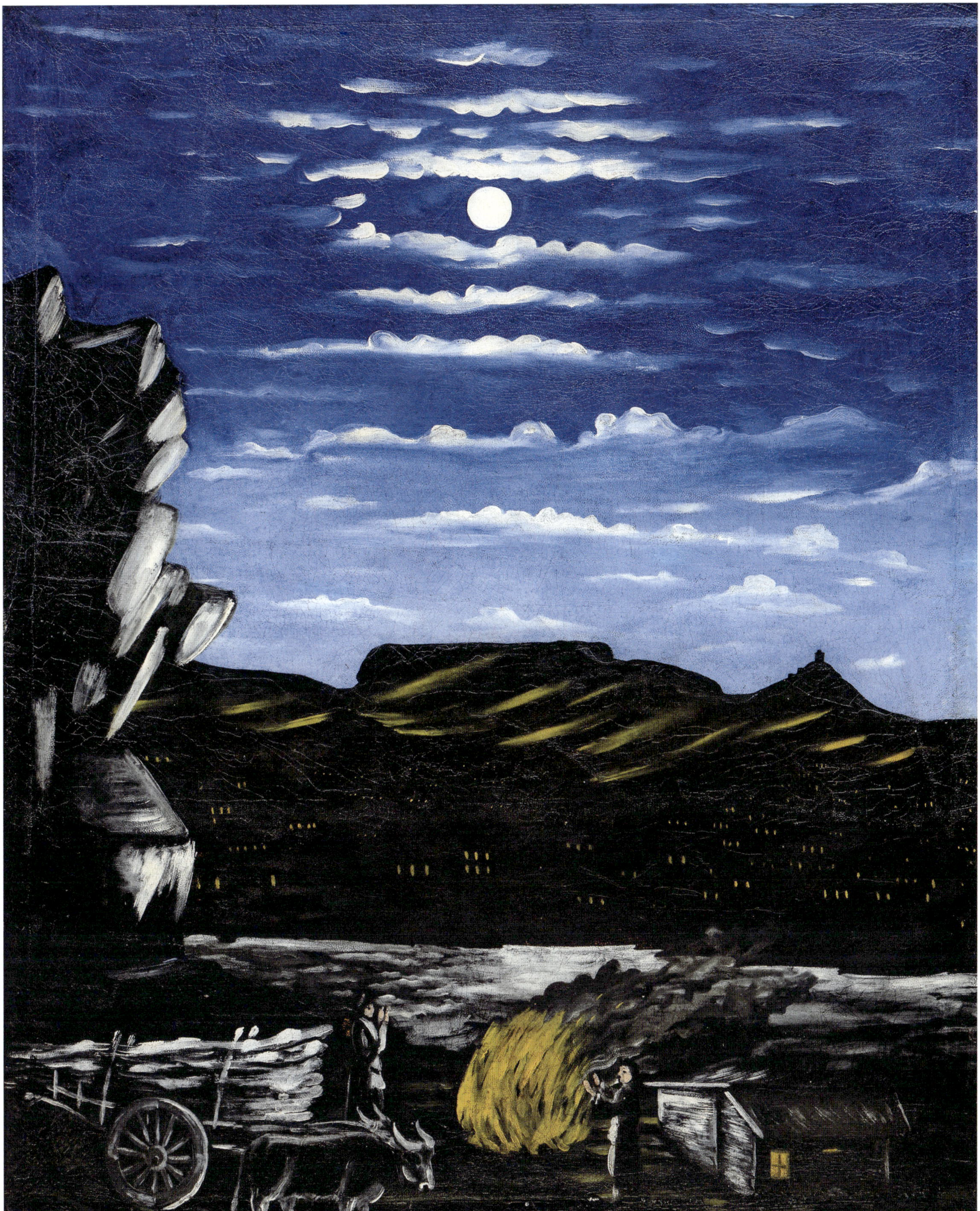

DB: So Pirosmani's oeuvre not only reflects its own time, but the time following his death in 1918. From 1928 it was constantly used for politics and ideology, and in the 1960s and 1970s he becomes a national *Soviet* artist?

NK: No, of course not Soviet, but he was loved by Soviets, putting the whole modernism and the avant-garde far away. They read and interpreted Pirosmani in their own manner, which had nothing to do with his own worldview and thus with his art. There are even many popular official songs on Pirosmani.

LC: Even one of the most popular Soviet songs ("Million alykh roz" (Million Scarlett Roses), 1982, about a painter courting an actress, *The Actress Margarita,* p. 77) is about him, by the famous singer Alla Pugacheva, the Russian Ella Fitzgerald. It is real kitsch.

NK: He was getting more and more popular, you could buy posters, postcards and so on. But nobody ever went to see the originals or realised the real value in them. Although some of them would hang in the National Gallery of Georgia, they were mixed with a lot of other paintings, even with socialist realism paintings, so that they were almost invisible. The real reason why he got popular was that almost every artist painted a Pirosmani painting, mainly his figurative paintings – peasants, workers, craftsmen, people of different subcultures, to stress social content. There were a lot of copies circulating and hanging in restaurants. Even carpets and tapestries were made and sculptures and wall paintings too.

DB: Did they find Pirosmani a typical Georgian, an artist from which you can build a national identity, a kind of the symbol of Georgianess?

NK: In the early 1910s, the Georgian avant-garde writer and artist who discovered Pirosmani, Ilia Zdanevich, was asked by the eminent, symbolist writer Grigol Robakidze what he and his fellow futurists had achieved. Zdanevich answered with one sentence published in his avant-garde newspaper *41°*, saying that they may had done nothing except discovering the national genius that was Pirosmani. So already Zdanevich presents Pirosmani in a national Georgian context.

THE POSSIBILITY OF ACHIEVING WHOLENESS

DB: What in the art of Pirosmani allowed the avant-garde this reading and understanding? And then again the same reading in the 1960s, 1970s, 1980s, and until today? Why was this possible?

NK: This is not an easy question. Let me try to answer. The avant-garde artists saw in him an alternative to fragmentation and the possibility of achieving the wholeness and fullness in his paintings. Zdanevich was always against fragmentation, which unfortunately was the reality back then as it is now. As you know, Zdanevich developed the concept of 'Everythingism', meaning that you can use the different modes and manners of past centuries: antiquity and the Middle Ages, East and West and put them together to create a whole and by this avoid the 'dark emptiness' of only one style, one artistic manner or one mode, as he said. Of course, this was unachievable, but he saw in Pirosmani the possibility of achieving this wholeness.

LC: He saw the epic dimension in Pirosmani's works.

DB: Many recent research projects by Georgian art historians show how Pirosmani learned and used many different sources to compose his paintings, from religious frescoes to folk art, silver ware, tombstones, everyday life and so on. He managed to bring it all together and produce powerful iconic pictures.

NK: And he created big, epic, paradise-like landscapes such as *Fête of St. George in Bolnisi* (pp. 68-69), which were very attractive for artists like Zdanevich and the modernists. Why? The thing is that you can't call them landscapes, much less specific landscapes. He was never interested in this kind of realistic landscapes. If you put together all of his so-called epic paintings, you'll find out that they depict Nature, not just specific pieces of the land, or of the mountains. For him nature, and not landscape, equals the universe and – all together, whole, entire, with good and bad, kindness and evil yet without any kind of valuation; with a definite structure oriented on the vertical, connecting the earth with the sky and Heaven.

He was the artist working for taverns in towns, mostly Tbilisi, but he never painted townscapes. He was not attracted by them, maybe they were quite chaotic, fragmented and with crowded streets. With town taverns, his paintings would expose Nature. The only time he ever painted Tbilisi was Mount Mtatsminda (Holy Mountain) and the funicular in the painting *The Tiflis Funicular*. I think he may have painted it because it shows the Mamadaviti Church halfway to the top, dedicated to one of the Assyrian fathers, St. David Gareji. Don't forget that he was a religious man and quite educated in this direction. But as a modern man, he had his individual point of view, his own worldview and own interpretation of the universal.

DB: But why would his art appeal to a modernist eye? Not only on the level of content, but also as form? What distinguished him from similar artists who may also have gone back to all sorts of sources?

NK: It was the method and the manner of the way he painted. It was very economical and at the same time very expressive and very strangely intense. If you look at the details, you see the abstraction.

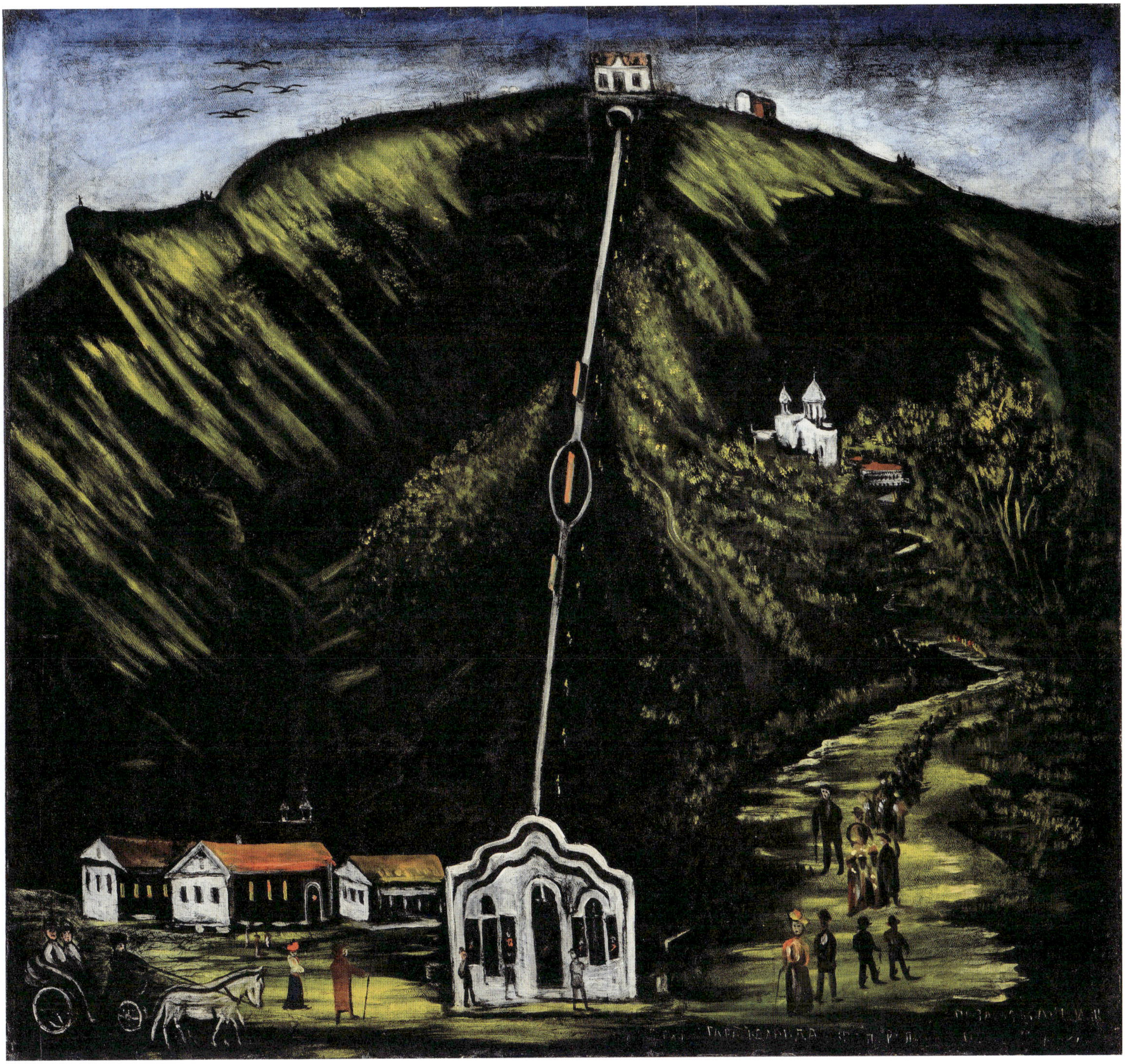

THE TIFLIS FUNICULAR

LC: The same way you see it in El Greco (1541-1614) or Francisco Goya (1746-1828). A very strange brush.

NK: Even or especially his attitude towards the canvas. He uses the black oilcloths, and the black turns into a colour, at the same time working as a support. He only uses a few colours, maybe seven or eight and does it all with this restrained palette. It's this black cloth, the black background that shapes everything, not the other way around. This was unseen, the exception were modernists. Even today, a very radical decision and method that he totally mastered.

DB: And enormous economy of means ...

LC: ... What you also see in Goya or El Greco, who both were (re)discovered only at the end of the 19th century. Nearly at the same time as Pirosmani.

DB: If you look at Pirosmani's paintings and the photographs or references on which they are based, what you see is how he 'edits' the picture, how he deletes everything that is not necessary to obtain a maximum impact. He would leave out all the information that photography would give, most of it being anecdotal. He is a master of condensing and concentration, and this must have been very appealing to a modernist eye – and still is to our eyes.

NK: He gets rid of everything that doesn't serve the idea of the picture and does it very purposely. Most of the time, the background behind a figure is just abstract with almost no information because it would only divert from the main topic: the person. Also, no shadows, or only very rarely, because there is not information there either.

If you look at his figures and then the animals, you see that they are alike. They are not just animals, but they are portraits of animals. He is the modern man; he treats them like personalities, that is important for him. Besides, he knows the medieval Bestiary books, which is also an interesting side of his paintings.

If you look at his landscapes, you can see the epic side of his works, how he displays different scenes in one painting to create a drama but also a harmony.

LC: If you look at Pirosmani's skies, they are very similar to El Greco's. They are both just a sky but also mystical, a Christian mystical zone. At the same time, they are plain colour as well, and this must have been appealing to the modernist.

DB: It's coded in multiple ways, it's not one or the other, it's both. And this again resonates with Zdanevich's idea of 'Everythingness'. Zdanevich was a multiple person himself, a researcher, an artist, an art historian of old Georgian churches, a writer, a founder of an alternative academy and a magazine editor and a publisher too. And he could sense the quality of Pirosmani's paintings as a place for many things. Pirosmani's paintings talk about its time, its turmoils and deep changes – while being at the same time so serene and good-humoured.

FRESCOS FOR A CHURCH WITHOUT RELIGION

NK: Pirosmani was a true modern artist. As I already said, most of his paintings were displayed in taverns, the so-called *dukhans*, around Tbilisi. Dukhans were not taverns in the European sense, they were almost sacred, yet secular places a little bit like in the East. There people from all social backgrounds gathered daily, like a ritual, like a church without religion. So, Pirosmani's paintings were like frescoes, if you like.

LC: This is also were the Georgian ritual of drinking and speaking comes from, the so-called *supra* with its famous figure, the *tamada* (the toastmaster, ed.), as the head of table or master of ceremony. The tamada has its origins in religion, even before Christian times, in Zoroastrian rituals.

Several times Pirosmani depicts the supra, the Georgian feast around a table with the tamada, as seen in *Five Princes Carousing* (pp. 90-91) from 1906. It involved telling poems, reciting verses, performing hospitality. It is a ritual from ancient times and later easily entered the dukhan.

NK: It somehow combined the Christian with the pagan, which had a very strong presence at the time, especially in the mountains ... The taverns were not just about eating and drinking but it was the place where poems were recited, and where discussions and debate would take place. The owner would often have handwritten literature about old legends like Prometheus before printing was easy to do. Yes, it was a tavern, but also an educational centre where many of Pirosmani's paintings were on display.

LC: It became legendary and was very liked by Russian visitors, writers and poets, by Polish, German, French visitors and travellers from the East – a very multinational place.

A PROJECTION SCREEN FOR FOLKLORE FASCINATION

DB: I have another question, which came up while researching Pirosmani, his art and its context. I observed how from the middle of the 19th century onwards, Georgia became the object of ethnographic studies for Western researchers and Georgian writers. It became a projection screen for ideas about authentic culture, an interest that was driven by a fascination with folk culture, and both embraced it as object and exoticised it. It created a certain image of Georgia and was, in my opinion, an important element in building the image of a national Georgian identity as an independent country distinct from Russia and Western Europe. One could argue that Pirosmani fit in there perfectly, still today: Pirosmani as the true Georgian artist and genius.

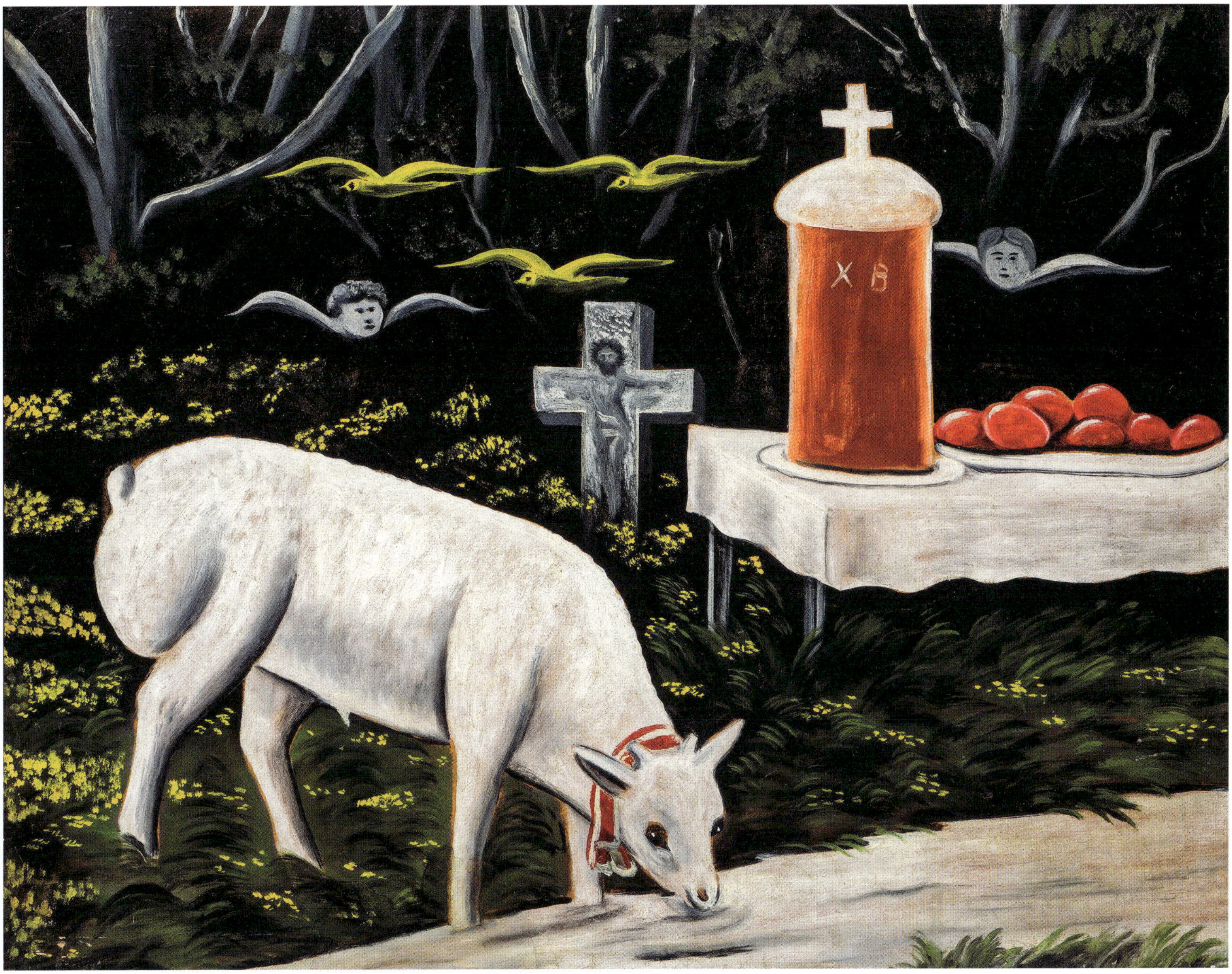

LAMBKIN AND EASTER TABLE WITH FLYING ANGELS

NK: The way literature and politics looked at Georgia can be divided into two camps. On the one side, as an exotic part of the Russian Empire. On the other side, the true researchers who really studied the history, the language, the culture.

DB: But could one say that the interest in folk art and Indigenous cultures was a way to differentiate Georgia from both the West and Russia? Culture as an identity-defining tool. And if yes, is a figure like Pirosmani part of this plan?

NK: No, I don't think so, because he was totally unknown until 1913 when he got discovered by the three young futurists, the two brothers Ilia and Kirill Zdanevich and Le Dentu. By then, Pirosmani was already advanced in age too. He was born in 1862, started with painting at the very beginning of the 20th century, but nobody ever noticed him till 1912.

DB: Sure, but why is there this great interest in him, beside him being an exceptional artist? Was he embodying the perfect mix of folk art, modernist ideals and Georgianess?

NK: Yes, because the question of the Georgian nation and of independence was indeed of huge importance at that time and for the leading figures of modernism too, for Kakabadze, Zdanevich, Gigo Gabashvili (1862-1936) and many others. To the same degree as the architecture of the churches, or literature going back to the 5th century and the great interest in the famous writer Shota Rustaveli (c. 1160-after 1220), the pre-eminent poet of the Georgian Golden Age. A lot of very detailed research took place in the 19th century about all this. One of the leading figures was Ilia Chavchavadze (1837-1907), the writer, journalist and politician, founder of the first Georgian bank and of two newspapers, the reformer of Georgian language, a fierce opponent of Russification and regarded as the Father of the Nation. Another leading role was played by the Society of Photographers, which built yet another version of Georgianess by transforming ethnographic research into pictures.

LC: Another important, Nietzschean figure, and Pirosmani knew him and his poetry, was Vazha-Pshavela (1861-1915). The researcher, art and literature critic, and also an artist himself, Vakhtang Kotetishvili (1893-1937) wrote about Nietzsche's influence on Vazha-Pshavela in 1910s, and also literature critic Kita Abashidze (1870-1917). Some didn't like him, because he used vernacular, archaic language in his poems. His answer to them was: "You must not be afraid when the cow moos from the mountains." He too was an intellectual and highly educated and ultimately respected even or especially by the avant-garde poets of the early 20th century.

DB: Another thing I was surprised by, was the way that photographers would portray Tbilisi and Georgia in a very touristic fashion. The way they look at the mountain people, the farmers, the merchants and shopkeepers was not about showing their life but getting them ready for the postcard, the cliche.

LC: One way for the Russian Empire to colonise the country was to transform it into ethnography and exoticism. This is what is not only happening with Georgians, but also with Ukrainians and many other countries and ethnicities. When they conquered the Kingdom of Georgia, it was presented as a collaboration, not as a conquest. As with Crimea or with Abkhazia. Once they had conquered Georgia, they began to present the country in an ethnographic and exotic way ... It is a proven way of provincialising and marginalising a country and its culture.

DB: ... The same happened to colonies all over the world.

LC: So, this is the why the Soviets then presented Pirosmani as a poor, drunken, talented artist. But not only that, it was about much more. They also used him to close or rather erase the entire period of modernism in Georgia and the time of independence already mentioned above, building an image of primitive Georgia to which modernity was brought by the Soviets.

DB: The legendary film *Salt of Svanetia* from 1930 builds on this same narrative and is, although extremely impressive and beautiful, a work of propaganda. So you not only had 'socialist in content, national in form', but even more so 'ethnographic by conquest'.

NK: My dissertation was researching this question of 'national by form', but at first it got rejected and only accepted ten years later, though I didn't change a single word in the text. I showed how, for instance, the way workers at the *kolkhoz* (collective Soviet farms, ed.) were depicted exactly in the same way as religious figures, saints, with the same gestures, poses and postures. The iconography of frescoes was turned into 'national by form' and used for social realism. Exactly this way of seeing was applied to Pirosmani as well, and now, after more than a hundred years, we really try to get away from it and find alternative understandings.

Nana Kipiani, PhD in art history theory, Georgia. The senior researcher at the G. Chubinashvili National Research Centre for Georgian Art History and Heritage Preservation in Tbilisi, Georgia. Specialist on modernism in Georgia and on Niko Pirosmani.

Levan Chogoshvili, artist, Georgia. An unofficial artist since 1973, known for including art history, historical time and its characters in his oeuvre.

Daniel Baumann (born 1967), art historian and curator, Switzerland. Since 2015 director of the Kunsthalle Zürich. Organised and curated yearly exhibitions in Tbilisi 2004-2009 together with, among others, Kipiani and Chogoshvili.

This conversation took place in Tbilisi in February 2023.

GEORGIAN WOMAN WITH A TAMBOURINE. 1906

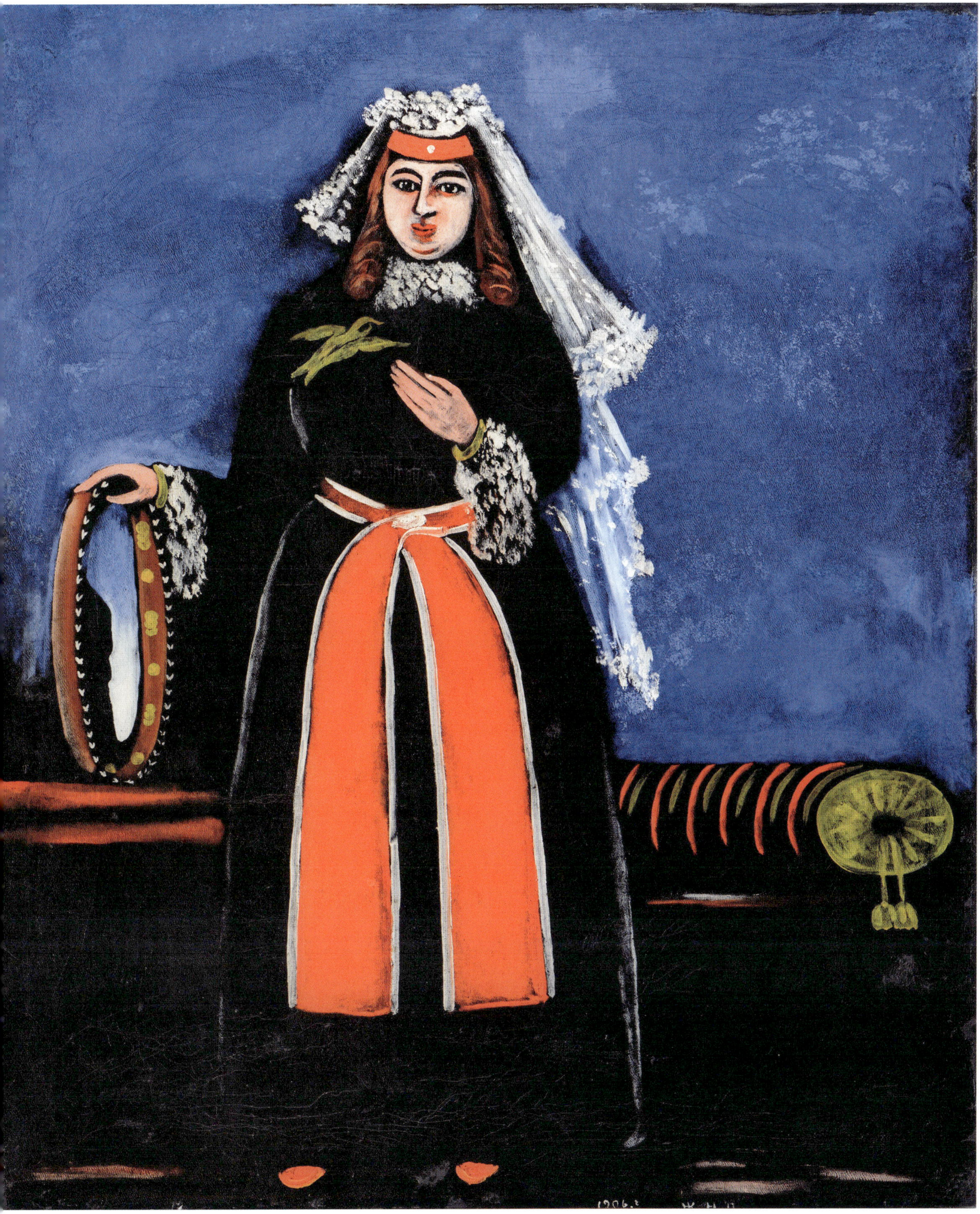

DOCTOR ON A JACKASS

>

ROBBER RUSTLING A HORSE

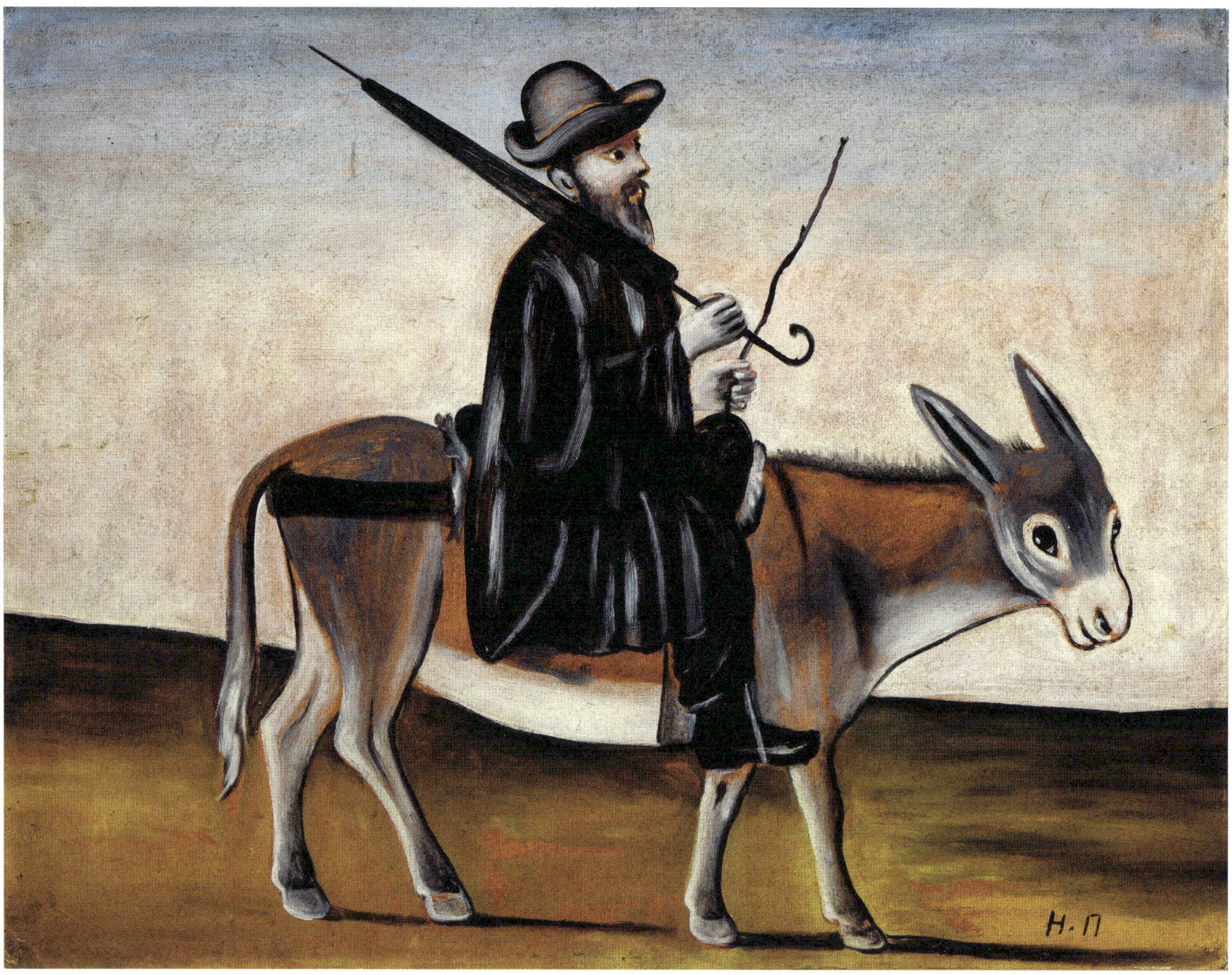

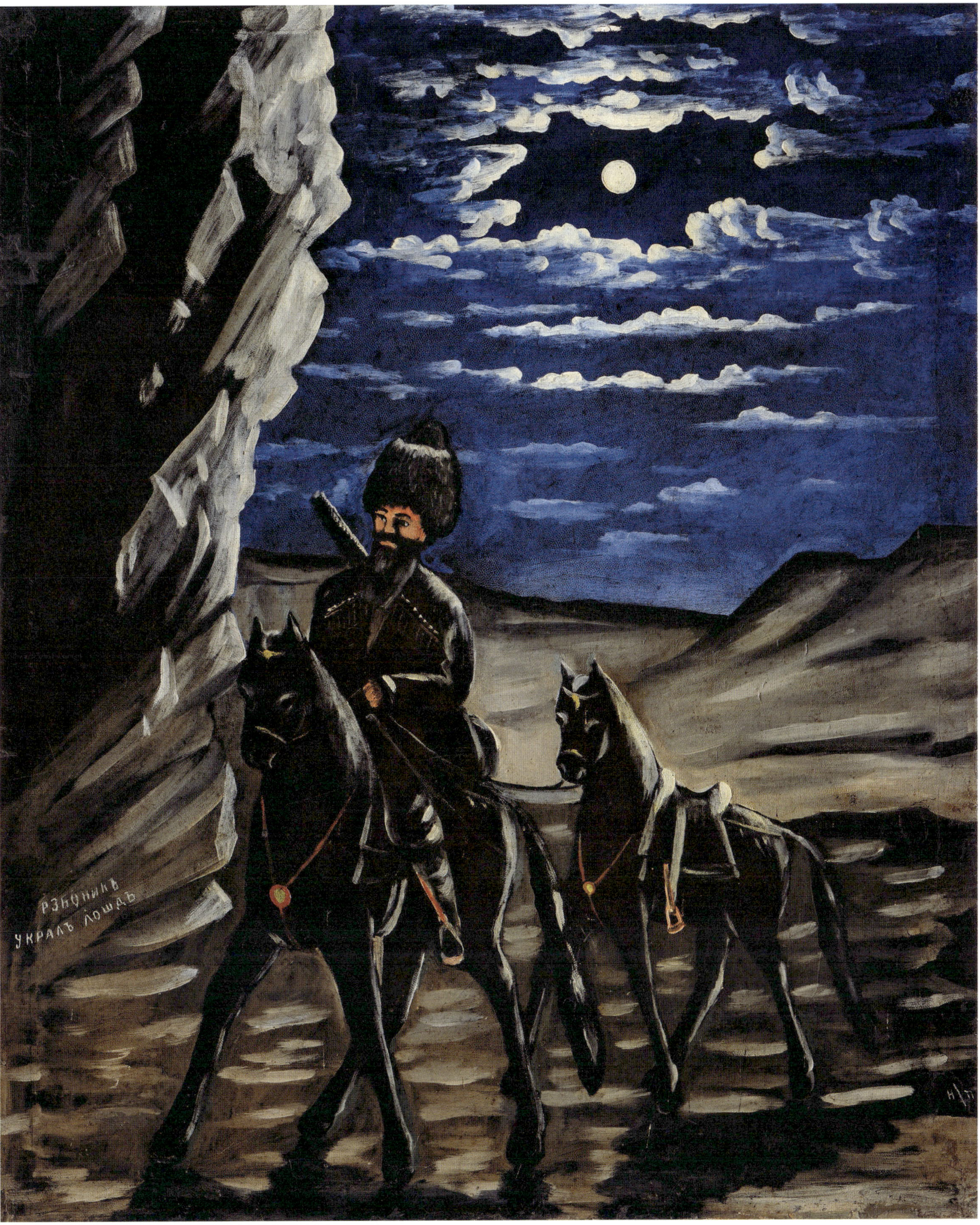
РЗБОНИКЪ
УКРАЛЪ ЛОШАДЪ

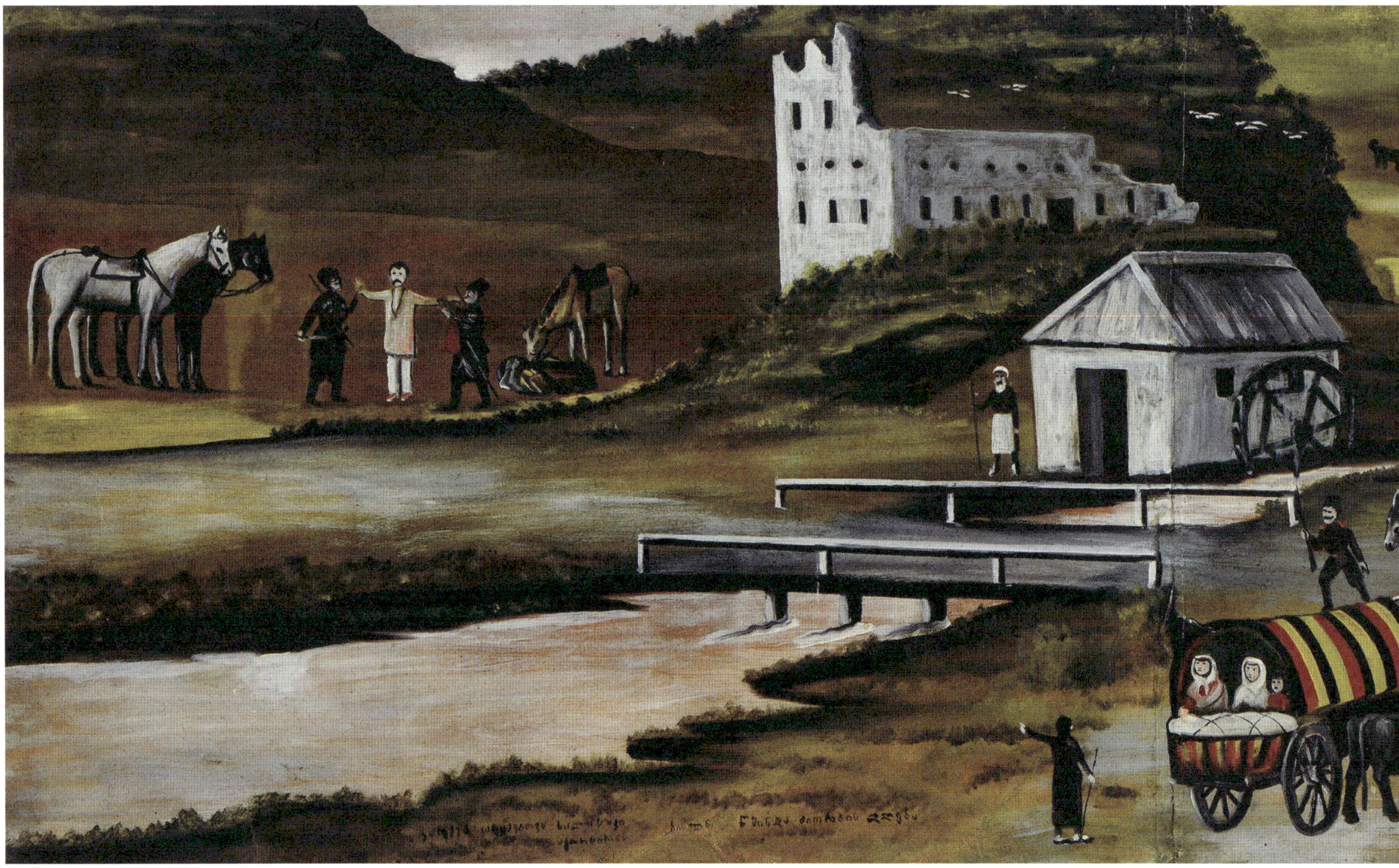

FÊTE OF ST. GEORGE IN BOLNISI

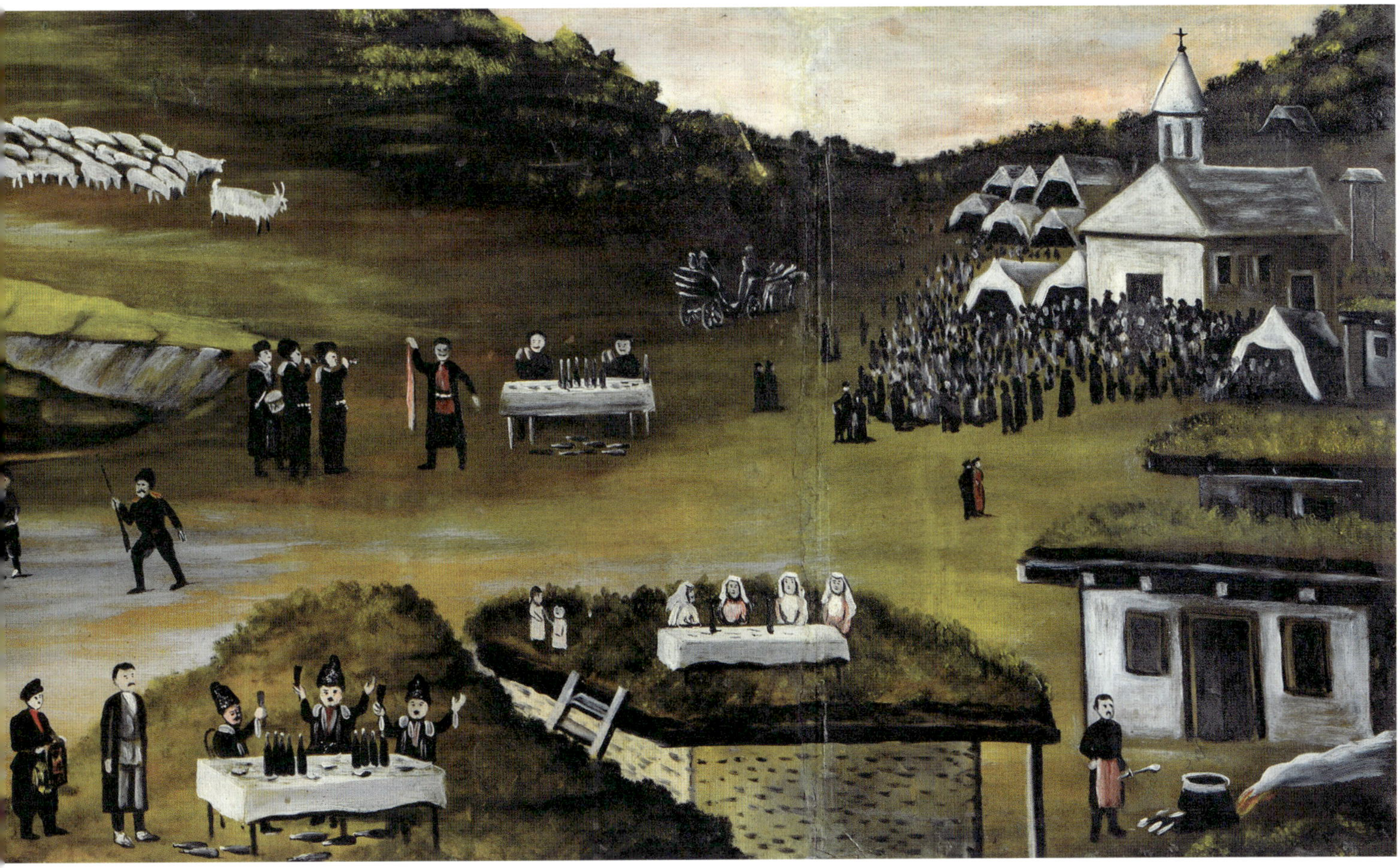

TATAR CAMEL DRIVER

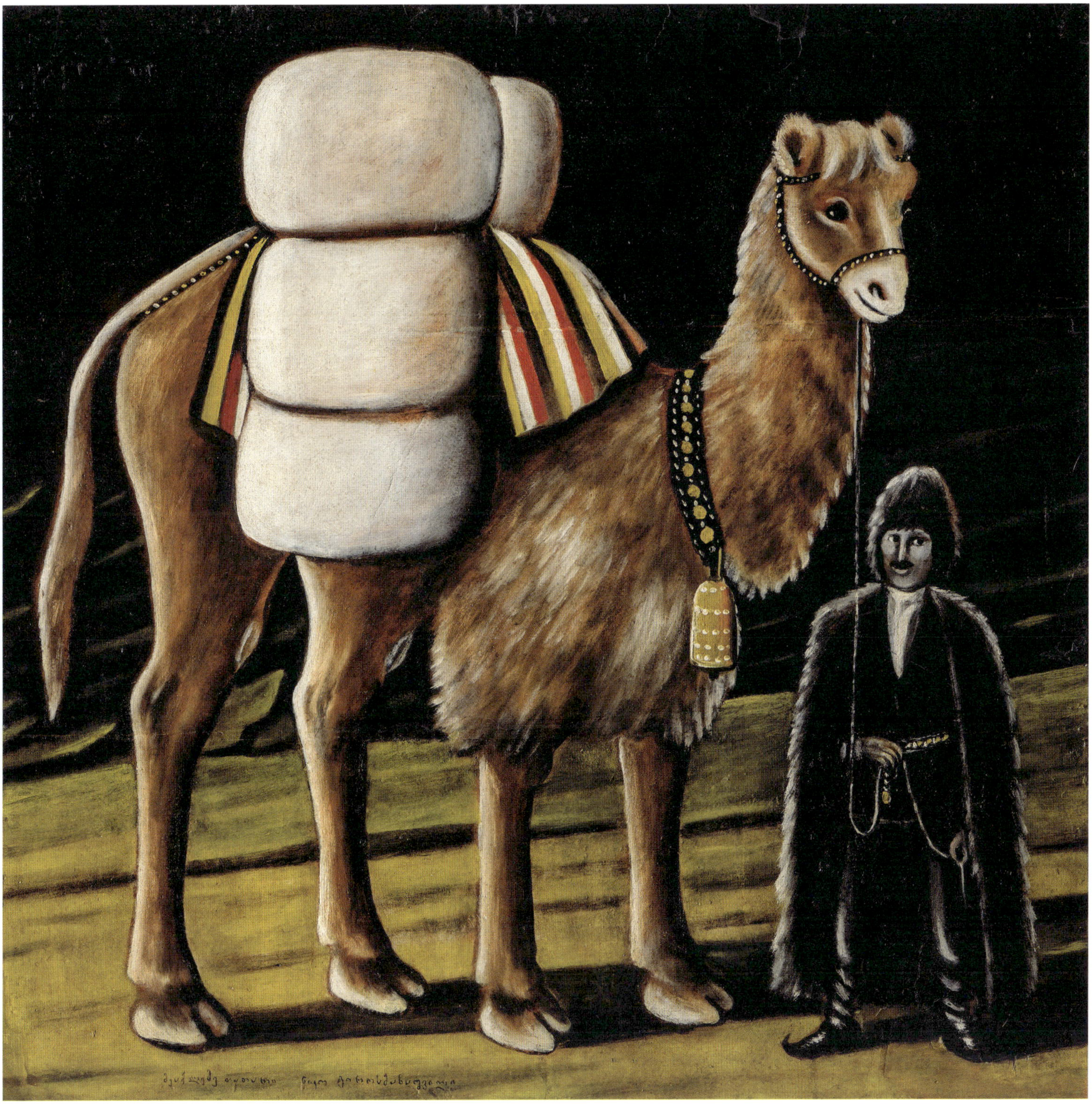

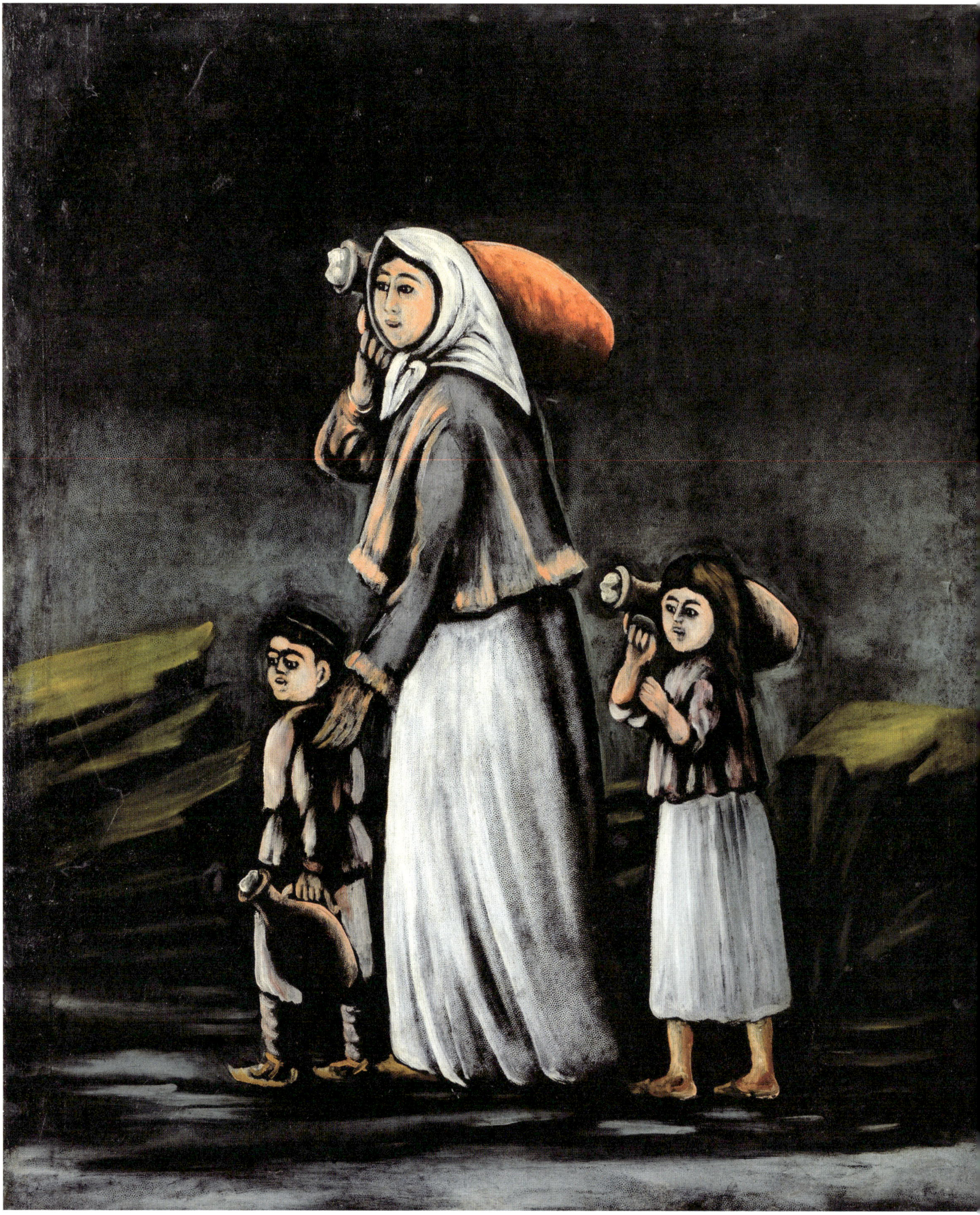

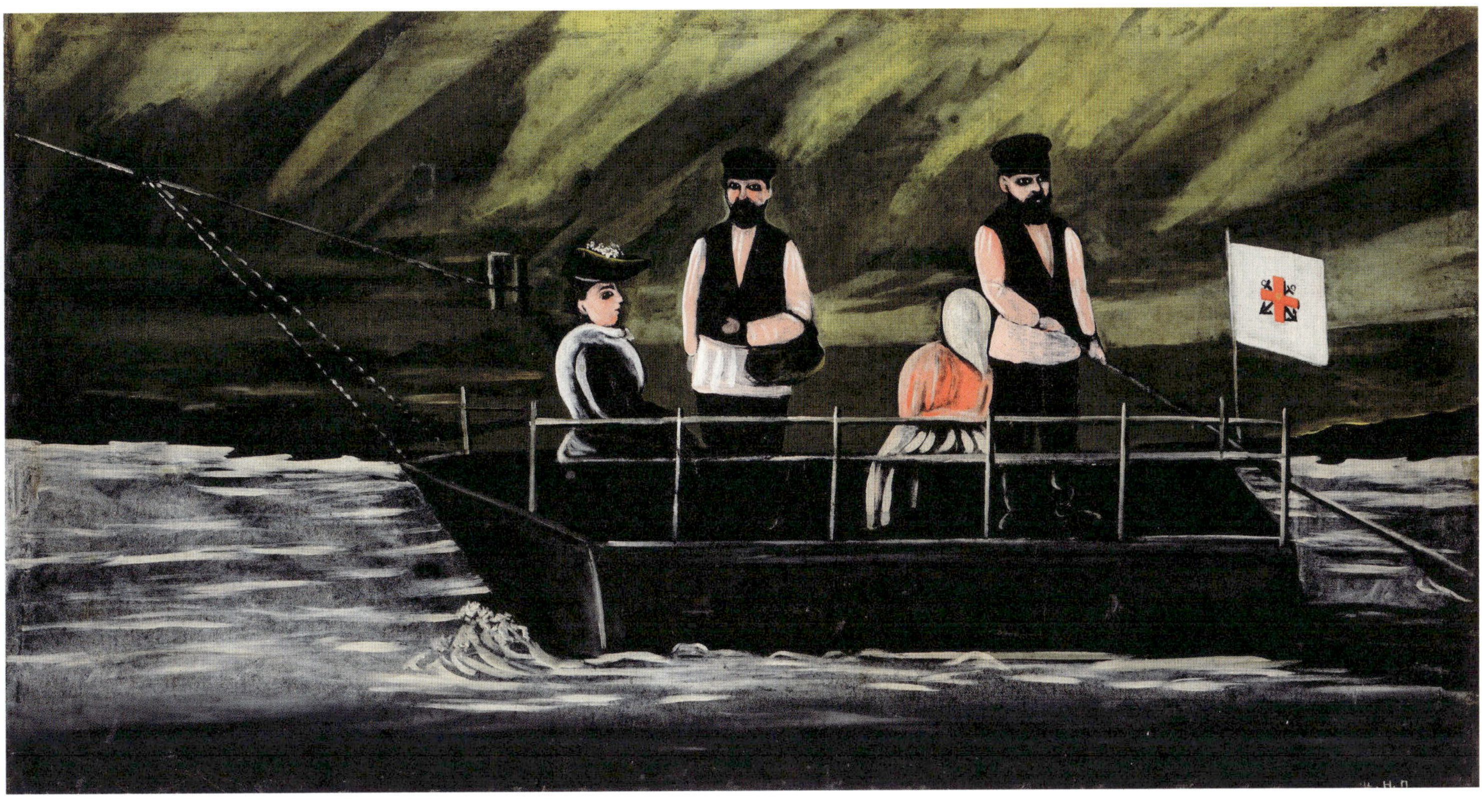

THE DIDUBE FERRY

<

PEASANT WOMAN WITH CHILDREN FETCHING WATER

The first time I came across Niko Pirosmani was in 2018. I was in Vienna to see a Pieter Bruegel the Elder (c. 1527-1569) exhibition (at the Art History Museum, ed.), and then the Albertina was showing his works. I believe I thought that he was a self-taught artist. With a very unusual expression. His works are quite unusual. They're done in a very childish way, but at the same time, they're actually quite ... skilful. He's sensitive. That's his strength.

As a painter it's very rare to discover a whole new oeuvre, actually. Above all, I was interested in the fact that he used very dark backgrounds; that he would always paint on a black oilcloth canvas. It's very unusual to start with a black background, so even though he uses rich colouring, his colours are quite subdued. It's really nice actually. I think his range of colour is quite unique. But he's also very erratic. Some of the paintings are really ugly; they just seem naive and shoddily made. But then the next picture is brilliant. He can paint a still life of meat products from a butchery against a dark background, and it's just fantastic.

I don't get the sense that he's the kind of artist who expresses his inner self. He's very much an observer. But on the other hand, he doesn't just portray things, such as sitting in a landscape or with a model; his paintings are very often based on memories, photographs and so on. He typically concentrates on just one thing for each painting: a hunter, an animal, a dinner table, a wedding or something like that.

As a painter, you try to work out what his method is. If you're interested, that is. If you find the painting interesting, you'll walk up close and study it.

I don't see him as an outsider artist who is completely disconnected from the rest of the world. He was orphaned as a young child and ended up living in Tbilisi with quite an affluent family. He learned to read and write both Russian and Georgian and was very interested in poetry and theatre. And in his youth, he would wear Western clothing. He 'got it'. And he was quite aware of what was happening in the art world. But at the same time, he was completely unaffected. He didn't really care for it.

Even though he's quite direct – he doesn't shade and detail his works like many others – he's credible. When he paints a landscape, you feel that you could walk around in it. And he's got a damn good sense of the way animals move ... You sense that he's taken part in hunting and farming. He has great range. Above all, he's a good observer. He paints humans as animals or animals as humans. I guess he sees humans that way. As a kind of animals. Probably.

I guess the reason why he chose the black background is that he probably began that way, and it made him feel safe. It's very much about feeling safe in everything you do. If you're a baker, and you have worked in a certain way, you want to keep doing it that way. If you're a fisherman, you know how to cast your net. You don't need to fix what isn't broken. And he's used to having the black background. I think it's as simple as that. But the big difference, to explain it from a painter's view: if you begin with a black canvas and don't use enough paint, the black will come through and make the colour darker. More dirty, simply. With a white canvas, the colours will shine a lot more. It gives it a different dimension.

The way he outlines his landscapes reminds me of the way it's done in Russian icons. They're often made on a dark background as well, especially dark wood. The motif becomes much more distinct and clearer that way. I've also noticed that he sometimes fills in with the black, so that it forms contours around his motifs. That he almost uses it like an outline. Because I don't get the feeling he uses sketches or preparations of any kind. It's just straight on. But he does utilise the black background really well.

He was born, and also died, the same year as Gustav Klimt (1862-1918), but he especially reminds me of Tivadar Kosztka Csontváry (1853-1919) from Hungary. They were not only contemporaries, both of them worked outside the art establishment. But an artist like Henri Rousseau (1844-1910) is also very close to him in style. I know that the LaM museum (in Lille, France, ed.) has a rather big collection of outsider art, and I believe you can find paintings with similar forms of artistic expressions there. They don't have much perspective, it's a bit imaginary in a way, and they shade the way they please to.

When the art world started taking an interest in that kind of art, it was because there was a need to move away from very perfect and observant art. They searched for something different. Without the guys from Saint Petersburg who discovered him, he might have been forgotten, even today still. But they made people aware that 'something is happening; here is a skilled painter.'

The Russians have these *lubok* prints (cheap woodprints, ed.) – I think I have some in my studio – they're based on folk art. But then again, artists have always been interested in that to some degree. It's our common origin. An artist like Pablo Picasso (1881-1973) struggled his whole life to become naivist, although he was incredibly skilful.

MAMMA ANDERSSON:

» HE'S SENSITIVE. THAT'S HIS STRENGTH «

TOLD TO MARC-CHRISTOPH WAGNER

I think there's definitely a connection between Pirosmani and folk art. He also depicts his people and their history in his paintings. His work is a bit like a time machine. The folk art becomes more easily accessible in a way, because there are no hidden messages there. There's no politics or psychology in it. It's very straightforward in a way.

We all have our roots, which has affected art in the long run – and even the art produced today, maybe. But I also think that people are quite tired of photorealistic art. It's not particularly interesting in the longer term. But an artist like Peter Doig (born 1959), for example, is a painter who makes quite simplistic paintings that people really like and embrace. He's not *that* different from Pirosmani. And an artist like Vincent van Gogh (1853-1890) is also related to him in a way. But both Doig and Van Gogh are very much a part of Western intellectual culture; there's another side to it which you won't find with Pirosmani.

But then he has something else, which is unique: his natural approach to painting. There's no resistance there. I think it is decisive that he has painted so many signboards for restaurants and hotels. That he painted every day. It is second nature to him. There was none of that experience that I have as a contemporary artist, where you get performance anxiety, and you have access to everything through the internet and can check up on it, you know the whole history of art. He was living in his own little world, and that's quite ... exceptional. He was never disturbed. He could really develop his own expression.

Mamma Andersson (born 1962) is a Swedish painter. Exhibitions include the 2021 solo show at Louisiana Museum of Modern Art, *Mamma Andersson: Humdrum Days*, and the 2023 joint show at Kunsten Museum of Modern Art Aalborg, Malmö Konstmuseum and Museum MORE (2024), *Tal R & Mamma Andersson – About Hill.*

The interview was originally made for Louisiana Channel and later adapted for print by Malou Wedel Bruun. Discover this and several other interviews with the artist at channel.louisiana.dk

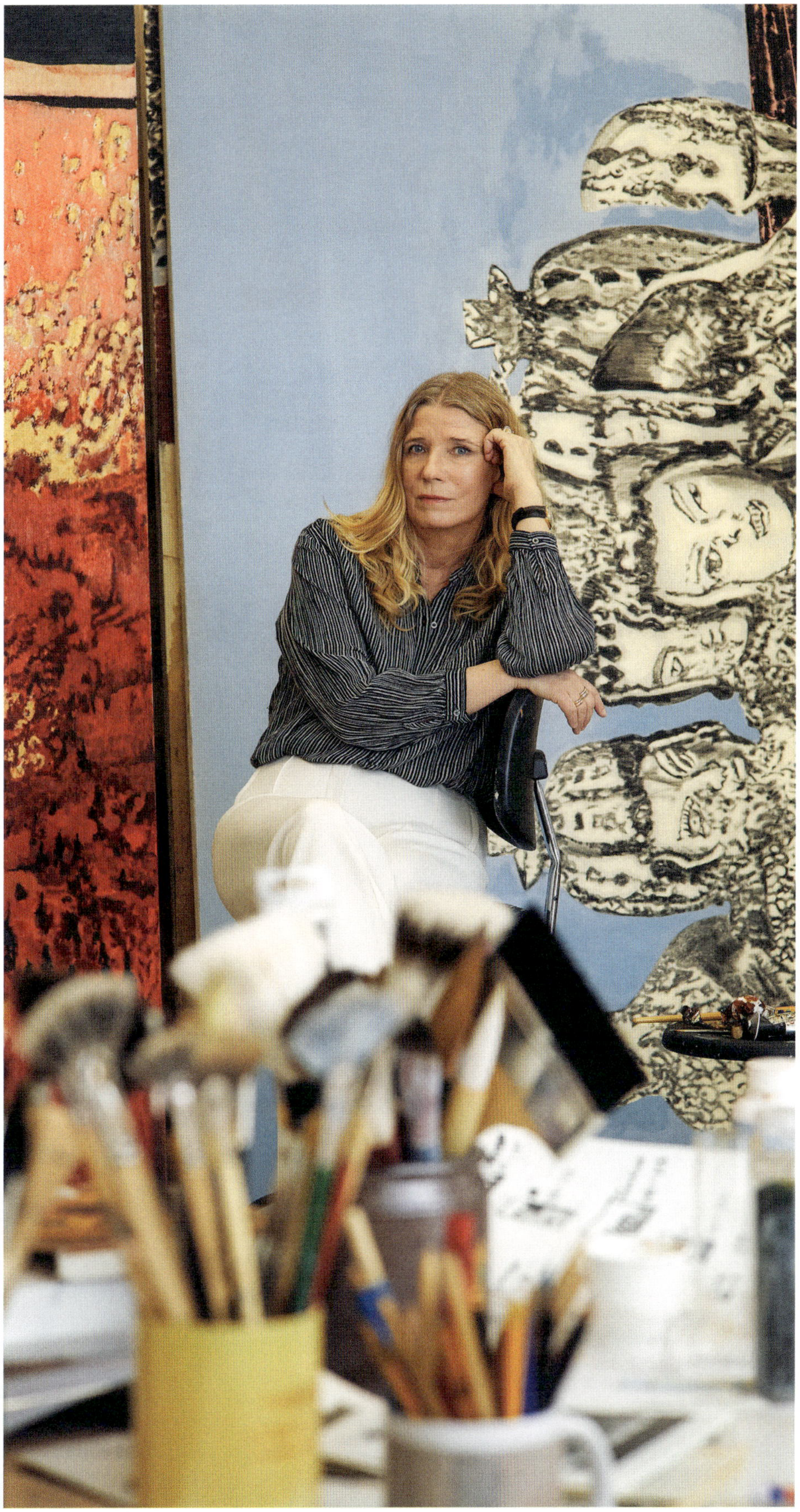

PHOTO: MATS LILIEQUIST

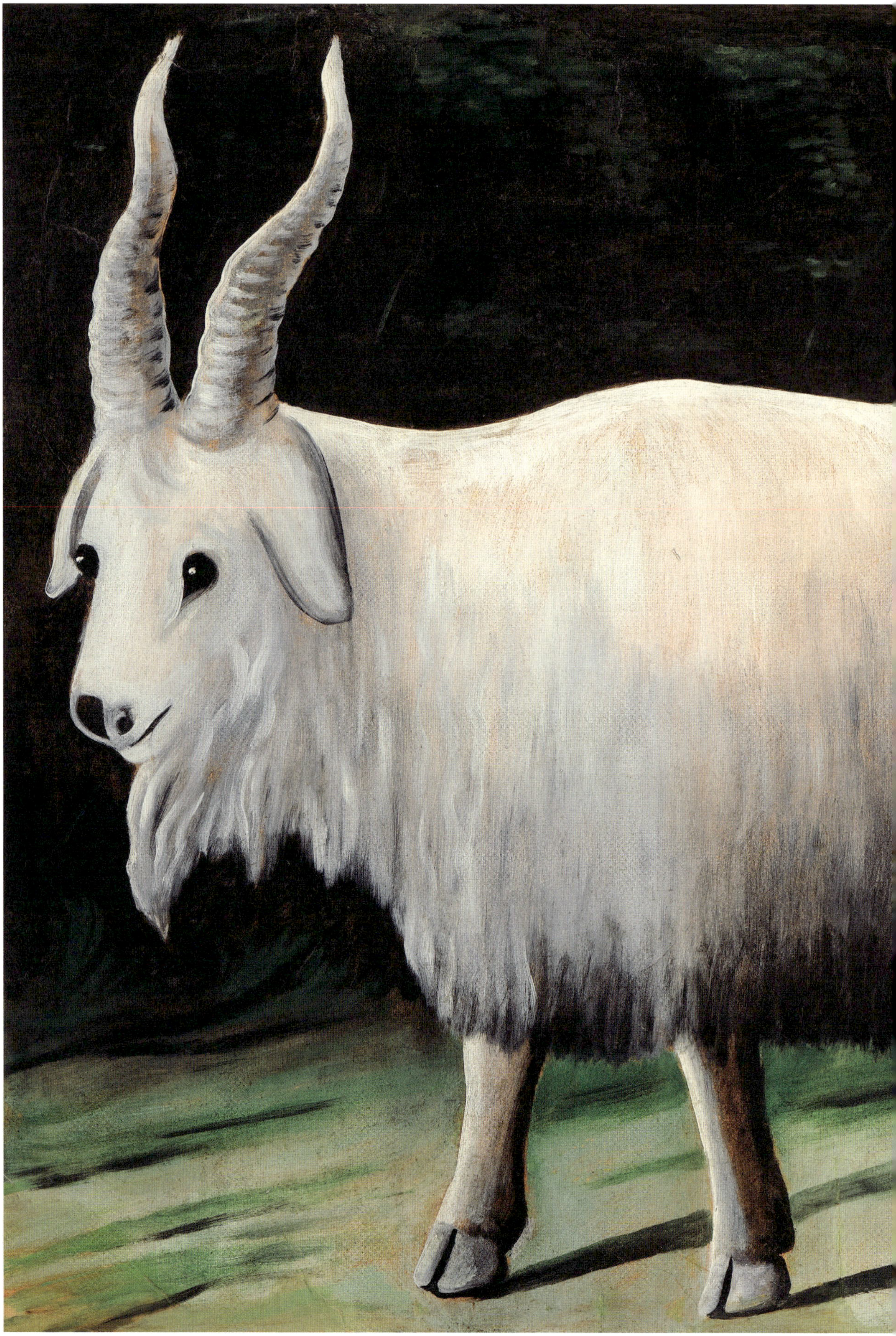

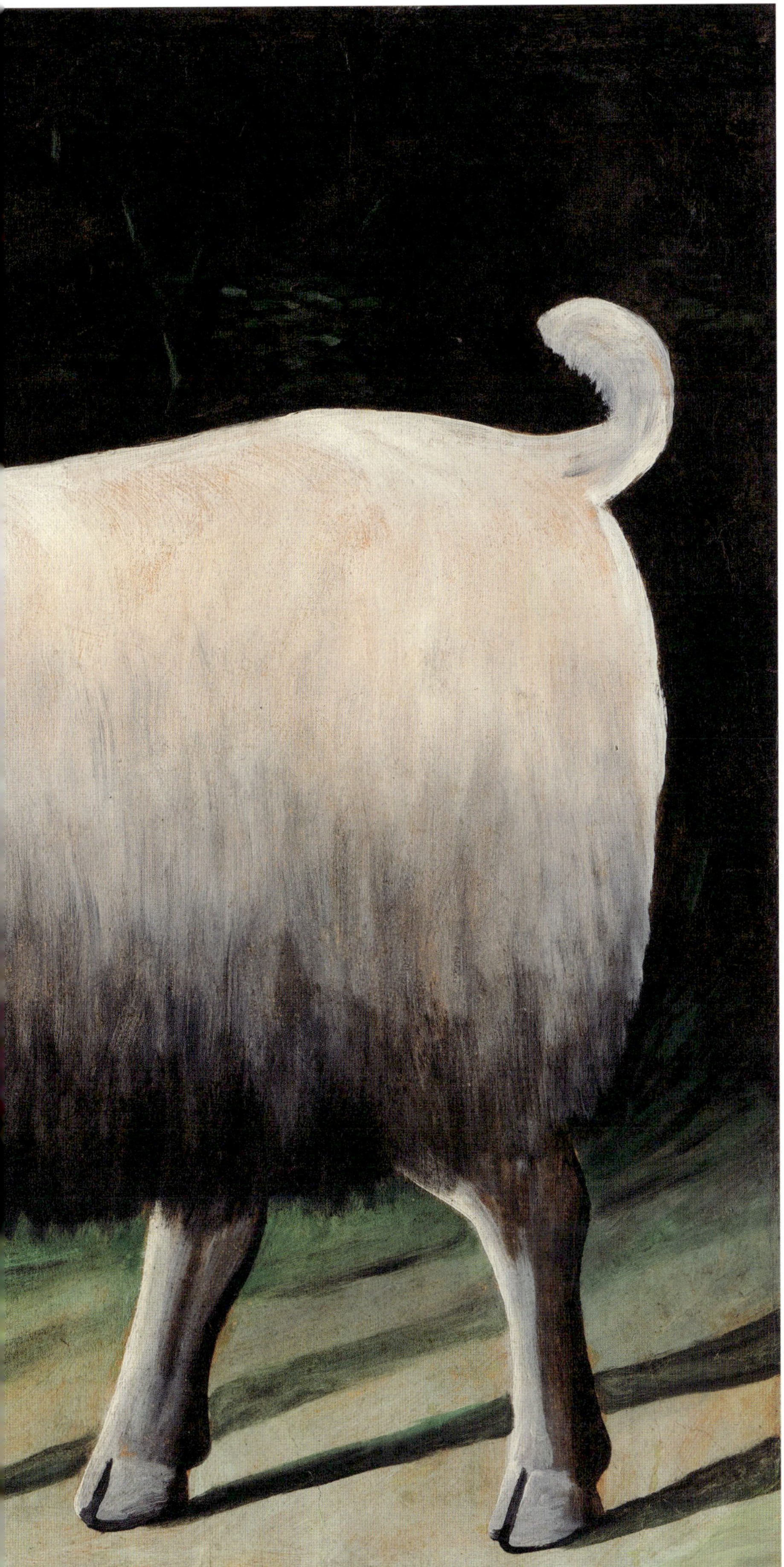

NANNY GOAT

NIKO PIROSMANASHVILI

PORTRAITURE
AND DIARY ENTRIES FROM 1926

KIRILL ZDANEVICH

This very famous historical text represents an important contribution to the cementing of Pirosmani's posthumous reputation. However, here the reader should be aware that Kirill Zdanevich (1892-1969) passes on certain information about the artist's life and work that has more to do with the mythmaking around Pirosmani than his actual life, for which we have few sources. Readers are therefore invited to compare this with the biography on pages 92-93 of this catalogue, ed.

The visual arts in Georgia came into being under the influence of the national cultures of its neighbours, the peoples of Assyria and Babylonia, Byzantium and Persia. Traces of the ancient culture of the Assyrians and Babylonians are still visible in bas-reliefs, the ornamental facades of ancient churches, the folk-sculptural forms found on tombstones and the architecture of watchtowers. The Byzantine influence can be discerned in church frescoes. Persia left its mark on Georgian miniature and book ornamentation. Yet the creative spirit of the Georgian people was able to transmute these ancient cultures, which, even as they enriched the nation, did not obscure its distinct contours.

The easel painter Niko Pirosmani (Nikolai Aslanovich Pirosmanashvili), an artist of inexplicable and miraculous power, reproduced in his work the full gamut of diverse cultures which contributed to Georgia's artistic image even as he gave lucid and original expression to the creative particularities of the Georgian people. Pirosmanashvili's success can be attributed to the fact that he gave voice to an inherited culture that was at once primitive and highly developed, while at the same time generating an idiom which convincingly reflected his own era. Pirosmanashvili's work is a classic of its own era: this is its local as well as its eternal significance. There exists no other or better way to convey pre-revolutionary Georgia, to grasp its life in all its fullness and force. Pirosmanashvili's stylistic choices seem the only possible solutions – as well as the best – to the artistic challenge posed by his epoch.

The cultures of the past found due reflection in Niko's paintings. The Assyrian bas-relief is resurrected in his *Black Lion* and *Giraffe* (p. 32); the Last Supper of Byzantium comes to life again in his *Carousal with Datiko Zemel, the Organ Grinder* (p. 39),[1] while the Persian passion for the graphic spot is evident in any number of Pirosmani's works.

Even as he delved deeply into the artistic roots of the people, Pirosmanashvili also rose to the level of the art of our own time, including innovations recently achieved in the West. The *Fisherman in a Red Shirt* (p. 95), with its spiral composition, straight lines and colouristic resolution, on an oilcloth barely painted over with still visible patches of primer, recalls the achievements of André Derain (1880-1954) and Henri Matisse (1869-1954). Even as he employed a unified mode of artistic expression, Pirosmanashvili did on some occasions resolve the complex compositional challenges he faced in different ways. On that basis we can divide the painter's artistic evolution into three periods. The painter's earliest works (1888-1906) are dominated by light green, yellow and grey and on occasion by black and dark blue, *Portrait Dinner* and *Hunting Scene with a View of the Black Sea* are distinguished by a fascination with the complexities of landscape, into which numerous human figures are inscribed, separated somewhat demonstratively from the background, their independent status deriving from the minute and variegated detail with which they are depicted.

The painter's second period (up to 1910) is marked by an increasing simplicity of composition: the painter depicts distinct human types against a reduced background, mostly on oilcloth. These are large monumental figures, drawn in broad generalising strokes. Among them we might note *Familial Company, The Actress Margarita, The Childless Millionaire and Poor Woman with her Children* (pp. 10-11) and others. These paintings, marked by their predilection for bright colours (intense yellow, black, deep blue, green and white), constituting a kind of still life dominated by a narrow palette, are among the greatest masterpieces Pirosmanashvili would ever produce.

The paintings Pirosmanashvili produced in his final period display a further simplification of compositional structure and colour range, depicting a range of near-white figures against a black background, with a few rare exceptions. Among the most significant works painted on cardboard during this time are such splendid works as *Bears* as well as *Cows*. In other works, such as *Boy Firewood Vendor* (p. 45), the artist elevates his use of black oilcloth (or more rarely tin or canvas) to a virtuoso level. We see the uneven use of a grey undercoat and subsequent formal elaboration through the use of a slightly tinted whitewash, around which the oilcloth has been left bare. Typical of this period is a sense of laconic or compressed expression, a new precision in the delineation of forms, a lightness of brush stroke and a more direct correspondence between individual details and the canvas as a whole.

THE ACTRESS MARGARITA

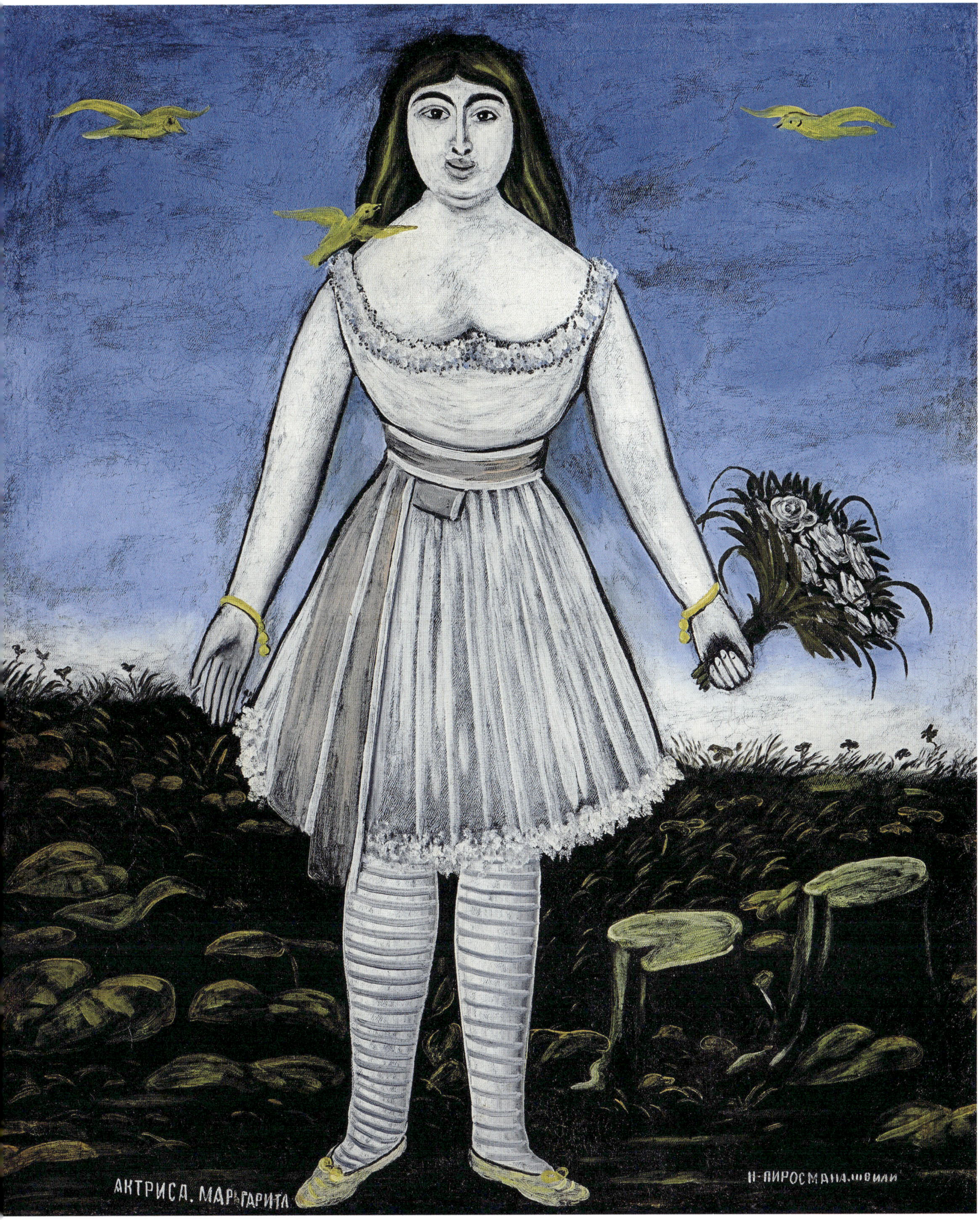
АКТРИСА. МАРЬГАРИТА
Н-ПИРОСМАНАШВИЛИ

All of this makes for an exceptional level of refinement, all the more astonishing in the case of an autodidact like Pirosmanashvili. The painterly techniques used in this period are varied. The paint applied is of varying density and consistency: faces are rendered smoothly and thickly; fabric – calico or velvet – in broad strokes while cliffs are rendered in short, jagged ones. The sky, the air, the body, wool, trees, bones: each object has its own means of expression. Pirosmanashvili deploys all manner of devices: perspective is dictated by the needs of composition: a coloured silhouette looms suddenly in the middle of a field, while human and animal figures serve to animate tree stumps, stones and large standing pitchers.

Pirosmanashvili painted on tin as well, the material from which shop signs were made. The refractory rigidity of tin lends a dry but sonorous quality to the small number of landscapes and still lifes found painted on this medium: their innate expressiveness becomes the very basis and condition of signage as an art form. In his final years (1914-1918) Pirosmanashvili worked chiefly on cardboard, a material which lends a certain woodenness to the texture of his works. His paintings were commissioned for specific sites and served as decorative panels. This explains why some of his works have a symmetrical or rhyming correspondence to one another (for example his diptych *Musha*[2] or *Porter*).

The very same reasons also drew Pirosmanashvili to themes whose innumerable variants go back to the festive culture of the Italian Renaissance, specifically Veronese's scenes of ceremonial festivity depicted against the variegated backdrop of everyday life. We witness banquet scenes, familial or official, involving peasants or princes, seated on the grass or at a table filled with a traditional repast of boiled chicken, fish, salad greens and wine; outdoor scenes of revelry set in fields or gardens (*Princes Seated in a Meadow; Feast During a Grape Harvest*), involving *kintos* or members of the sect of Molokans, which often contain background

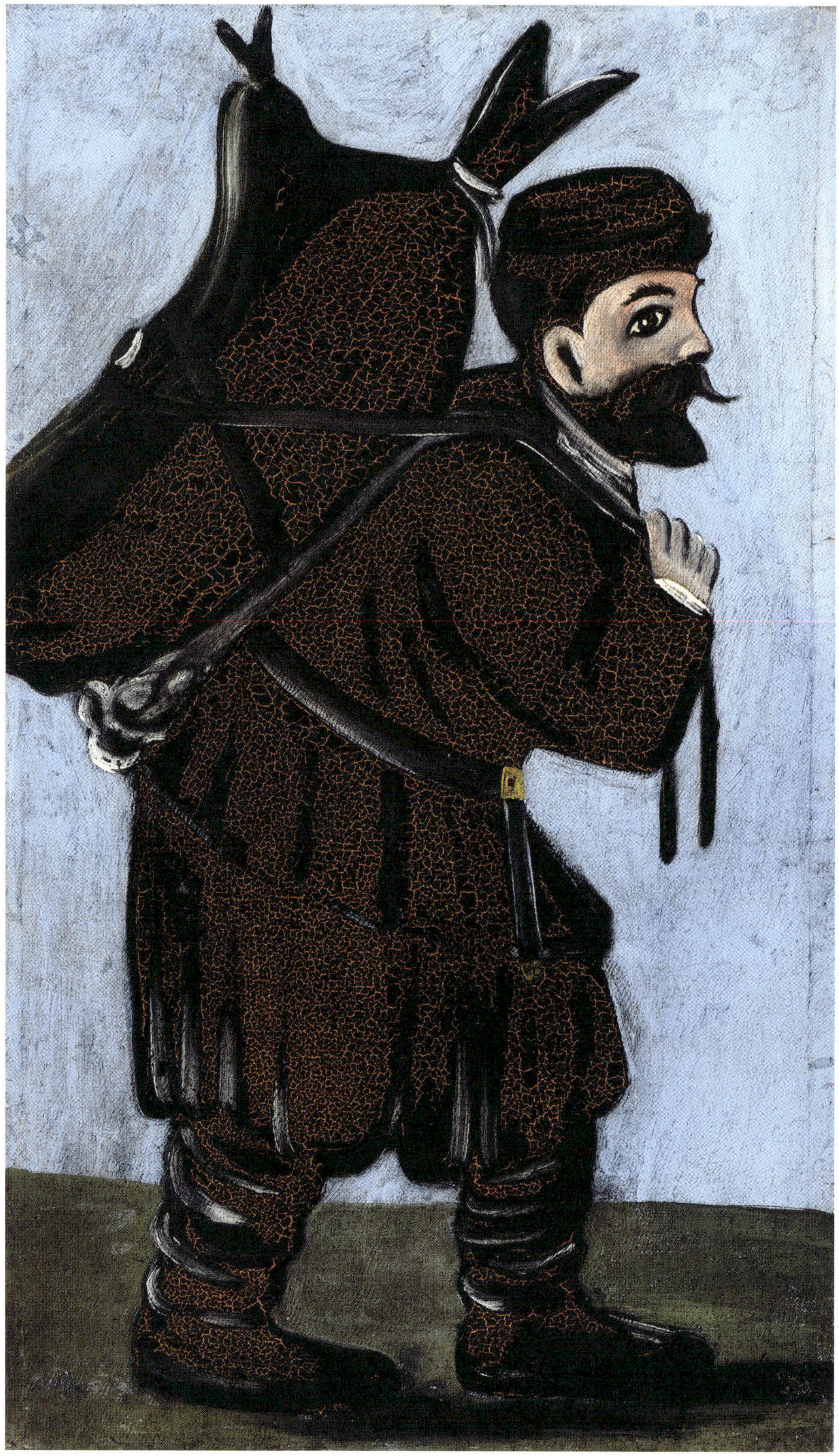

MUSHA WITH A WINESKIN (HALF OF DIPTYCH)

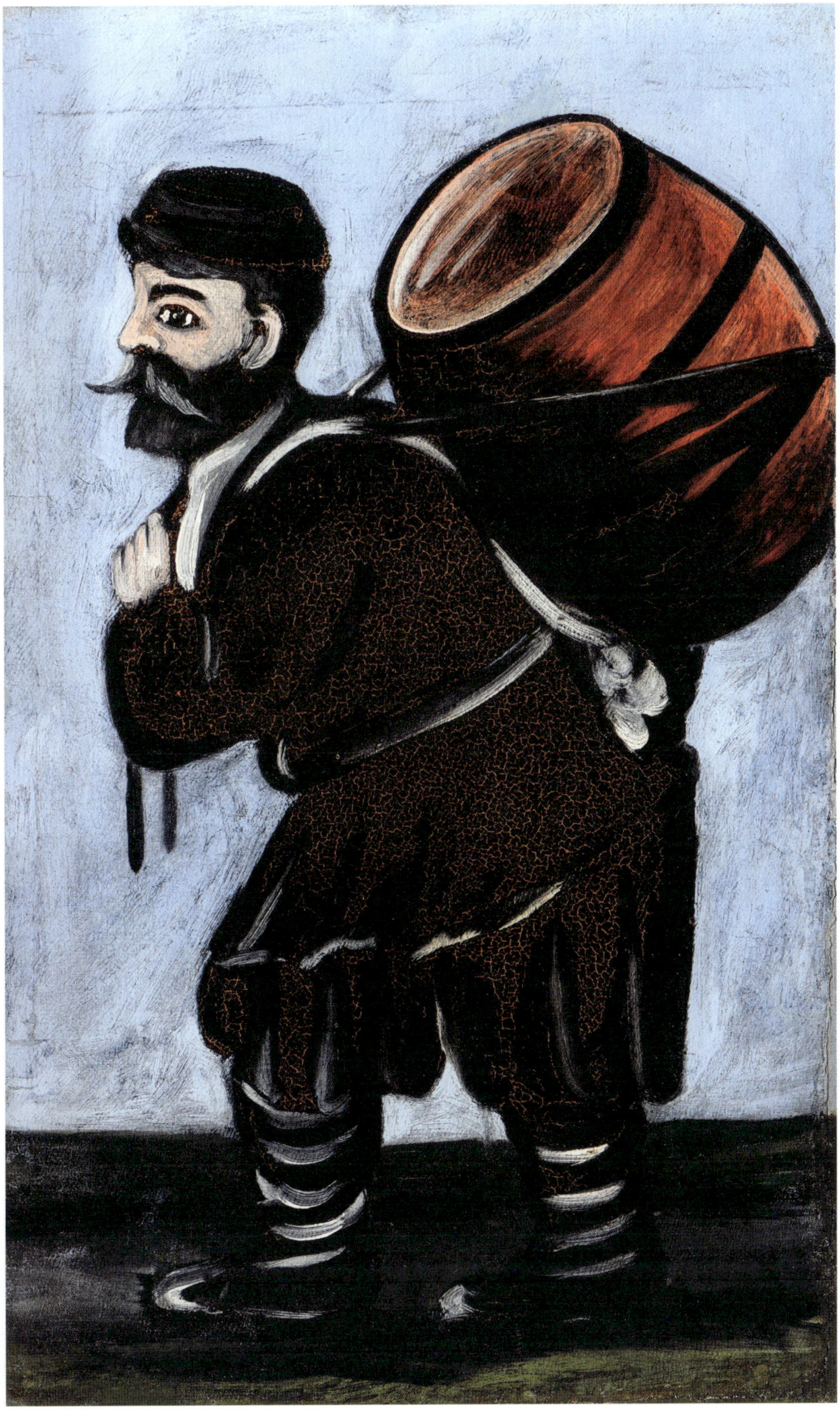

MUSHA WITH A KEG (HALF OF DIPTYCH)

vignettes of brigands pillaging, pilgrims riding on bullock-carts, peasants harvesting grapes, or people celebrating church holidays. A sense of merriment, of a happy and fruitful life, pervades these works.

Historical themes *(Saakadze Saves Georgia from its Foes; Shamil and his Bodyguard* and others), diverse theatrical spectacles, scenes of travel, ritual and peasant labour embrace and supplement the works of festive revelry, thereby delineating the full gamut of Georgian life before the revolution, from half-forgotten customs to contemporary types. In every painting Pirosmanashvili shows himself to be an artist of the people, entirely devoid of any sense of seclusion or interiority. In his constant concern for the needs of the viewing public, in his desire to make his work pleasant and accessible to the people, Pirosmanashvili everywhere remains an artist bound to tradition, one whose painterly devices can be readily understood. His intuitive links to the commercial shop-sign, to the Georgian fresco, to the Georgian artisanal crafts of toy making, embroidery and ornamentation are clearly evident. Largely devoid of mystical intimations, his work more commonly displays a concern, Cézannesque and essentially realist, to bring to light whatever appears readily comprehensible to the artist as artist.

Sunshine, glare or shade are almost entirely absent in Pirosmanashvili, who prefers an even spread of light which seems to emanate from somewhere within his paintings. Shadow serves to express form rather than as a way of conveying light.

Pirosmanashvili painted quickly. Each one of his paintings was completed in two or three sittings, within a few hours. Take the painting *Little Kinto,* completed by Pirosmanashvili in half an hour in the presence of a large group of people clamorously expressing their appreciation both of the painting's resemblance to its subject and of the speed with which Pirosmani executed the work.

I have already mentioned the fact that Pirosmanashvili's themes varied greatly. In his work we find representations of folk customs, battle scenes, typological portraits, genre paintings, still lifes, landscape and innumerable animal figures.

The dimensions of Pirosmanashvili's paintings range from five meters in length to fifteen centimetres. Their composition is largely determined by the dimensions of the canvas. They are painted on oilcloth, more rarely on canvas or on tin and finally on cardboard. Pirosmanashvili authored a colossal number of paintings: more than a thousand. Regrettably not many survived. For this we can blame careless owners, the poor conditions – such as cellars – in which they were kept, and more generally the conditions of a transitional era.

Pirosmanashvili lived an ordinary life, yet his creative accomplishments are remarkable. Working in taverns and storefronts to earn a meager meal and glass of vodka, suffering from extreme privation and need, the artist became a martyr to his craft.

The artist Mikhail Le Dentu (1891-1917) and the Zdanevich brothers Ilia and Kirill (the undersigned, ed.) first discovered Niko's paintings in the spring of 1912. This joyful discovery prompted them to seek out other paintings by Niko, as well as the artist himself. The search for paintings and painter proved successful: we tracked down the artist. We came to a building on Molokan Street where Niko was pointed out to us. He was standing on the pavement with a brush in his hand, busy painting the word "Dairy" on the wall. He turned to us, gave a dignified bow and continued working, sustaining the conversation we had initiated with infrequent replies.
The visual details of this meeting remain etched in my mind to this day: the artist standing by a white wall, dressed in a torn black jacket and a soft felt hat, tall in stature, carrying himself with an air of calm independence – his responses nonetheless betraying a sense of hidden bitterness. (Acquaintances would jokingly address him as "count").

Pirosmanashvili's father, a peasant fruit-grower, lived in the eastern Georgian province of Kakheti, where Niko himself was born in 1863 in the village of Mirzaani. Upon his father's death, between the ages of six and eight, Niko was sent to Tiflis (later known as Tbilisi, ed.)[3], where he lived at the home of a certain soldier named Kalantar. It was here that Niko first attempted to paint in watercolours.
On reaching maturity Niko was asked by his guardian what he would like to be. He replied: "An artist". The answer didn't go down well, and the young man was sent to work as a railway conductor, a profession he pursued for eight years until he fell ill. Niko then ran a dairy business for a time, decorating his store with pictures of cows. His store was first located on Olginskaia Street, then in Soldiers' Bazaar. He gradually attained a level of prosperity. People who knew Niko from that time recall him as successful, kindly, a lively dinner companion with plenty of money to spare, irascible but quick to forgive. He would paint and readily give his paintings away to friends and acquaintances. One episode from this period reflects the painter's growing popularity. In 1902-1903 the Persian consul in Tiflis wrote a letter to a local newspaper about Niko's paintings. The painter responded in kind, generating a polemic that awoke the interest of the townsfolk (I regret to say I have been unable to ascertain any details regarding this). This cycle ended in a catastrophe precipitated by Niko's tragic love for the "French" vaudeville performer, the actress Margarita. In the space of one year Niko, now bankrupt, was cast onto the street. Thus began his vagabond existence as a professional artist who now lacked even a room to call his own. The half-starved artist lived year after year among the taverns and stores of the city. Pirosmanashvili's work arose in precisely these conditions, his talent in no way diminished by the daily struggle he experienced. In time Niko changed, losing the easy laughter of his youth. He withdrew into himself, projecting an air of severity and calm.

He would wander the city in search of work, moving from one cellar to another with a suitcase containing his work tools and meagre wardrobe. The cover of his suitcase contained a drawing of a man in a top hat.

The circle of Niko's friends and admirers gradually expanded and, with it, interest in the artist's life and work grew. Below I provide lengthy extracts from notes taken by eye-witnesses. Having commissioned a portrait of himself from Pirosmanashvili, Ilia Zdanevich[4] kept an account of his daily visits:

Sunday 27 January, 1913. I went this morning to Meskhiev (on 70 Cherezovskaia St.), from whom I purchased the portrait of the boy. From there I went to see Nikolai [Pirosmani]. Nikolai remained seated during my visit while he painted my portrait. He asked about the painting I had purchased. A preliminary outline of my portrait now exists, while the deer (which I also commissioned) is largely complete: it is magnificently executed, apart from the background which is not fully done. First Nikolai took me aside and said: "As for the exhibition, if someone gave me a room to work in and canvas to paint on, I would be able to paint ten to fifteen paintings in a month, better than those I have done until now, even better than *Sheremetev Gardens*." He then added: "People keep spoiling my paintings. Take a look at this painting, for example. There's a hare in it. Why? Who needs a hare? But they asked for it: 'Please,' they said, 'do it for our sake.' I draw these things so as not to get into a quarrel. People spoil all my paintings this way."

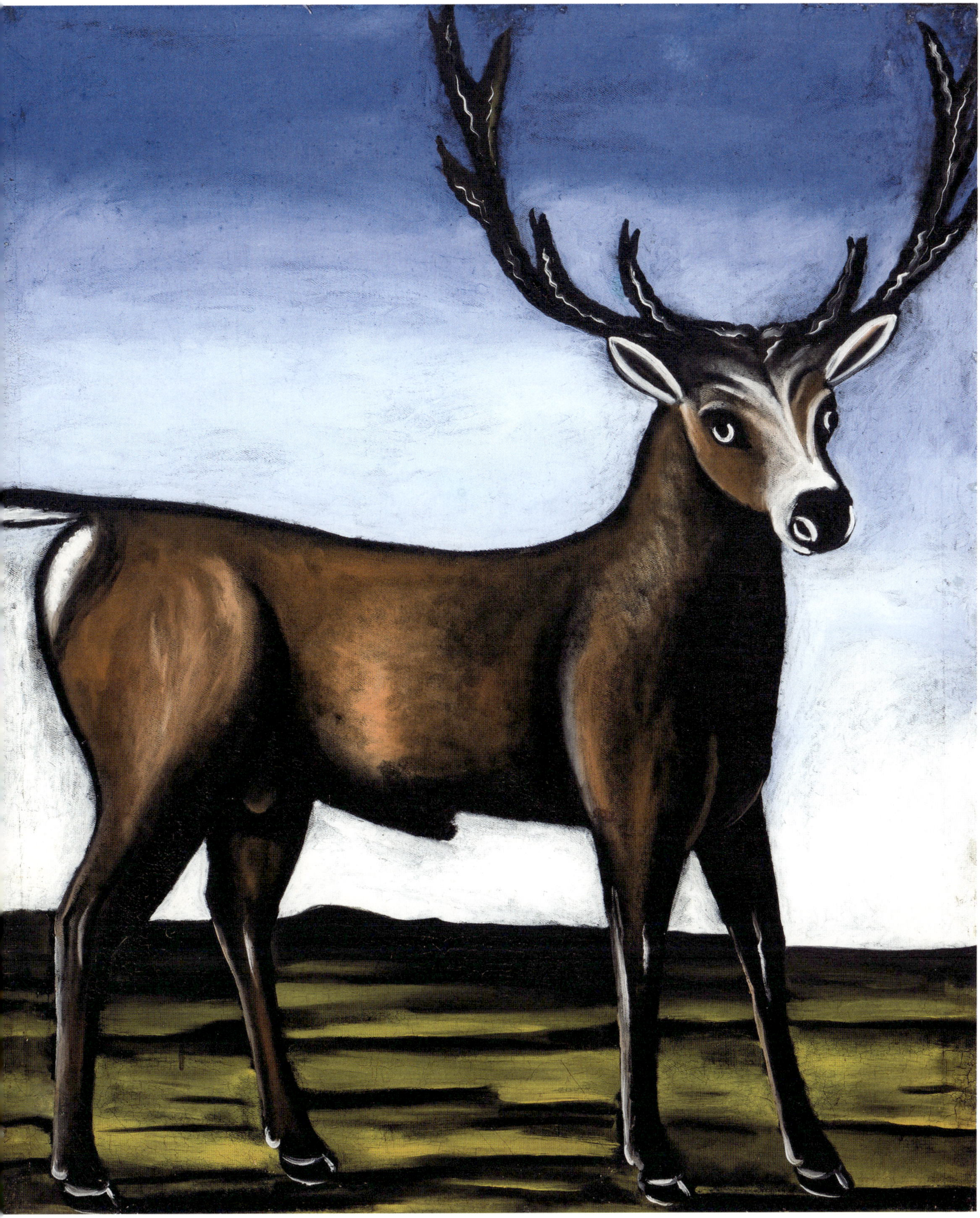

In response to my question as to whether he painted icons, he said: "An icon, a painting or a house: each one is different. I have never painted an icon. Just once I painted Saint George. Painters are like calligraphers. They can't draw." He then began to lament his terrible poverty, his shabby clothes, as well as the ignorance of his customers, while asking for my help. He begged me not to tell any of the tavern keepers about the fact that he needed a room. "The room should be bright," he said. "Here it's dark." When he paints, he places his left hand underneath his right to stop it from shaking. He said he had taught himself Russian: "I bought a Georgian book translated into Russian." And then: "I can't work here. They keep making me drink." He told me he had done a self-portrait once – "in a nice suit, not like this one" – but he had sold it to somebody. Yesterday he said: "There are different kinds of paintings. You can paint for a whole month, or even a whole year, and still have material left over." Then he added: "I must confess I am not wild about the paintings at Beradze's. I can do better."

28 January. I was with Nikolai this morning. He had been drinking. My portrait now has a tree, and he has added some grass to the deer painting. He told me has was upset with me for coming late. He had just received a new commission for which he would be paid 60 kopecks: this was going to keep him busy. I asked, "What kind of commission?" He then showed me a house lantern on which he had to paint the words "Molokan Street, Number so and so." That was the entire order. "So what?" he said. "If we can't fulfil ordinary requests, how can we do more elevated subjects?" I had to agree with him. Then Nikolai said that he had worked as a delivery man for the railways and that he had never completed his military service. Before dinner I dropped by to see Nikolai again, but didn't speak to him. He was asleep.

I then went to Bego Iaskiev's tavern on 40 Peskovskaia Street, where I bought a still life for one rouble fifty, after which I went back to Nikolai. The owner of the establishment, Sandro Kochelashvili by name, told me that he wouldn't have paid even five kopecks for such a thing. Then we began to discuss Nikolai in general. Among other things Sandro said, "He wanted to draw a tree stump and place your hand on it as well as a pile of books. But I told him to draw a table. As for the deer, that's what you need a tree for, so that the deer can be seen leaning against it." I said that Nikolai can paint whatever he wants and that I couldn't make him do anything. Then we started discussing the painting they wanted to present to me as a gift. Sandra began praising it fulsomely, saying: "This is going to be the best piece in your exhibition.[5] It shows a prince capable of drinking three buckets of wine at the dinner table."

We then woke Nikolai up. He came out and said: "My talent tired itself out waiting for you. I waited for you in the morning. You were late." He asked me for two roubles. He looked over the still life and said: "I remember it. Why not: it was one of my best works. I painted it for myself. So what if it's small. It's bound to be worth a hundred roubles."

29 January. I was at Nikolai's. in the morning posing for my picture. The deer is done. Nikolai has done fifteen paintings for Bego Iaskiev for no remuneration other than meals. He has works hanging in the White Tavern on the highway to Manglisi, as well as in the city's outer neighbourhoods. Sandra Kochelashvili keeps interfering and asking Nikolai to paint trees, leaves and such. It's hard to make him see reason. In general it would appear that Nikolai is unable to complete a single piece on his own without being goaded on by someone else. "If I had a hundred roubles," he tells me, "I would get some decent clothes, rent a room, and then start painting."

I told him I was going to write an article about him in the papers. As I took my leave he said: "Drop by later. I am going to paint some flowers." Then he added: "My best commission was for Qipiani, a stationmaster on the Baku railway line. He paid me thirty rubles. Sometimes the mechanics who work in small shops also pay me. Generally, though, I work for food."

30 January. I was with Zyga Waliszewski[6] this morning. They brought in *Three Princes on a Meadow.* We almost got into a fight with Sandro's acquaintances, who didn't want to sell the painting. Nikolai said the following about the frame: "If the wall is brightly coloured, then a black frame is best. If the wall is painted dark, then a bright frame is better. Otherwise the painting doesn't stand out. It took me nine days to paint *Three Princes.* That's Prince Gulbatov and his cousins, the Chavchavadze princes. He was upset he hadn't shaved: that's why his face doesn't bear a strong likeness to him." Then some other fellow came along and asked: "How much do you charge for a portrait?" Nikolai replied: "Thirty rubles." He sat down and posed: the likeness was striking. He will finish the painting tomorrow. I said: "In Moscow any cafeteria owner will buy your work. Just be careful not to ask for too little. If you need something, write to me. I will send you whatever you need." Then Ziga and I began visiting various taverns in search of Nikolai's paintings. At the Varangian we were offered *Queen Tamara* for three roubles. In the evening I went back to see Nikolai for the second time, this time with my brother [Kirill]. When we arrived, Nikolai was sitting at the back of the tavern on a bench, warming his hands by some smouldering coal embers. When he heard that Kirill was an artist, he began to ask: were his paintings any good?

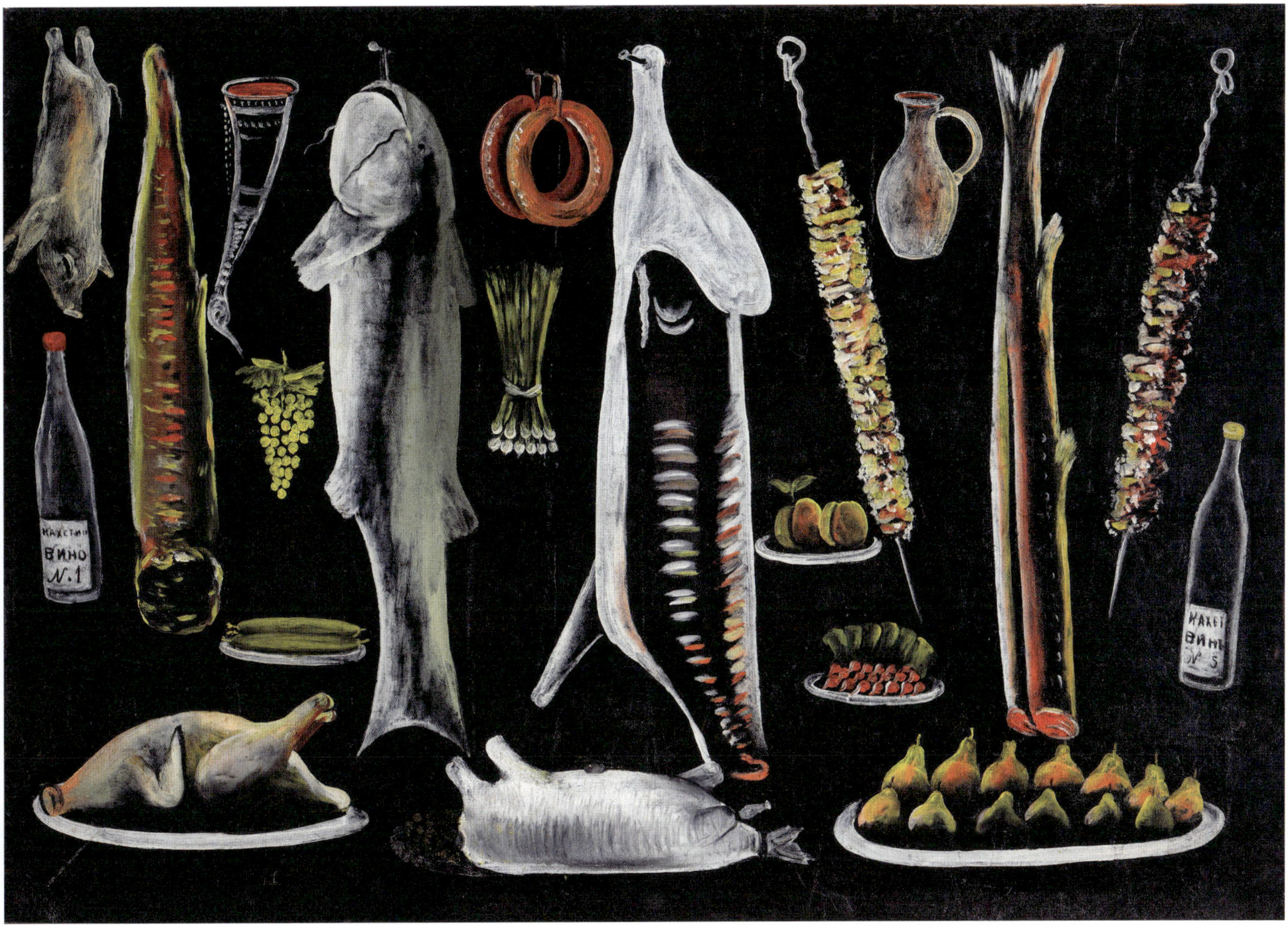
КАХЕТИН
ВИНО
N.1
КАХЕТ
№ 5

The owner Sandro then inserted himself into the conversation, commenting on the quality of my portrait as well the deer and insisting that a moon was required. Nikolai declared that it didn't need any moon and began to get angry. He asked for his brushes. Then he asked us to show him at least one work by my brother. We invited him to come visit us.

31 January. I visited Nikolai this morning and posed for him. The portrait is almost ready. He has also added a sky to the painting of the deer. I then went to the editorial office of *Zakavkazskaia rech,*[7] where I asked if my letter regarding the artist Pirosmani had been accepted for publication. They told me it would be published tomorrow. From there I went to see Nikolai again. He started telling me about his life, his professional career in the railways and then as a merchant, up to his ruin. In 1904 he had rented a room in Prickly Ravine, but for the past nine years he had not even had that and was living exclusively off his painting. "I used to be rich," he said, "but now I don't even own any decent clothes." His father had left him land in Kakheti, but he didn't want to live there since he wasn't, as he said, an "agriculturalist." As I was leaving some other people showed up and began to criticise my portrait. Nikolai said: "Don't listen to them. They're fools. They don't understand anything."

1 February. I was with Nikolai this morning. The portrait is done. For the Gulbatov portrait I will have to pay Sandro two roubles which he claims to have given to his friends to calm them down. Nikolai discretely reminded me of his request (the Moscow commission). In the evening I was with the artist T. and the journalist A. We looked over Niko's paintings. The artist said: "He reminds me of the Persians, but he is cruder and lacks any sense of colour. In general I don't see anything remarkable about him." Overall their response was indefinite and indifferent. I might add that in this they are a rare exception: those intellectuals who have actually seen his work have been uniformly praising it.

2 February. I went to fetch my portrait and the deer. Nikolai began to protest: "Don't give me anything for the deer, that's fine. If there are any commissions in Moscow, write to me." When I informed him that his paintings were going to be displayed in an exhibition, his hopes were rekindled and he brightened up. I take leave of everyone and go to the railway station

The train departs, but there, in the depths of the vast city, by a pile of smouldering coal embers sits a man with an anguished expression on his face, a solitary wanderer and a major artist, who has made a deep impression on me. After making Nikolai's acquaintance I now know what life is.

(Here the extracts from
Ilia Zdanevich's journal end.)

During the war years those who had known Niko left Tiflis and lost touch with him. Others took up his cause.[8] They sought him out in 1916 and invited him to a gathering at the Georgian Artists' Association, where he declared: "This is what we need, brothers. In the middle of the city, for easy access to all, we need to build a large wooden house where we can gather. We will buy a large table, a large samovar, drink tea, drink a lot, talk of painting and art. You don't want this. You keep talking about other things." He ended on a quiet and wistful note. That was the last time Niko attended a session of the Association.[9] Then the painter Lado Gudiashvili[10] tracked him down to a Didube courtyard,[11] living in a shoebox of a room below the staircase of a small building. Have you come as friend or as foe?" Niko asked him, examining him with a "haunted" look in his eyes. After striking up a conversation, Niko asked him: "Will we build a house? Did you know that all the cellars in Tiflis were painted by me?" Niko appeared sad and tired. His health had been shattered.

Soziashvili (the owner of the wine cellar Niko frequented) describes the painter's final years as follows: "He would come to me every day and seat himself at a table. He was never seen in company, and he never accepted food or drink from anyone. He knew Georgian literature, had a great fondness for Vazha-Pshavela,[12] wrote verse himself and was a poet. His notebook of verse has been lost. He loved Georgians, but disliked those in power, policemen and the like. He would complain, albeit seldom, that he had been forgotten."

So the years passed, Archil Maisuradze[13] relates the following: "In the spring of 1918, as evening approached, Pirosmanashvili entered the cellar of No. 29 Molokan Street and lay down to sleep on the floor. He was already ill. Three days later, I happened to go down there and found Niko lying in the cold dark room. Initially I didn't recognise him and called out: "Who's there?" "It's me," Nikolai answered, and I knew him at once from his voice. He didn't recognise me, however, saying: "I'm unwell. I've been lying here for three days and can't leave." I immediately brought along a horse-drawn cab. Ilia Mgalobashvili (now deceased) took him – if I'm not mistaken – to the Aramiants hospital where he passed away after a day and a half. He left no property behind. I believe he is buried in Peter and Paul Cemetery."

More years passed. Soviet Georgia, having realised the value of a singular artist of the people and overcome considerable difficulties, is now publishing this monograph[14], a worthy monument to Niko Pirosmanashvili. The study of his work is a fruitful exercise for contemporary Georgian art. His legacy can enrich and give new strength to young artists. The memory of this man, gifted from birth, has survived, along with so many of his works. So Niko Pirosmanashvili's labour lives on, for the sake of the future.

Notes

1 Besides Datiko Zemel the carousal also features *kintos*. The Georgian author Grigol Robakidze (1880-1962) defines the kinto as a member of "an utterly singular breed of déclassé street peddlers whose sole goal in life was a kind of singular artistic merriment". **2** *Musha with a Keg* and *Musha with a Wineskin*, ed. **3** Louisiana Museum of Modern Art's note: The *Danish Lexicon by Salmonsen* states, in 1927, about Tiflis: "A peculiarity of modern T. is that there are far more men than women, and that so many people live here without a permanent home. In connection to this it has earned its reputation as a lively but corrupt city." **4** Ilia Zdanevich (1894-1975), along with his brother Kirill (1892-1969) and their mutual friend, art student Mikhail Le Dentu (1891-1917), "discovered" Pirosmani in the summer of 1912, Ilia subsequently returned during his winter holidays to Tbilisi, during which time he sat for a portrait he had commissioned from Pirosmani. The diary entries which follow, written by an 18-year-old gifted enough to lecture in Moscow on the poet and ideologist Filippo Tommaso Marinetti's (1876-1944) futurist manifestos that very year, describe Ilia's daily encounters with Pirosmani during January and February 1913. **5** Thanks to the efforts of Le Dentu and the Zdanevich brothers, four of Pirosmani's works found their way that same year to Moscow, where they were displayed as part of *Mishen* (The Target), a major exhibition of March-April 1913 organised by the artist Mikhail Larionov (1881-1964) to reflect the culmination of the neoprimitivist phase of the Russian avant-garde. Displayed alongside works by Larionov, Natalia Goncharova (1881-1962), Kazimir Malevich (1879-1935), Marc Chagall (1887-1985), Aleksandr Shevchenko (1883-1948), Mikhail Le Dentu and Kirill Zdanevich, as well as children's art, old *lubok* prints and shop-signs, these paintings – which included the portrait discussed above, as well as *Woman with a Tankard of Beer, Still Life* and *Deer* – would be the first public showing of Pirosmani's works during his life. Pirosmani thus entered the art world framed by the aesthetic and ideological presuppositions of the Russian avant-garde. **6** Zygmunt (Zyga) Walizsewski (1897-1936), an artist of Polish origin active in Tbilisi's cosmopolitan modernist milieu during the 1910s and 1920s. Alongside Le Dentu and the Zdanevich brothers, Walizsewski participated in the 'discovery' of Pirosmani in 1912-1913; after the revolution in 1917 he was involved in the upsurge of futurist avant-garde creativity unfolding in the cafes and cabarets of the Georgian capital. He moved to Poland in 1920, pursuing a career in the visual arts between Poland and France until his death. **7** *Zakavkazskaia rech* (The Transcaucasian Voice), a Russian-language daily financed by progressive members of the Georgian elite, published in Tbilisi between 1910 and 1917. **8** A reference to the Georgian artists Dimitri Shevardnadze (1885-1937), Davit Kakabadze (1889-1952), Lado Gudiashvili (1896-1980) and Mikhail Chiaureli (1894-1974), who together founded the Society of Georgian Artists on 31 March 1916. Pirosmani's brief association with the Society might be considered emblematic of the *third* stage in his circulation history. If the first stage involved Pirosmani's prolonged immersion in the popular urban milieu in which he lived and worked, and the second saw his 'discovery' by the neoprimitivist avant-garde, the third stage – following shortly after the second – involved Pirosmani's embrace by the most enlightened members of the new generation of the Georgian national intelligentsia.
A one-day exhibition of over fifty works by Pirosmani at the Zdanevich family home in Tbilisi on 5 May 1916 – the second and last exhibition of Pirosmani's works to take place in his lifetime – unleashed a vigorous discussion of the artist and his work at two meetings of the Society of Georgian Artists that same month. **9** The meeting, which took place on 25 May 1916, led to a wider awareness of Pirosmani's work among the Georgian population. Nevertheless, Pirosmani's status in Georgian circles remained sharply contested. This is evident from a widely circulated cartoon published on 10 June in *Sakhalkho purtseli* (The People's Leaflet) which showed a critic bearing a striking resemblance to Grigol Robakidze addressing Pirosmani thus: "You need to study, brother! A man your age can still create something ... Orphic. In around twenty years you could become a decent artist. Then we will send you to an exhibition of young artists." The cartoon, which appears to have precipitated Pirosmani's withdrawal from public life, throws a curious light on Robakidze's subsequent article. The article reads as a disavowal of the sentiments ascribed to him in the cartoon. **10** Lado Gudiashvili (1896-1980), 20th century Georgian painter, a native of Tbilisi, who sought to reconcile the vernacular and regional cultural idioms of the Caucasus with modernist currents emanating from Paris. His final meeting with Pirosmani took place in the summer of 1917. **11** A neighbourhood on the outskirts of Tbilisi. **12** Vazha-Pshavela (1861-1915), arguably the most original Georgian poet of the late tsarist era, wove visual and ethnographic elements drawn from his native alpine region of Pshavi into a distinctly modern – at once tragic and neoromantic – sensibility. **13** A shoemaker, Pirosmani's neighbour during his final months. **14** This refers to the book *Niko Pirosmanashvili* (1926), published in Georgian, French and Russian at the same time by a group of poets, authors, journalists and artists, from which this text originates.

Kirill Mikhailovich Zdanevich (1892-1969), Georgian avant-garde artist, scenographer and book designer, known for his love of colour and his broad interest and commitment to modern art and his concept of *Vsiochestvo*, or Everythingness. Educated at the Saint Petersburg Academy of Arts 1911-1913. Visited Henri Matisse (1869-1954) and Pablo Picasso (1881-1973) in Paris in 1913. Enlisted in the Russian army 1914-1917 in East Prussia. Settled in his native Tbilisi in 1917. Founded the Futurist group 41° to promote avant-garde poetry with his brother, the jurist and playwright Ilia Zdanevich (1894-1975) and the poets Aleksandr Kruchenykh (1886-1968) and Igor Terentyev (1892-1937). In the aftermath of the Second World War, he was convicted of being a Formalist and sent to a labour camp in Siberia for ten years. Published books on Georgian art and artists from the late 1950s until his death. Along with Ilia and the artist Mikhail Le Dentu, he was the person who 'discovered' Niko Pirosmani in 1912.

Originally published in Russian in Tabidze, Titsian, Grigol Robakidze, Geronti Kikodze, Kirill Zdanevich and Kolau Cherniaysldi, *Niko Pirosmanashvili* [Tbilisi: Gosudarstvennoe Izdaltestvo Gruzii, 1926], Alys Moody and Stephen J. Ross eds., trans. Harsha Ram, *Global Modernists on Modernism*: An Anthology (Bloomsbury Academic, 2020).

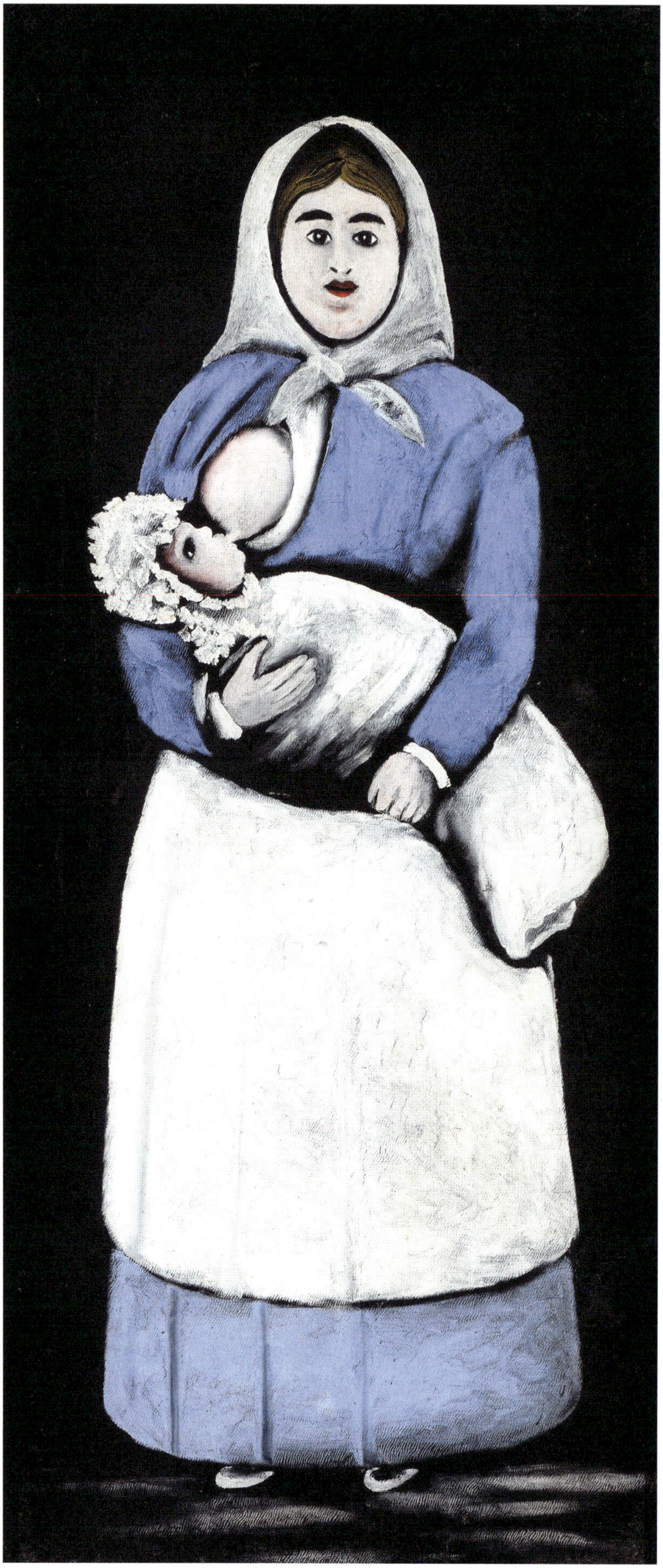

WETNURSE WITH A CHILD
>
POLAR SHE-BEAR WITH CUBS

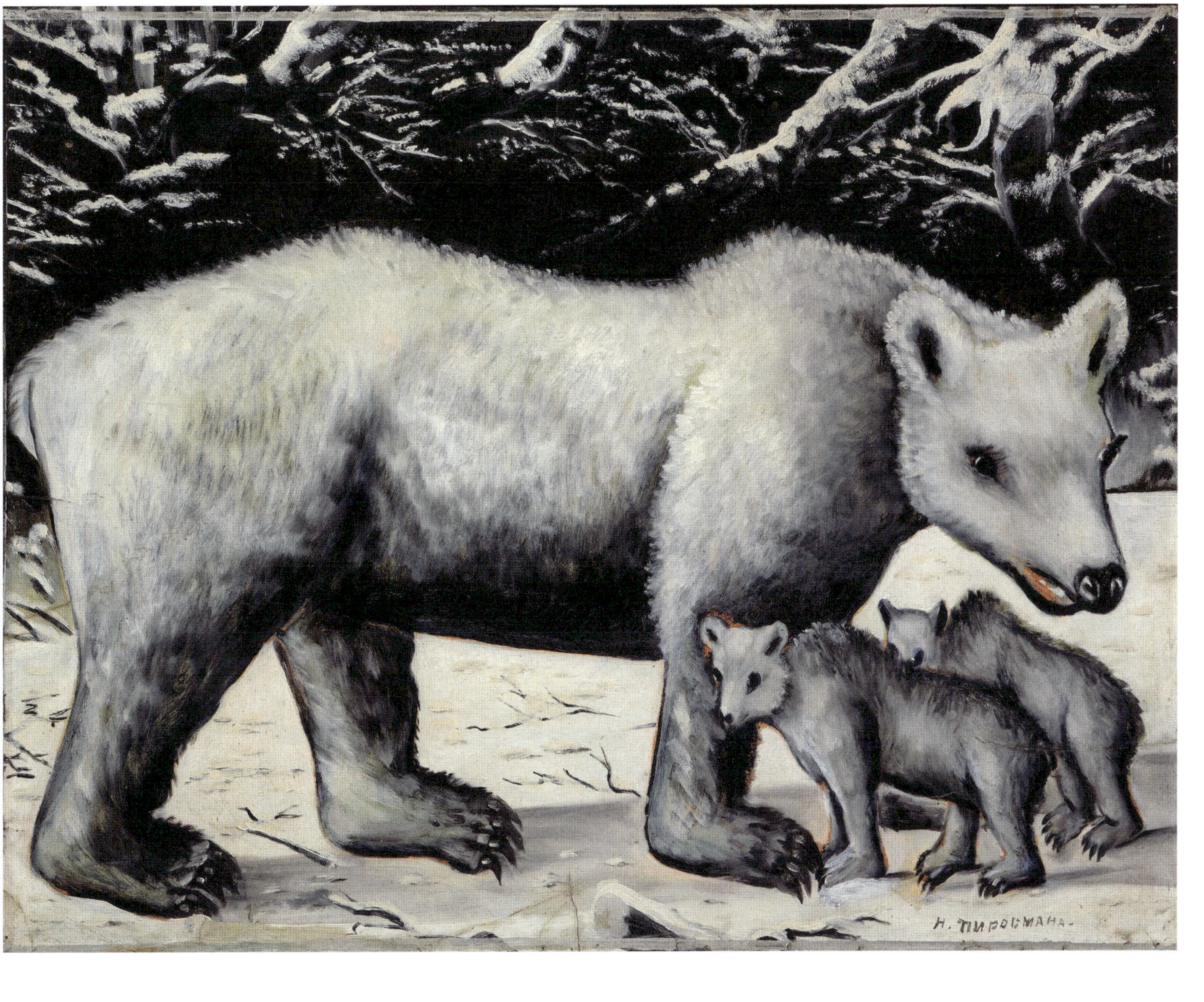
Н. ПИРОСМАНА.

I first saw the work of Pirosmani in a Georgian restaurant in Tel Aviv. I was sitting with a menu card, and then I saw a tiny black and white image of somebody having a banquet. And ... I tore it out. The grand thing about attraction is that you can always invent reasons afterwards, but the hand is just much faster. It picks up stuff that there might be many reasons for. I didn't know it was him, but I stole this small image and put it in my pocket because I loved that image so much. The thing is, I had been watching it upside down, so when I went back to the studio, then, out of some kind of weird courtesy to the unknown artist, I painted it upright. So, when people look at it (*The Sohum*, 2014), they can't just read it in a normal way. They kind of enter – weirdly – the table and then they fall over the figures.

I didn't need to know his name, and I haven't spent any time reading about him. It doesn't matter to me. Everything I need to know is in the paintings and will always be in the paintings. All the stories? I leave that to other people. I just thought it was a brilliant image, and I think great paintings; if you see them on a postcard or a stamp or on a menu card, even a badly-done black and white reproduction, they're still great. They still shine and you stretch your hands out and then it's too late. You think you're taking it, but it's actually taking you.

For Pirosmani, as for almost every artist, the greatest achievement of the last 500 years is the invention of the camera. That's the best thing that ever happened for painting. Historically we know that painting was liberated from the state, from noble people, from the church, whatever. But actually, the bigger liberation was that artists could just give in to imagination. There's a difference between being in fantasy and being in imagination. Fantasy is more selfish, freewheeling, or you just drift away like a cloud. But imagination? You are still somehow humble, connected to what you see. And there is this weird connection to what he sees and this weird distance, like he's kind of a tourist. You have a feeling that he looks at the animals, but he has never really seen them, which makes his work even stronger because if it's not about just reproducing the correct animal, then you cannot separate your experience of the animal and your misunderstanding of the animal. Most great art is actually not done out of knowledge. It's done out of misunderstanding ...

The great thing also about his paintings is that they look like something that happened much later. They kind of look like illustrations. He is quite similar to Henri Rousseau (1844-1910); you can always count the elements. Of course, there are several figures, but there is very often a wolf in the foreground, a ruin in the background and the moon. Or just a goat, a demon goat, where its body is half the size of the canvas, so it almost brings conflict to the middle of it; the body of the goat almost becomes a painting in the painting. Or think of the very beautiful painting of the woman in a red dress (*Woman with a Tankard of Beer,* p. 31). From a mug the same colour as her dress, it looks like she's drinking a beer mixed with flowers. That's the most brilliant painting.

You could offend art history by saying that there is a line between this very early kind of illustration and a cartoon, even pop art. I think there's also a weird link to artists like Francis Picabia (1879-1953). Picabia is just a dandy in a world that Pirosmani or Rousseau or others are more 'real' in. I think it's a really interesting discussion about something being 'naivist'. I think a naive artwork is where the artist is trying to be some kind of puppet master. They put in all those symbols that they have, and they are in total control and everything is calculated. But to make a painting happen? I don't think that's naive. And no matter how many grand academies artists go to, in the end they are all self-taught. Because the deep knowledge you need as an artist is to look at other people's work. Maybe it's the people who sit in the academies that create this hierarchy. They get offended that somebody is great without passing through the academy, and then they call them self-taught.

Different works clearly have something to do with Georgian folk culture. And I find them interesting because the compositions he tries are more complicated. There are more beautiful failures in them, more kinds of honey in them, great honey, great sugar. I think it's quite obvious in his painting that there's always a 'what is here,' and then there's always something about travellers. And there's always an animal that appears to not exist there; always this feeling of somewhere else. Clearly, it's an area with lots of tales because people travelled over the mountains, far away, all the way to China.

When he portrays animals, there's no real separation between animals and people. It's just this breathing 'something'. Like his *Giraffe* (p. 32), you have eye contact with that painting, just like with any person. And every animal is like that. Sometimes he paints the animal twice with the animal in a peaceful situation and in a more threatening one, which is quite interesting to put in the same painting.

TAL R:
» PIROSMANI MADE ME STEAL «

TOLD TO ROXANNE BAGHESHIRIN LÆRKESEN

And if you translate this onto a human, you have a character that looks calm, attractive, and then looks very, very angry and attractive. I think that's a great idea. So there's a lot to learn from the structure in this work.

I think also you could make a whole study out of this: he paints onto black. Of course, people before him have painted on a very black background, but in his case, it's really not to create drama. It's more like the painting used to be black, and then, out of the black, somebody steps out to stand there for a second and you get this feeling, that when you leave, they pull back into the black. And as a viewer, you just feel grateful that they will step out of the black for a second. Like the image appears and says, "I'm here for a second. And then I run back into the mountains, into black, into 'no language anymore.' "

So I look at the work and I immediately feel jealous, because I think they are really beautiful. And there's just something I want to get from them. But then I look at them more kind of cold-blooded and I try to count, understand, see structures and see places to move in. Understand the discussion he's in. That's all you do as an artist, I think. Try to understand the discussion.

The great thing about art is that from one perspective the work is 100 years old. But from where I see it, it's just five minutes ago, and it's possible to walk into them like that. Maybe the folktale paintings are more placed in that time, but his paintings of just people or food or animals? They're not even five minutes ago, they are just around the corner. You can just go around the corner. It's there.

Tal R (born 1967) is a Danish-Israeli artist. Exhibitions include the 2017 solo show at Louisiana Museum of Modern Art, *Academy of Tal R*, and the joined 2023 show at Kunsten Museum of Modern Art Aalborg, Malmö Konstmuseum and Museum MORE (2024), *Tal R & Mamma Andersson – About Hill.*

The interview was originally made for Louisiana Channel and later adapted for print by Malou Wedel Bruun. Discover this and several other interviews with the artist at channel.louisiana.dk

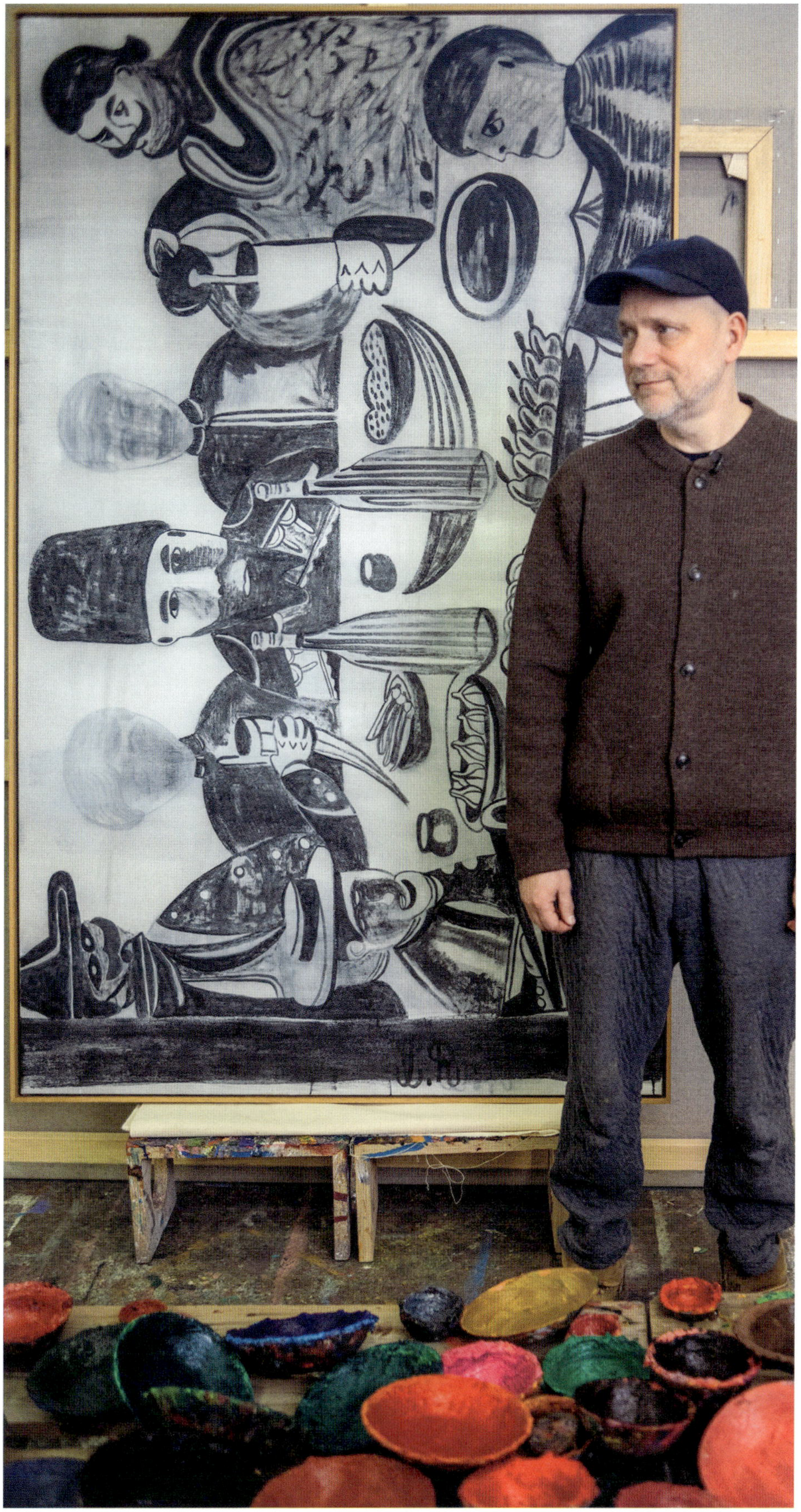

PHOTO: SIMON WEHYE

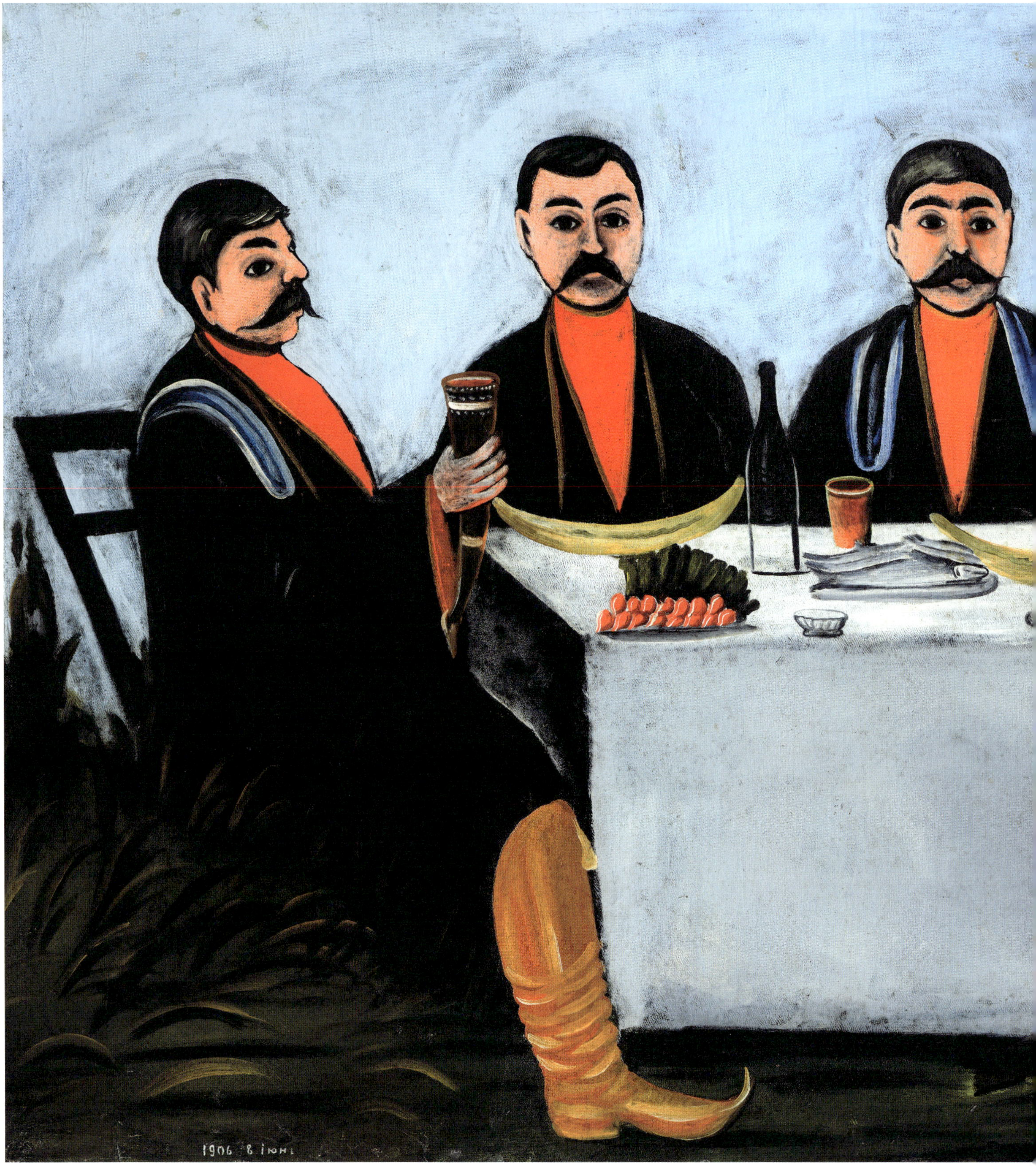

FIVE PRINCES CAROUSING. 1906

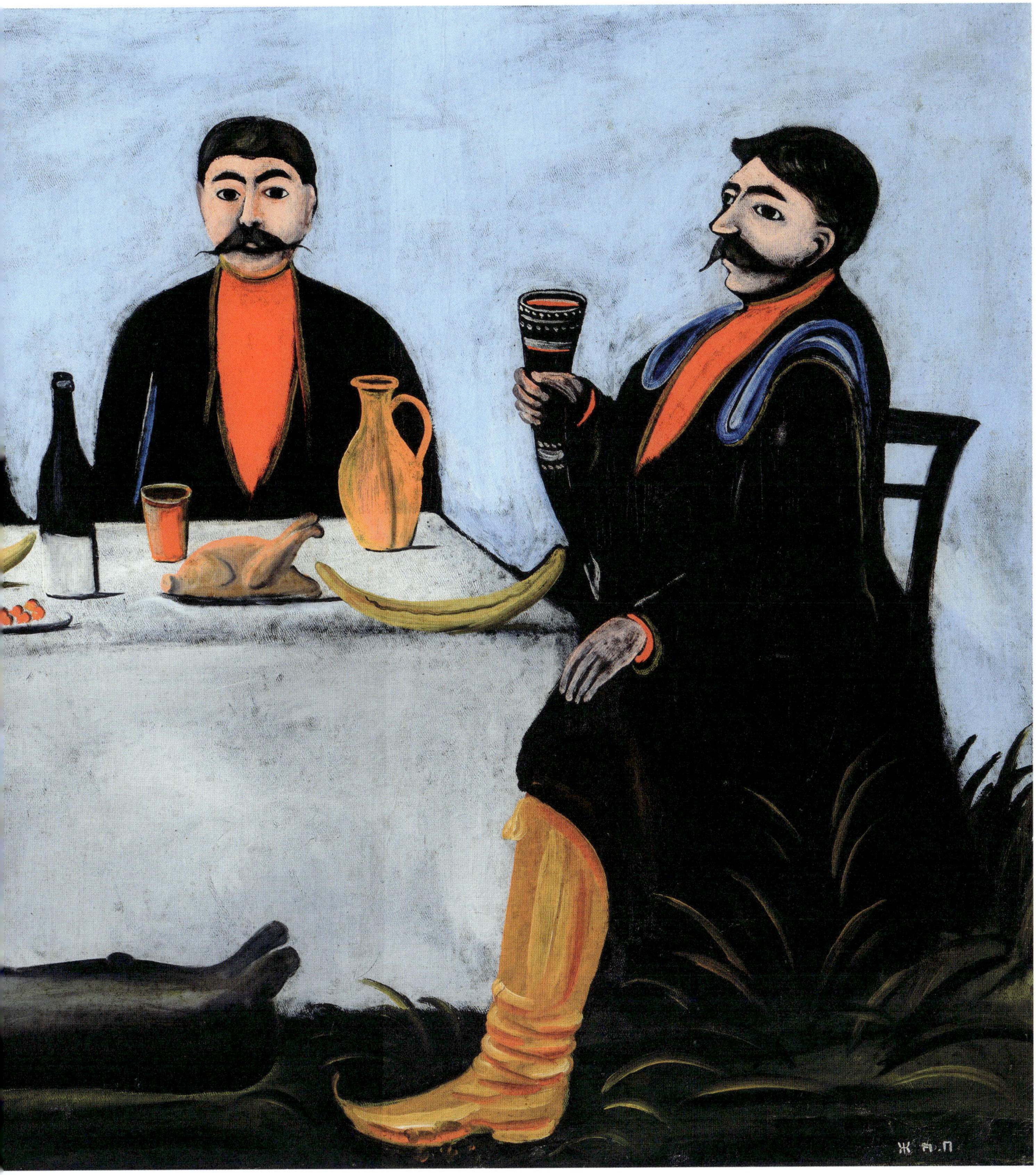

1862/1863 Nikala Pirosmanashvili (later known as Niko Pirosmani) is born in the village of Mirzaani in the province of Kakheti, eastern Georgia, on 5 May according to legend, the youngest of four children; two daughters and two sons.

1863 Aslan Pirosmanashvili, Pirosmani's father, is a poor farmer, and due to a lack of work the family is forced to move to the village of Shulaveri in southern Georgia. There his father works for the Kalantar family, owners of a vineyard.

1870 Pirosmani's brother and parents die within a short period of time. The Kalantar family takes Pirosmani in and he lives with them for the next fifteen years, first in Shulaveri and then in the capital, Tbilisi. There he learns to read and write in Georgian and Russian. Also during this period he begins to paint watercolours and is given some instruction in drawing.

1883-1884 Pirosmani trains as a typographer, although he never makes a career of it.

1888-1893 Pirosmani opens a studio together with the self-taught painter Gigo Zaziashvili (1868-1952) and attempts to sell some of his paintings, but is not successful. He works as a cook, and from 1890 is employed by the Transcaucasus Railway as a brakeman. The work takes a toll on his health and he applies for medical leave. Pirosmani leaves the railway at the end of 1893.

1894-1898 Pirosmani and a friend open a dairy shop in Tbilisi. He decorates the shop with pictures and painted signs. The business grows and is successful, and with the money he earns Pirosmani builds a house for one of his sisters in Mirzaani, their hometown. He continues to paint throughout this period.

1899-1904 His plans to marry a woman from Mirzaani come to nothing, and his partner's young daughter dies. Pirosmani becomes withdrawn and begins to drink. He gives up his business and begins a nomadic existence, making a living through occasional work and painting portraits of railway workers and people at taverns, who give him meals in return.

1905-1911 Pirosmani lives with the innkeeper Bego Iakashvili in Tbilisi. He helps in the kitchen and paints. The myth goes that he endures a stormy but unrequited love for the French vaudeville actress Marguerite de Sèvres (Margarita), whose portrait he paints. In the summer of 1910, Pirosmani lives at the Eldorado restaurant in the Ortachala Gardens near Tbilisi, where he paints 13 pictures, including his famous giraffe and a number of portraits. He subsequently resumes his itinerant lifestyle.

1912 The Georgian Zdanevich brothers – artist Kirill (1892-1969) and writer Ilia (1894-1975) – and the Russian artist Mikhail Le Dentu (1891-1917) see Pirosmani's paintings in a tavern in Tbilisi. They are thrilled by the works and buy several of them. In Moscow, they tell the Russian avant-garde artist couple Natalia Goncharova (1881-1962) and Mikhail Larionov (1881-1964) about Pirosmani.

BIOGRAPHY

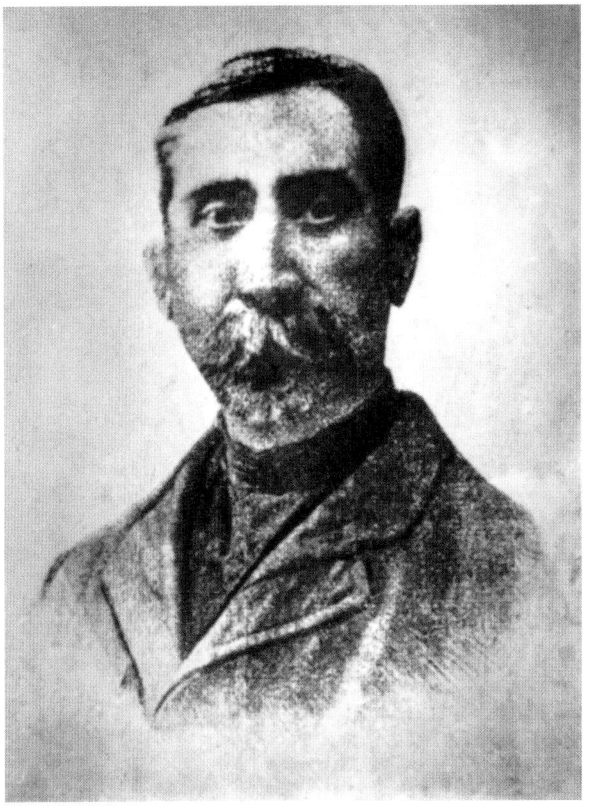

1913 In January, Ilia Zdanevich meets Pirosmani for the first time in Tbilisi as Pirosmani is painting a sign. Zdanevich has his portrait painted and writes about their conversations in his diary. Back in Moscow, he writes about Pirosmani in an article entitled "A Self-Taught Painter" and gives four of Pirosmani's works to Goncharova and Larionov. In March and April, the paintings are shown at the landmark exhibition *Mishen* (Target) alongside works by Kazimir Malevich (1879-1935) and Marc Chagall (1887-1985), among other artists. Meanwhile, Pirosmani is living in a Tbilisi inn.

1914 Ilia Zdanevich publishes an article praising Pirosmani and admonishing Georgian artists and critics for not recognising the quality of his work. There are plans to hold a solo Pirosmani exhibition in Paris, but the outbreak of the First World War in August prevents this. From the outbreak of the war until his death, Pirosmani paints mainly on cardboard due to shortages.

1916 Ilia Zdanevich opens a one-day exhibition of Pirosmani's works in his studio in Tbilisi on the occasion of Pirosmani's birthday, 5 May. There is now increased attention on Pirosmani. The symbolist playwright and author Grigol Robakidze (1880-1962), for example, writes an article entitled "A Georgian Primitivist: On the Exhibition of Works by N. Pirosmanashvili". But there is little recognition from official institutions and artist associations. Pirosmani lives in poverty. A caricature of him and Robakidze which is printed in a newspaper hurts him deeply, and although he continues to paint, he withdraws from the spotlight. He now lives in a small room beneath a flight of stairs.

1917 The Russian Revolution causes turmoil in Tbilisi as artists, writers and intellectuals flee to the Georgian capital from Russia. Pirosmani receives a small donation from the Georgian Art Society.

1918 At the beginning of April, Pirosmani is found unconscious in his room under the stairs. He dies soon after, on his birthday, 5 May, according to legend. His place of burial is unknown. Georgia declares independence on 26 May; this lasts until 1921, when the country is invaded and incorporated into the Soviet Union.

AFTERMATH Following his death, Pirosmani's stardom continues to rise. From having been a self-taught outsider, he was now seen as a key figure, initially by the avant-garde and then in broader and broader circles, ranging from a biographical feature film and an old favourite song based on the myth of his love for Marguerite de Sèvres, to exhibitions in Paris, Vienna and Tokyo. Today he is a Georgian national icon, primarily represented at the National Gallery of Georgia (AMG) in Tbilisi.

There are many versions of Pirosmani's life and times. This biography, written by Kaspar Thormod, is primarily based on Ilia Zdanevich expert Régis Gayraud's research presented in the work *Niko Pirosmani: Wanderer Between Worlds* (2018).

PORTRAIT OF PIROSMANI PRINTED IN THE NEWSPAPER *TSNOBIS PURTSELI* (THE MESSENGER) ALONG WITH ONE OF HIS WORKS IN 1916.

Deer [p. 81]
Oil on waxcloth
138.2 x 113 cm

Carousal with Datiko Zemel, the Organ Grinder. 1906 [p. 39]
Oil on waxcloth
105.6 x 198.3 cm

Fisherman in a Red Shirt [p. 95]
Oil on waxcloth
111 x 89.5 cm

Musha with a Keg (half of diptych) [p. 79]
Oil on waxcloth
61.3 x 37.6 cm

Musha with a Wineskin (half of diptych) [p. 78]
Oil on waxcloth
60.7 x 37 cm

Still Life [p. 8]
Oil on tinplate
36 x 73 cm

Ortachala Belle (half of diptych) [p. 50-51]
Oil on waxcloth
52 x 117.6 cm

Ortachala Belle (half of diptych) [p. 46-47]
Oil on waxcloth
52.5 x 118 cm

Woman with a Tankard of Beer [p. 31]
Oil on waxcloth
112.6 x 90 cm

Janitor [p. 44]
Oil on waxcloth
107 x 47.6 cm

Wetnurse with a Child [p. 86]
Oil on waxcloth
110.5 x 48 cm

Ortachala Belle with a Fan [p. 5]
Oil on waxcloth
110 x 49.5 cm

Cook [p. 55]
Oil on waxcloth
105.7 x 44.7 cm

Lambkin and Easter Table with Flying Angels [p. 61]
Oil on cardboard
80.4 x 99.9 cm

Nanny Goat [pp. 74-75]
Oil on cardboard
83.4 x 101 cm

Polar She-bear with Cubs [p. 87]
Oil on cardboard
80.4 x 99.8 cm

Ambling Hind [p. 43]
Oil on cardboard
68 x 80.4 cm

Fox [p. 18]
Oil on cardboard
38 x 80.8 cm

Roe Deer by a Stream [p. 12]
Oil on cardboard
80.2 x 99.6 cm

Boy Firewood Vendor [p. 45]
Oil on waxcloth
113 x 90 cm

Robber Rustling a Horse [p. 65]
Oil on waxcloth
112.8 x 89.4 cm

Giraffe [p. 32 and cover, back]
Oil on waxcloth
137.4 x 111.7 cm

Arsenal Mount at Night [p. 57]
Oil on waxcloth
110.5 x 87.5 cm

The Kakhetian Train [pp. 22-23]
Oil on cardboard
70 x 141 cm

Yellow Lion Sejant [p. 9]
Oil on cardboard
100.2 x 80.5 cm

Eagle Seizing a Hare [p. 16]
Oil on cardboard
100 x 80.8 cm

Boar [pp. 52-53]
Oil on waxcloth
55.7 x 74.5 cm

Girl with a Toy Balloon [p. 19]
Oil on cardboard
65.3 x 41.5 cm

Bear on a Moonlit Night [p. 13]
Oil on cardboard
99.9 x 80 cm

Peasant Woman with Children Fetching Water [p. 70]
Oil on waxcloth
112.3 x 92.6 cm

White Sow with Piglets [p. 21]
Oil on cardboard
80 x 99.5 cm

Roe Deer and Landscape. 1913 [p. 3]
Oil on cardboard
98.5 x 70.5 cm

The Childless Millionaire and Poor Woman with her Children [pp. 10-11]
Oil on waxcloth
114.5 x 156 cm

The Tiflis Funicular [p. 59]
Oil on waxcloth
109 x 116 cm

Tatar Camel Driver [p. 69]
Oil on cardboard
99.3 x 99.3 cm

The Didube Ferry [p. 71]
Oil on waxcloth
105.2 x 198.3 cm

Portrait of Alexander Garanov. 1906 [p. 20]
Oil on waxcloth
110.5 x 91 cm

Fête of St. George in Bolnisi [pp. 66-67]
Oil on cardboard
78.3 x 265 cm

Five Princes Carousing. 1906 [pp. 90-91]
Oil on waxcloth
104 x 195 cm

Still Life [p. 83]
Oil on waxcloth
100.5 x 136.7 cm

Fête on the Bank of the Tskhenistskali River [pp. 14-15]
Oil on waxcloth
114.3 x 202.3 cm

Doctor on a Jackass [p. 64]
Oil on cardboard
79.4 x 99.6 cm

The Actress Margarita [p. 77 and cover, front]
Oil on waxcloth
115.9 x 94 cm

Georgian Woman with a Tambourine. 1906 [p. 63]
Oil on waxcloth
110.4 x 89 cm

Still Life with a Loaf of Sugar (fragment of signboard for a wineshop in Didube) [p. 40]
Oil on tinplate
53 x 59 cm
Niko Pirosmanashvili State Museum of Mirzaani

Three Deer by a Stream [p. 42]
Oil on cardboard
103.3 x 81.4 cm

Rooster and Brooder with Chicks [p. 17]
Oil on cardboard
68 x 77.7 cm

Woman with Flowers and Parasol [p. 41]
Oil on waxcloth
112.7 x 53 cm

LIST OF WORKS

THE COLLECTION OF SHALVA AMIRANASHVILI MUSEUM OF FINE ARTS OF GEORGIA

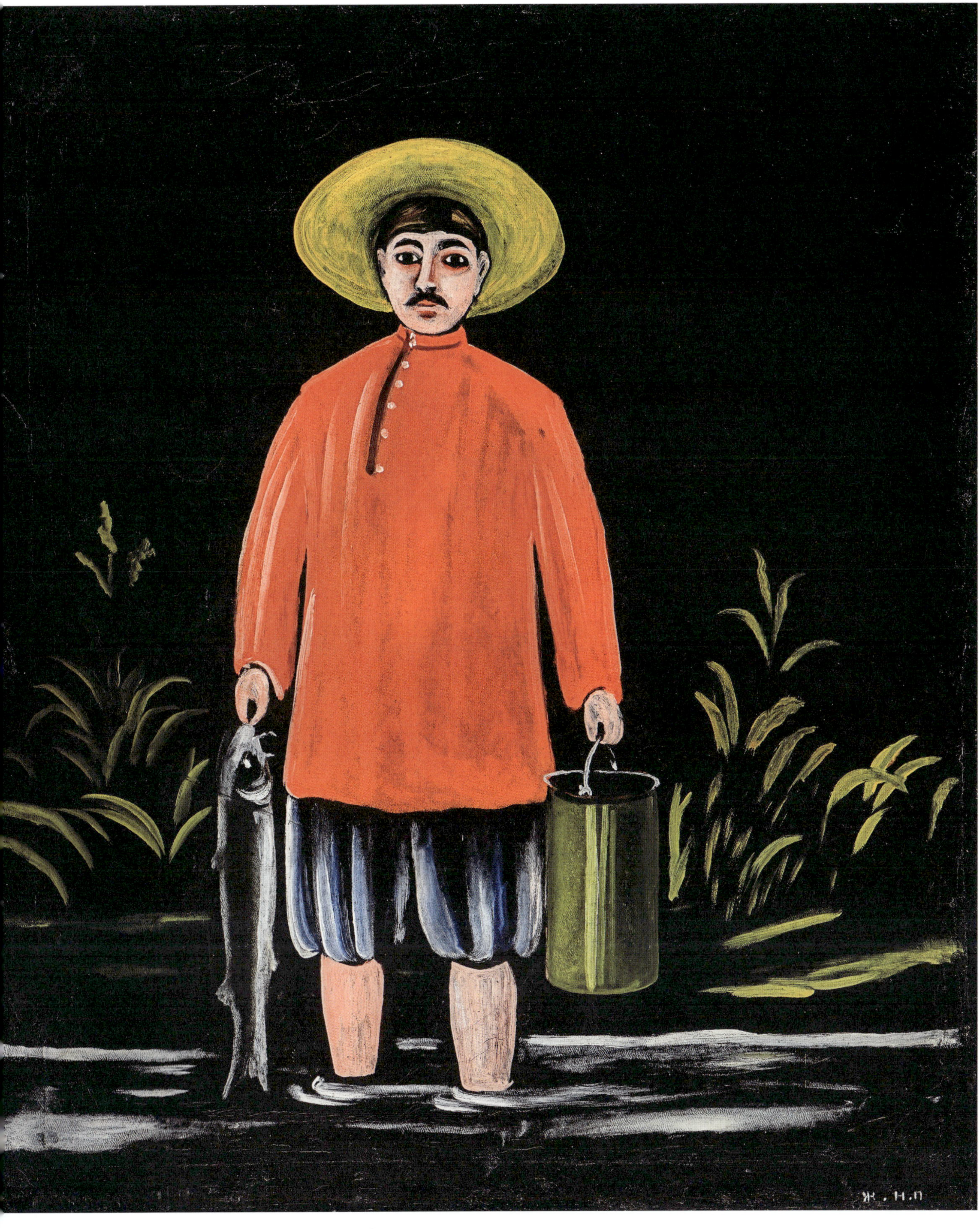
Ж. Н.П

NIKO PIROSMANI
BLACK LIGHT

Edited by Malou Wedel Bruun and Poul Erik Tøjner
Graphic Design: Michael Jensen
Editorial assistance: Pernille Gøtze Johansson
Translations: Adam King
(Poul Erik Tøjner, Kaspar Thormod, Biography),
Harsha Ram (Kirill Zdanevich)
Proofreading: Henry Broome
Photo Editor: Kim Hansen

Cover, front: *The Actress Margarita*
Oil on waxcloth, 115.9 x 94 cm
Cover, back: *Giraffe*
Oil on waxcloth, 137.4 x 111.7 cm
Inside cover, front and back:
Ortachala Belle (parts of diptych, details)
Oil on waxcloth, 52 x 117.6 / 52.5 x 118 cm

Photos: P. 49 (Thea Djordjadze): Rasmus Quistgaard
P. 75 (Mamma Andersson): Mats Liliequist
P. 89 (Tal R): Simon Wehye
P. 93 (Niko Pirosmani): The Digital Library "Iveriel"
of The National Parliamentary Library of Georgia

Litho/Print: Narayana Press
ISBN: 978-87-93659-66-7
Printed in Denmark 2023
www.louisiana.dk

Svanemærket tryksag, 5041 0562

MIX
Paper
FSC FSC® C010651

This catalogue is published
on the occasion of the exhibition
Niko Pirosmani
Louisiana Museum of Modern Art, Humlebæk, Denmark
4 May – 20 August 2023

Curator: Poul Erik Tøjner
Curatorial Assistant: Kaspar Thormod
Curatorial Coordinator/Registrar:
Marianne Ahrensberg
Conservator/Exhibition Producer:
Jesper Lund Madsen
Graphic Design: Marie Lübecker

The exhibition is organized jointly by Louisiana Museum
of Modern Art and Fondation Beyeler, Riehen/Basel, Switzerland,
and realised in cooperation with Georgian National Museum
and the Ministry of Culture, Sports and Youth of Georgia.
With generous support from Infinitart Foundation.

GEORGIAN NATIONAL MUSEUM

MINISTRY OF CULTURE, SPORTS AND YOUTH OF GEORGIA

INFINITART FOUNDATION

Main Corporate Partner
FRITZ HANSEN

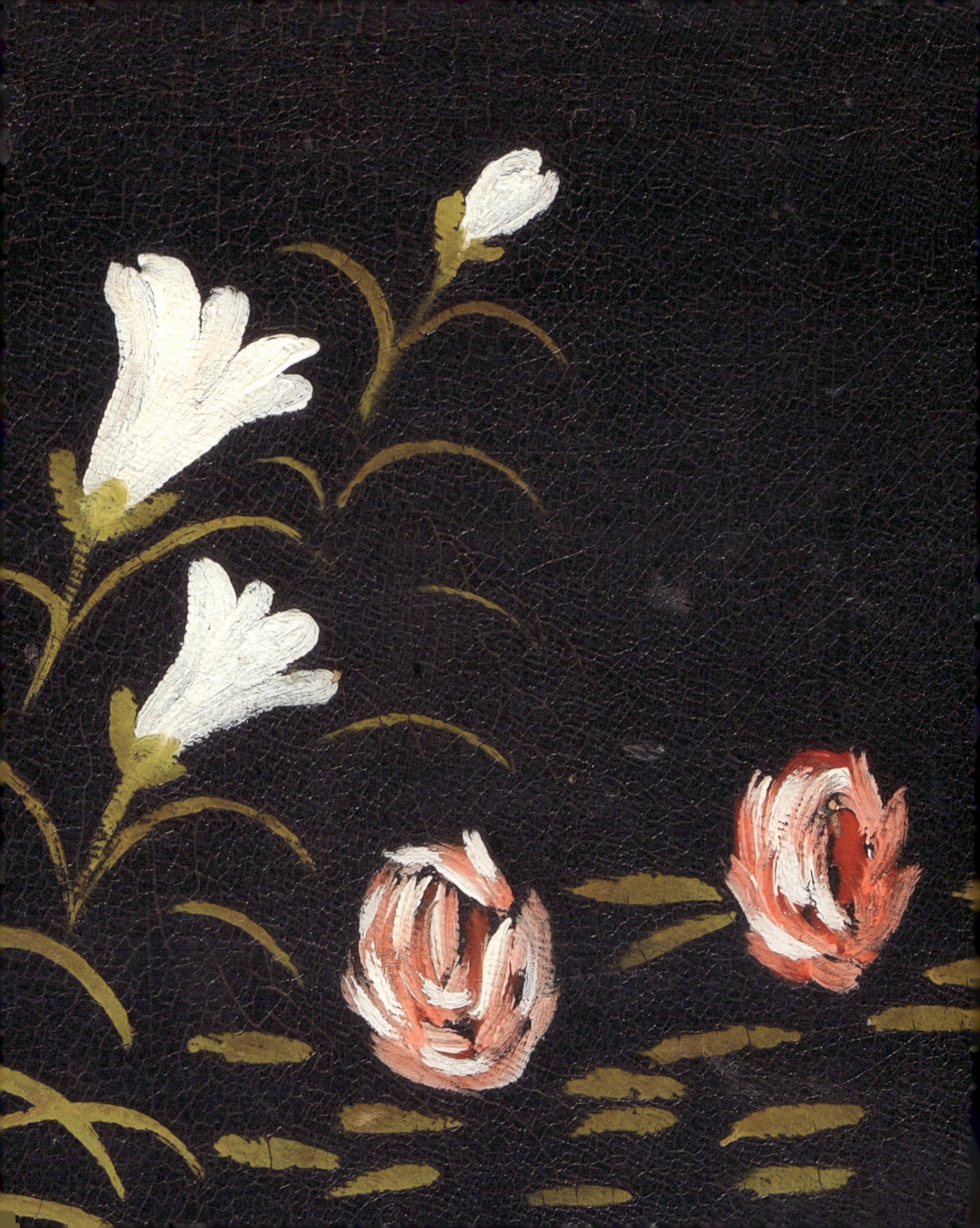